MW00856862

Consciousness and Fundamental Reality

PHILOSOPHY OF MIND

SERIES EDITOR
David J. Chalmers, New York University

Consciousness and Fundamental Reality

PHILIP GOFF

OXFORD
UNIVERSITY PRESS

OXFORD
UNIVERSITY PRESS

Oxford University Press is a department of the University of Oxford. It furthers
the University's objective of excellence in research, scholarship, and education
by publishing worldwide. Oxford is a registered trade mark of Oxford University
Press in the UK and certain other countries.

Published in the United States of America by Oxford University Press
198 Madison Avenue, New York, NY 10016, United States of America.

© Oxford University Press 2017

All rights reserved. No part of this publication may be reproduced, stored in
a retrieval system, or transmitted, in any form or by any means, without the
prior permission in writing of Oxford University Press, or as expressly permitted
by law, by license, or under terms agreed with the appropriate reproduction
rights organization. Inquiries concerning reproduction outside the scope of the
above should be sent to the Rights Department, Oxford University Press, at the
address above.

You must not circulate this work in any other form
and you must impose this same condition on any acquirer.

CIP data is on file at the Library of Congress
ISBN 978-0-19-067701-5

For Emma

CONTENTS

ACKNOWLEDGMENTS

I want to begin by giving special thanks to three people who have been especially important in my intellectual development: Galen Strawson, David Papineau, and David Chalmers.

From my first year as a philosophy undergraduate, I was utterly convinced of the inadequacy of physicalist accounts of consciousness. However, I couldn't find anyone who agreed with me, and so by the end of my three years of undergraduate study I was on the verge of giving up my anti-physicalist convictions. This all changed in my first week as a postgraduate student at the University of Reading. The new professor Galen Strawson believed all the things I had been taught were unbelievable: the irreducibility of consciousness, the grounding of thought in consciousness, and the reality of natural necessity. Galen inspired me to think the unthinkable, and our conversations over the last 15 years have been crucial to my intellectual development.

If the importance of Galen in my intellectual life was due to our agreement, the importance of David Papineau was due to our disagreement. Before I met David, I basically thought physicalists were crazy consciousness deniers. David gave me a deep sense of the motivation for his view—type-B physicalism—and over several years helped me develop arguments against it; these arguments form the bulk of the first half of this book. He has been an ever-present source of wisdom and guidance in my philosophical life.

I first met David Chalmers in conferences in Tucson and Sydney toward the end of my PhD, where we immediately started arguing about the best way to formulate the case against physicalism. I have never met anyone better to argue with. You have to take a deep breath before starting; it all happens very quickly, and if you pause for too long Dave will have moved on. But nobody is better for coming up with devastating objections (which force you to start from scratch after working on a paper for three months). The arguments in this book would be a good deal weaker without his razor-sharp critiques. I would also like to thank Dave for coming up with the title of this book.

I started writing this book during a sabbatical while I was working for the University of Liverpool in winter term of 2014, after having presented many of the ideas in my third year philosophy of mind course the previous semester (I am grateful to Garrett Mindt, Greg Miller, Hat Milsted, and all the students who participated in that course). The following academic year (2014–15) I began my current job at Central European University in Budapest and was lucky enough to spend the first term teaching only one course: on my book manuscript! I am grateful to Hanoch Ben-Yami for allowing me to do this, and to Howard Robinson (who co-taught the course), Mel Freitas, and all the students who participated for their input and suggestions. I would also like to thank Tim Crane, David Pitt, and my colleagues at CEU for their contributions to a work-in-progress session that year on one of the arguments from chapter 9.

I submitted the initial manuscript to Oxford University Press in July 2015. I couldn't have hoped for two better reviewers: Geoff Lee and Adam Pautz. Each was able to combine an open mind to the unorthodox views I defend with a rigorous examination of the arguments, and their extensive and insightful comments resulted in a much improved book. I would also like to thank Peter Ohlin and Andrew Ward from Oxford University Press for advice and editorial guidance, Shalini B. for managing the production process, Nino Kadić for putting together the index, and Garrett Mindt for additional help with the index.

After receiving comments from Lee and Pautz in April 2016, I presented revised versions of crucial arguments from the end of chapter 9 and from chapter 10 at the "Monism" conference at Jean Nicod Institute (run by Uriah Kriegel), the "Consciousness and Grounding" Conference at the University of Birmingham (run by Naomi Thompson and Darragh Byrne), and at a talk for the Templeton funded "New Directions in the Philosophy of Mind" project at the University of Cambridge (run by Tim Crane). I recall especially useful comments from Jonathan Schaffer, Uriah Kriegel, Terry Horgan, Khai Wager, David Papineau, Galen Strawson, David Chalmers, David Pitt, Emma Bullock, Angela Mendelovici, Darragh Byrne, Tim Crane, Kati Farkas, David Bourget, Laura Gow, Kit Fine, Alex Grzankowski, Umrao Sethi, James Tartaglia, Peter Epstein, and John

Henry Taylor. I received extremely useful comments on the manuscript itself from Hedda Hassel Mørch, Sam Coleman, Tom McClelland, Torin Alter, Luke Roelofs, Miri Albahari, Itay Shani, Nino Kadić, Forest Schreik, Adrian David Nelson, Greg Miller, and John Henry Taylor. After a long summer of hard work, I submitted the final manuscript in September 2016.

I am very grateful to Jessica Wilson for recommending the artwork of Christian McLeod (http://www.christianmcleod.com/) for the cover, and to Christian himself for kindly letting me use his piece "PERHAPS THE TERRACE OF THIS GARDEN OVERLOOKS ONLY THE LAKE OF OUR MINDS."

In developing the arguments of this book, I received a great deal of support and critical engagement from the growing panpsychist and Russellian monist community: Hedda Hassel Mørch, Luke Roelofs, Itay Shani, Bill Seager, Pat Lewtas, Tom McClelland, Greg Miller, Miri Albahari, Derk Pereboom, Yujin Nagasawa, Torin Alter, Tom Winfield, Keith Turausky, Khai Wager, Greg Rosenberg, Michael Blaumer, Matteo Grasso, Guilio Tononi, David Skrbina, Angela Mendelovici, David Bourget, Godehard Brüntrup, Ludwig Jaskolla, Alexander Buck, Ludwig Gierstl and everyone in the "Mind-Dust" group at the Munich School of Philosophy, and most especially my friend and comrade-in-arms Sam Coleman. I also benefited from vigorous discussions with my physicalist opponents, including John Henry Taylor, Robert Howell, Robert Kirk, Frank Jackson, Michael Tye, Katalin Balog, Barry Loewer, David Rosenthal, Daniel Dennett, Keith Frankish, Alyssa Ney, Brian McLaughlin, Nick Humphrey, and most especially my arch nemesis (and good friend) Esa Diaz-Leon. And of course many of the discussions that have shaped this book have been with people who don't neatly fit into either category: Martina Nida-Rümelin, Paul Coates, Jonathan Schaffer, Helen Yetter-Chappell, Kit Fine, Howard Robinson, Jessica Wilson, Paul Noordhof, Uriah Kriegel, Michelle Montague, Barry Dainton, Jonathan Simons, Daniel Stoljar, John Heil, Benj Hellie, Francis Fallon, Tom Winfield, Rob Hoveman, Péter Rauschenberger, Linda Lázár, Shamik Dasgupta, and David Pitt. I am especially grateful to Kati Farkas and Tim Crane, who as well as helping me develop these ideas have been an important source of guidance and friendship throughout my professional life.

On a more personal note, I am grateful for support and encouragement from my mum and dad, my siblings Helen, Clare, and Simon, and my close friends John Houghton and Philip Mudd. Discussions of the mind-body problem with Simon and John have been deeply significant in the development of my thought.

Most of all, I am grateful to my wife, colleague, and best friend Emma Bullock. We have had endless conversations on all aspects of this book, and her insights and sharp criticism are all over it. Without her unconditional support, especially during the horrible final month of writing, I think it would have taken another ten years.

1

The Reality of Consciousness

Mind and matter don't seem to fit in the same world; this is the essence of the mind–body problem. Space-filling solid stuff doesn't seem to belong with invisible inner-experiencing. The neural processing of the brain is best known through third-person scientific investigation, while the subjective first-person perspective of the mind is best known through introspection. How are we to make sense of these seemingly incongruous things being unified aspects of a single reality?

One option is to avoid the clash altogether by denying the existence of mind-independent matter: this is the *idealist* solution to the mind–body problem. A second option is to accept that mind and matter are utterly distinct but equally fundamental features of reality: this is the *dualist* solution to the mind–body problem. I don't think we should rule out either idealism or dualism as possibilities. But it is prima facie desirable to have a unified picture of nature that doesn't deny either the reality of the conscious mind or the observer-independent existence of the external world; such is the aspiration of the *anti-idealist monist*.

The aim of this book is to make sense of anti-idealist monism. I focus on two forms: *physicalism*, one of the most popular views in contemporary philosophy of mind, and *Russellian monism*, a new and radical alternative to physicalism. The first half of the book is spent arguing against physicalism. The latter half is spent exploring and defending Russellian monism.

In this first chapter I will briefly describe each of these views, and outline the main claims I make about them. Before doing that, however, I will outline my fundamental methodology and "big picture" perspective on the issues we will be dealing with.

1.1 The Big Picture

1.1.1 The Datum of Consciousness

A thing is conscious just in case there's something that it's like to be it; if it has an "inner life" of some kind.[1] There's something that it's like for a rabbit to be cold, or to be kicked, or to have a knife stuck in it. There's nothing that it's like, in contrast, for a table to be cold, or to be kicked, or to have a knife stuck in it (or so we ordinarily suppose).[2] There's nothing that it's like *from the inside*, as it were, to be a table. We mark this difference by saying that the rabbit but not the table is conscious.

It is important to note that consciousness so defined—sometimes called "phenomenal consciousness" to distinguish it from other notions— is not something cognitively sophisticated, such that we might be reluctant to ascribe it to non-human animals such as sheep or hamsters. In this respect the standard philosophical definition of "consciousness" differs from a common meaning of that word in science and everyday life, where it is often used to mean something like an awareness of self or even an ability to reason. In some sense a rabbit is aware of the world around it, but it is doubtful that it is able to think reflectively about itself as an occupant of that world. The lack of self-awareness does not bar the rabbit from enjoying a rich inner experience. Thus, the rabbit is "conscious" in the phenomenal sense.

While "phenomenal consciousness" is a technical term, the property it refers to is part of our common-sense picture of the world. Almost everyone believes that there is something that it's like to be a hamster, but there is nothing that it's like to be a rock or a planet. Common sense also leaves a grey area. Is there something that it's like to be a fly? When a fly bangs repeatedly against a window, is it experiencing some very crude form of suffering and frustration, or is a fly just a mechanism with no kind of inner experience whatsoever? Such questions are not easy to answer, but the ease with which we grasp them illustrates that having an inner life—having phenomenal consciousness—is an essential part of our common-sense conceptual scheme.

---

[1] Most people trace this way of defining consciousness back to Nagel (1974), although it appears earlier in Sprigge and Montefiore (1971).

[2] As will become clear in later chapters, I am in fact open to the possibility that tables are conscious. Nonetheless, my purpose at this point is simply to clearly articulate the concept of consciousness, and I do this with reference to common-sense views about which things do and which things do not have consciousness.

Phenomenal consciousness is a general property that comes in specific forms: pain, anxiety, and the forms of experience involved in seeing red, or smelling gasoline, or tasting coffee. Specific forms of phenomenal consciousness are variously called *conscious states*, *experiential properties*, or *phenomenal properties*; I will use these terms interchangeably. And the concepts we deploy when we think about conscious states as such, that is, when we think of them in terms of *how they feel* or *what it's like* to have them, are known as "phenomenal concepts." For example, if I am in pain, and I attend to my pain and think about it in terms of how it feels, I thereby form a phenomenal concept of my pain.

My methodological starting point is that phenomenal consciousness is a hard datum that any adequate theory of reality must accommodate. Moreover, consciousness must be accommodated *unrevised* in the following sense:

> *The Consciousness Constraint*—Any adequate theory of reality must entail that at least some phenomenal concepts are satisfied. (A concept is satisfied when it truly corresponds to reality, for example, the concept of God is satisfied if and only if God exists).

This principle does not entail that we never make mistakes about consciousness, even in one's own case. Consider the following example. You are extremely anxious during a visit to the dentist. The dentist applies pressure to the inside of your mouth. The combination of anxiety and pressure leads you to think that you are feeling pain when in fact you're not. This may be a case in which you mischaracterize your own conscious experience: you think you are feeling pain when in fact you are feeling anxiety and a sensation of pressure.[3] The Consciousness Constraint tells us merely that *some* phenomenal concepts are satisfied and so is consistent with the fact that we apply the wrong phenomenal concepts in certain cases.

Nonetheless, the Consciousness Constraint is a very significant constraint on metaphysical enquiry, as it tells us that one of our ordinary pre-theoretical concepts *gets the world exactly right*. In general, we should be happy to revise our ordinary notions to make them fit with our best

---

[3] I will argue in chapter 5 that certain judgments about our experience do involve something close to certainty, but this is not true across the board.

scientific theory of the world. We have a common-sense notion of solid-ity according to which solid objects are *all filled in*. Science has shown us that nothing is solid in that sense: the chair you are sitting on is mostly empty space. This doesn't mean nothing is solid. It just means we have to revise our pre-theoretical notion of what solidity is. Einstein told us some weird things about the nature of time, and we revised our concept of time to accommodate them. In some cases, we are even happy to elimi-nate from our ontology certain common-sense entities. Perhaps our sci-entific world view is incompatible with the existence of free will, and as a result philosophers ought to conclude that there is no such thing.

Matters are different when it comes to consciousness. I cannot rule out for certain the possibility that I am in the Matrix and my entire expe-rience of the external world is an illusion. But it seems that I can rule out the possibility that I have no inner life whatsoever; the evil computers couldn't be making me think I'm conscious when in fact I'm not.[4] And it's not simply that I know that there's something that vaguely resembles our common-sense notion of "consciousness," as might be the case with our common-sense notion of "solidity." When I entertain the proposi-tion <there is something that it's like to be me>, I know with a very high degree of justification, greater than my justification that the external world exists, that *that very proposition* is true—not merely that propo-sition or some revision of it containing slightly different concepts. The Consciousness Constraint has profound implications for scientific theo-rizing, setting strict limits on its potential for rewriting our conceptual scheme. If it turns out that our scientific world view is inconsistent with the reality of inner experiencing—according to our ordinary notion of inner experiencing—then it is the scientific story rather than conscious-ness that must budge.[5]

The Consciousness Constraint is my fundamental axiom, the Archimedean fixed point around which all else revolves. Readers who do not share my non-negotiable commitment to the reality of phenom-enal consciousness may nonetheless be interested to see what picture of the world is compatible with that commitment. I am inclined to think that appeal to the Consciousness Constraint is a much-neglected tool in

---

[4] As Tom Winfield pointed out to me, in some Matrix-style scenarios the computers are benefi-cent rather than evil. I maintain my epistemic right, however, to feel ill at ease with them.

[5] Accepting the Consciousness Constraint is compatible with accepting the fallibility of our phil-osophical intuitions and second-order judgments concerning phenomenal consciousness and what is required for phenomenal concepts to be satisfied.

metaphysics, and in the final chapter I outline a way forward for meta-physics rooted in it.

With the Consciousness Constraint understood, we are now in a posi-tion to reformulate the aim of this book: to find an anti-idealist monistic conception of the world that respects the Consciousness Constraint.

1.1.2 Science and Metaphysics

Philosophers, including myself, pour much time and effort into techni-cal arguments. But most of us are motivated by a "big picture": a funda-mental commitment that the philosopher is not going to dispense with unless she *really* has to (and even then she probably won't!).

Here's one quite popular "big picture" approach:

> *Methodological naturalism*—The lesson we should draw from the success of natural science is that we should look to, and only to, the third-person scientific method (i.e., rigorous empirical inves-tigation of what is publicly observable) to tell us what reality is like.[6]

Let us spell out this "big picture" in a little more detail. In the last five hundred years or so the project of natural science has gone extremely well. From the movement of the planets, to the evolution of life, to the fundamental constituents of matter, natural science seems to be an unstoppable juggernaut of explanation. For the methodological natural-ist, what this shows is that we've finally found something that *works*, something we can put our ontological faith in. For thousands of years before the scientific revolution philosophers struggled to find out what reality is like and got nowhere. Since the scientific revolution, natural sci-ence has enjoyed success after success after success.

From this perspective, philosophers who look somewhere other than third-person empirical science to try to work out the nature of the brain, or of matter in general, are "old school," trying to drag us back to the dark ages. They are to be equated with folk who believe in magic, or deny climate change, or think that the world was created in six days. One of the most fervent defenders of methodological naturalism is Patricia Churchland. In her recent book *Touching a Nerve* she dismisses those who

---

[6] Ladyman et al. (2007) defend a form of methodological naturalism.

doubt the potential of wholly empirical methods to explain consciousness as "naysayers":

> Well into the nineteenth century, the scientific consensus was
> that light is a fundamental feature of the universe, never to be
> explained by anything more fundamental. What happened? By
> the end of the nineteenth century, Clerk Maxwell had explained
> light as a form of electromagnetic radiation. . . . Imagine a pre-
> diction made in the year 2 CE saying that no one will ever under-
> stand the nature of fire. . . . Or imagine a prediction in year 1300
> that science will never understand how a fertilized egg can end
> up as a baby animal. Or a prediction in 1800 that no one will ever
> succeed in making something that controls infections. Suppose
> someone predicted in 1970 that science could never find a way to
> record levels of activity in a normal human brain without open-
> ing the skull. Wrong. This technical achievement flowered in the
> 1990s as functional resonance imaging (fMRI) was developed.
> To the degree that the nay-saying rests on an unsubstantiated
> prediction, it need not deter us from moving forward.[7]

The picture is clear. Methodological naturalists are pioneering into the
future. Their "naysaying" opponents are dragging us back to the past.

There are a number of problems with the picture Churchland paints of
her opponents. Firstly, opponents of methodological naturalism are not
necessarily giving up on trying to explain consciousness; they simply find
it plausible to go beyond the exclusive appeal to (third-person) empirical methods of investigation. There are some philosophers, perhaps most
famously Colin McGinn, who argue that human beings are by their very
nature unable to explain consciousness.[8] But this is by no means an
orthodox position among the opponents of methodological naturalism.
The charge of "naysaying" is a caricature.

Churchland implies that the opponents of methodological naturalism
hold that consciousness is fundamental, by equating their position with
the mistaken view that light is fundamental. Again, this is a caricature. In
later chapters we will explore the views of *constitutive panpsychists*, who
try to explain human consciousness in terms of more fundamental forms

---

[7] Churchland 2013b: 57–8.
[8] McGinn 1989.

of consciousness involved in simpler systems in the brain, and *constitutive panprotopsychists*, who try to explain consciousness in terms of more fundamental qualities of matter. Far from being instances of "naysaying," these are systematic attempts to explain.

Of course, some opponents of methodological naturalism do take human consciousness to be fundamental; in later chapters we will examine arguments in favor of this view. However, it is not unknown for science to postulate new fundamental properties. Indeed, while Maxwell did not take light to be a fundamental kind in its own right, he did introduce new fundamental physical ontology—electromagnetic charge and electromagnetic forces—to account for electromagnetism; and to this extent Churchland's appeal to Maxwell is misplaced.[9] All things being equal, a sparser ontology is better, but there are many and various criteria a good scientific theory must satisfy, and sometimes expanding fundamental ontology is, on balance, called for. What we are looking for is the most simple, elegant, unified theory that accounts for the data, and there is no obvious a priori reason to think the best theory won't postulate consciousness as a fundamental feature of the universe.

In the context of explaining consciousness, methodological naturalism often leads to a kind of *neuro-fundamentalism*: the view that the only way to make progress on explaining consciousness is to do more neuroscience. Naturally, Churchland is a passionate evangelist for neuro-fundamentalism. She ridicules the methods of David Chalmers, one of the most well-known opponents of neuro-fundamentalism, with the following piece of cutting rhetoric:

> No equipment had to be designed and maintained, no animals trained and observed, no steaming jungle or frozen tundra braved. The great advantage of nay-saying is that it leaves lots of time for golf.[10]

Putting on one side the caricatured charge of "naysaying," this quotation suggests that Churchland has an exceedingly limited view of how science operates, as though it's simply a matter of doing the experiments and recording the data. In fact, many significant developments in science have arisen not from experimental findings in the lab but from a radical

---

[9] Chalmers (1995) makes this point.
[10] Churchland 2013b: 60.

reconceptualization of our picture of the universe formulated in the comfort of an armchair. Think of the move in the Minkowski interpretation of special relativity from thinking of space and time as distinct things to the postulation of the single unified entity spacetime, or the move in general relativity from thinking of gravity as a force to thinking of it as the result of curvature in spacetime. My hunch is that progress on consciousness will involve this kind of radical reconceptualization of the mind, the brain, and the relationship between them, and the Russellian approach explored in the second half of this book looks to be a promising way of doing this.

The neuro-fundamentalist may reply that the conceptual innovations referred to previously were ultimately tested empirically; general relativity, for example, was eventually shown to fit the data better than its Newtonian predecessor. But developments in science are not always a matter of fitting the data better; sometimes they involve improvement in the internal virtue of the theory. Special relativity is a case in point. Special relativity and its Lorentzian predecessor are *empirically equivalent*: both predict, for example, the Michelson–Morley finding that the speed of light is measured to be the same in all frames of reference. Einstein didn't account for some data that Lorentz was unable to account for; it's simply that he found in his imagination a more elegant way of accounting for the data.

Indeed, in formulating special relativity, Einstein wasn't out doing experiments; he wasn't "designing equipment" or "braving jungles"—the kind of activities Churchland maintains are required for "proper science." He was sitting in an armchair wondering whether it would be possible to ride alongside a beam of light and figuring out what would follow if it were possible. Einstein's fundamental motivation in formulating special relativity was to bring greater internal unity to physics by ensuring that a principle of relativity held both in the older science of mechanics and in the new science of electromagnetism. In our enthusiasm for empirical methods, we must not forget that *deep thought* has a crucial role to play in science; at this point the boundaries between science and philosophy start to blur.

Moreover, if we accept the Consciousness Constraint outlined in the previous section, then there is a non-empirical datum that any adequate theory of reality must accommodate (at least if we understand "empirical data" as publicly observable): *the reality of phenomenal consciousness*. Suppose we have a theory that accounts for all the data of third-person observation and experiment, including human behavior and cognitive processing, but that cannot account for the fact that some phenomenal concepts are satisfied. We should reject such a theory as falsified, just as we would a theory that is inconsistent with empirical data. We know that there is phenomenal consciousness, and hence any theory inconsistent with its reality cannot possibly be true.

For this reason, there is an indispensable role for philosophers in the project of finding out the nature of fundamental reality. There is no experiment that will tell us what is required from reality for phenomenal concepts to be satisfied.[11] Working this out is a philosophical not a scientific task, and so we must turn to our best philosophers to tell us how to interpret the Consciousness Constraint. This is not ideal, as philosophers presently profoundly disagree on what is required from reality for phenomenal concepts to be satisfied. But, unfortunately, we have no other option. We just have to hope that the slow and careful process of rigorous academic activity eventually leads to consensus.

I am not presuming here that satisfying the Consciousness Constraint requires *adding* to the reality that is postulated to account for the data of observation and experiment. It could turn out—although I will argue against this—that the kind of things postulated to account for (third-person) empirical data happen to be sufficient to also account for the reality of consciousness. But that can't be assumed from the start; part of the task of working out what will satisfy phenomenal concepts is working out whether empirical postulates will suffice.

It has not been properly articulated in the public mind, nor in the minds of many philosophers, that the reality of consciousness is a datum in its own right, a datum distinct from the data of third-person observation and experiment. I think this in part explains the dismissive reaction by people who consider themselves to be "scientifically minded" or "hard-nosed naturalists," to some of the theories that are taken seriously in this book—in particular, to panpsychist views according to which the fundamental constituents of the world have conscious experience. Third-person observation and experiment do not give us grounds for thinking that electrons have consciousness, and on this basis many conclude that we have no reason to accept such a view. Properly internalizing the imperative to account for phenomenal consciousness—as a datum in its own right—is epistemically transformative: one becomes open to

---

[11] At the very least we need philosophical reflection to tell us which experiments or observational data will help shed light on this.

peculiar theories of reality that have the potential to account for the reality of consciousness in the same way that most people are open to the peculiarities of relativity and quantum mechanics given their potential to account for the empirical data.

I do not mean to say that most people are happy to deny the reality of phenomenal consciousness; this is a radical and extremely rare position.[12] I just mean that most people—most philosophers and the vast majority of those outside of philosophical academia—do not explicitly recognize the unrevised reality of phenomenal consciousness as a datum in its own right, nor have they thought through how this impacts upon the project of trying to work out what reality like. As a result, the general public assumes that it is the job of scientists to tell us what reality is like, and the job of philosophers to make us feel a bit better about the world that science has resigned us to.

I am cautiously optimistic that this is a phase of history that we will one day move beyond. It results I think from the visceral effect of technology on metaphysical belief. The wonders of modern technology incline educated women and men to place their metaphysical trust in, and only in, the scientific method. As Woody Allen's lead character in *Deconstructing Harry* put it: "If it's between the Pope and air conditioning, I choose air conditioning." It has come to be thought that respect for the empirical sciences demands not only that we concede them authority on their own terms, but that we grant them authority on the complete metaphysical—sometimes even the complete ethical[13]—truth.

However, so evident is the reality of consciousness that I can't believe that consciousness-denial, or even consciousness-revision, will ever get much of a grip on those serious about truth. And sooner or later it will surely become generally appreciated that this entails taking consciousness seriously as a datum in its own right.

Things are moving in the right direction. Consciousness has gone from being a taboo topic for the "scientifically minded" to being seen as a "hard problem" for science. However, despite the subtitle of the book in which David Chalmers popularized the phrase, the "hard problem of consciousness" has generally been interpreted as a tricky puzzle that will one day go

---

[12] See Frankish (2016) for a very interesting defense of eliminativism about phenomenal consciousness.

[13] See, for example, Harris (2010).

away if we just do a bit more neuroscience.[14] The next stage is for people to see consciousness not as something to be squeezed into the world we already know about from science, but as an *epistemic starting point* on a par with the epistemic starting points we get from observations and experiments. Consciousness is not a "mystery"; nothing is more familiar. What is mysterious is *reality*, and our knowledge of consciousness is one of the best clues we have to working out what that mysterious thing is really like.

1.1.3 The Philosophical Foundations of Physics

I finished the last section with some brave hopes for the future. But for the moment, the methodological naturalist's narrative about the success of science, and the accompanying claims about the morals we should draw from it, is a powerful motivating force for many. I want to suggest an alternative way of thinking about the history of science, which may motivate us in a different way.

One of Galileo's most important contributions to the foundations of the scientific revolution was his assertion that the language of natural philosophy should be exclusively mathematical, a view he expressed in this well-known passage from *The Assayer*:

> Philosophy [by which he means "natural philosophy," which became physical science] is written in this grand book, the universe, which stands continually open to our gaze, but it cannot be understood unless one first learns to comprehend the language and read the letters in which it is composed. It is written in the language of mathematics, and its characters are triangles, circles, and other geometrical figures, without which it is humanly impossible to understand a single word of it; without these, one wanders about in a dark labyrinth.[15]

What is less often focused on is the *metaphysical picture of reality* that underwrote the Galilean research program. Before Galileo, philosophers took the world to be full of *sensory qualities*: colors, smells, tastes, sounds. And intuitively one cannot capture the redness of a tomato, the spicy taste of paprika, or the sweet smell of flowers in the austere, abstract

---

[14] Chalmers 1996. Actually, the phrase "hard problem of consciousness" was coined in his 1995 article.

[15] Galileo 1623: 237–8.

language of mathematics. Galileo got around this problem by stripping the world of such qualities and locating them in the soul.[16]

For Galileo, the spiciness of the paprika isn't really in the paprika; rather it's in the soul of the person tasting the paprika. The sweet smell of the flowers isn't really in the flowers; rather it's in the soul of the person smelling them. Even colors for Galileo resided not "out there" on the surface of objects but within the human soul. By stripping external objects of any qualities other than shape, Galileo created a metaphysical picture of the material world in which it could be exhaustively described in mathematical geometry:

> Now I say that whenever I conceive any material or corporeal substance, I immediately feel the need to think of it as bounded, and as having this or that shape; as being large or small in relation to other things, and in some specific place at any given time; as being in motion or at rest; as touching or not touching some other body; and as being one in number, or few, or many. From these conditions I cannot separate such a substance by any stretch of my imagination.
>
> But that it must be white or red, bitter or sweet, noisy or silent, and of sweet or foul odour, my mind does not feel compelled to bring in as necessary accompaniments. Without the senses as our guides, reason or imagination unaided would probably never arrive at qualities like these.
>
> Hence I think that tastes, odours and colours, and so on are no more than mere names as far as the object in which we place them is concerned, and that they reside only in the consciousness. Hence, if the living creature were removed, all these qualities would be wiped away and annihilated.[17]

We can see then that it was a change in our *philosophical conception* of the world that made mathematical physics possible, and that change was a matter of placing the sensory qualities we encounter in conscious experience outside of the material domain studied by physics.

---

[16] In contrast to Descartes, Galileo conceived of the soul in Aristotelian terms, as the principle of animation in the body (*corpo sensitivo*). See chapter 3 of Ben-Yami (2015) for more discussion of this.

[17] Galileo 1623: 274–7.

This is the start of mathematical physics, which subsequently proved to be a great success. Once we can capture nature in mathematics, we can start to frame *laws of nature* in mathematical language. A short while later we had Newton's laws of motion and gravity. And five centuries of developing more and more accurate mathematical models of the behavior of matter has enabled us to manipulate the material world in all sorts of extraordinary ways, giving us lasers and microwave ovens and flights to the moon.

It is tempting to take this success as evidence for methodological naturalism, or even a kind of *physics-fundamentalism* according to which the great success of physics shows that physics is on its way to giving us a complete account of fundamental reality. But this is the wrong conclusion to draw. The success of mathematical physics resulted from *limiting the scope of enquiry*; by putting the sensory qualities we encounter in conscious experience—colors, smells, tastes, sounds—outside of the domain of the physical sciences, we are able to give a purely mathematical description of what's left over. But those qualities that Galileo took out of the material world still exist *somewhere* and must still be accounted for *somehow*. If the spicy taste of the paprika isn't really in the paprika then where is it? Galileo thought it was in the soul, but if we don't want to believe in souls then we need to find a place in the natural world for the sensory qualities.

But do these reflections on the *origins* of science really tell us very much about its *potential*? Isn't the great success of Galilean physics evidence that it's fundamentally on the right lines and will one day explain even the sensory qualities which Galileo thought were beyond its reach? This line of reasoning is confused, as can be seen in the following analogy. In my first year as an assistant professor, the head of department kindly let me off administration duties, allowing me to focus exclusively on teaching and research. The fact that I did well when I didn't have to do administration obviously gives us no reason to think that I would be good at administration.[18] Similarly, the fact that physical science has done well since sensory qualities were put outside its domain of enquiry gives us no grounds for thinking it has the potential to adequately deal with sensory qualities themselves.

And so there is no good reason to think of the anti-physicalism I defend in this book as pushing against the onward march of science.

---

[18] Sadly I wasn't.

The anti-physicalist can perfectly well appreciate that physics is sovereign in its own domain—mapping in mathematical models the behavioral dispositions of basic matter—while maintaining that there is more to reality than can be captured in the austere mathematical vocabulary of physics.[19]

Galileo took the sensory qualities out of the material world to make mathematical physics possible. But we know with something close to certainty that these sensory qualities exist; their reality is evident in our experience. If redness doesn't exist "out there" on the surfaces of tomatoes, then at least it exists in my mind as a form of conscious experience. At some point those qualities need to be put back into our metaphysical picture of the world. That is precisely the aim of this book.[20]

Having hopefully given the reader a sense of where I'm coming from, I turn now to the views we shall be exploring.

1.2 Physicalism and Russellian Monism

1.2.1 Physicalism

Physicalism is the view that fundamental reality is entirely physical. Despite the popularity of this view, it is actually quite tricky to spell out exactly what it amounts to, as we will explore in detail in the next chapter. To simplify matters somewhat, the view I focus on in the first half of the book is an unadulterated form of the physicalist position, which I call "pure physicalism." Pure physicalism involves the thesis that the complete nature of fundamental reality can in principle be captured in the vocabulary of the physical sciences. I go on to show (in chapter 6) how the argument can be applied to more diluted forms of physicalism.

My charge against physicalism is a familiar one: physicalism is unable to account for the reality of phenomenal consciousness. In other words, physicalism is unable to respect the Consciousness Constraint. Although familiar, my argument differs significantly in detail to those that have been given previously.

---

[19] As we shall discuss in the next chapter, the vocabulary of physics also involves nomic notions, such as the notion of a *law of nature*.

[20] I am inclined to think that if Galileo were to time-travel to the present day and be told about the "hard problem of consciousness," his response would be: "Of course physical science can't explain the qualities we find in experience. I created physical science by taking them out of matter!"

Probably the two most discussed arguments against physicalism in recent times are Frank Jackson's version of the knowledge argument and David Chalmers' version of the conceivability argument.[21] In Jackson's knowledge argument, we hear about Mary, the brilliant neuroscientist raised in a black and white room from where she learns everything there is to know about color experience. One day Mary sees red for the first time and learns something new: what it's like to see red. The moral of the story is that there's more to the conscious experience of color than physical science can ever convey. In Chalmers' conceivability argument he tries to demonstrate that "zombies"—physical duplicates of human beings that lack any kind of conscious experience—are conceivable, in the sense that no contradiction or incoherence can be found in the idea of such a thing. He goes on to argue that if zombies are conceivable, then they're possible, and if they're possible, then the physical facts cannot account for consciousness.

I have concerns with both of these arguments. The knowledge argument plausibly demonstrates an *epistemic gap* between the physical facts and the facts about experience, but more needs to be done to transform it into a metaphysical gap. My worry with Chalmers' conceivability argument is that it rests on highly contentious semantic assumptions—those assumed by the "two-dimensional" semantic framework in terms of which the argument is posed—which in my view Chalmers has never adequately justified.

In my discussion of these arguments I try to show that what is really needed to make these kinds of arguments work is a commitment to *Phenomenal Transparency*: the thesis that phenomenal concepts are transparent. To understand this thesis we need to understand a distinction that is central to this book: the distinction between transparent and opaque concepts.[22]

A concept is *transparent* just in case it reveals the nature of the entity it refers to, in the sense that it is a priori (for someone possessing the concept and in virtue of possessing the concept) *what it is for that entity to be part of reality*.[23] A plausible example is the concept <sphericity>. For

---

[21] Jackson 1982, 1986; Chalmers 1996, 2009.

[22] I have developed this distinction in a number of papers, beginning with Goff (2011). Martine Nida-Rümelin (2007) has a very similar critique of physicalism, rooted in the thesis that through introspection we are able to grasp the essence of phenomenal qualities.

[23] The form of reality will depend on the kind of entity. For an individual to be part of reality is for it to exist; for a property to be part of reality is for it to be instantiated (Platonists might want to

the property of sphericity to be instantiated is for there to be something with all points on its surface equidistant from its center; if you possess the concept of sphericity, and you're clever enough, you can work that out from the armchair.

A concept is *opaque* just in case it reveals little or nothing of the nature of the entity it refers to, that is, very little of what it is for that entity to be part of reality is a priori accessible (for someone possessing the concept and in virtue of possessing the concept). The concept <water> is a plausible example of an opaque concept. For there to be water is for there to be stuff composed of H_2O molecules, but this cannot be found out from the armchair.[24] In contrast to sphericity, you have to actually do some science to find out the essential nature of water.

Phenomenal Transparency, then, is the thesis that phenomenal concepts reveal the nature of the conscious states they refer to. By thinking about, say, a particular pain in terms of what it's like, you can thereby come to know what it is for that pain to be instantiated. In this respect, the concept <pain> is more like the concept <sphericity> than it is like the concept <water>.

Suppose that Phenomenal Transparency is true. According to physicalism, a physical state like pain has a wholly physical nature; perhaps—to continue with the hackneyed and empirically implausible example favored by philosophers—for something to feel pain is for its c-fibers to fire. If this were the case, then—assuming that phenomenal concepts are transparent—the physical nature of pain would be accessible to anyone who has felt pain (and thereby has a phenomenal concept of pain); merely feeling pain would allow you to know that for something to feel pain is for its c-fibers to fire (or whatever the specific physical nature is). But it is clearly not the case that anyone who has felt pain knows its physical nature—neuroscience isn't so easy!—and hence physicalism must be false. If we can secure Phenomenal Transparency, we have a strong case against physicalism.

Now suppose that phenomenal concepts are opaque: that they reveal to us nothing about to the nature of the states they refer to. It follows, or so I try to argue, that we can't possibly have philosophical grounds for

distinguish a property's existing from its having concrete reality); for an event to be part of reality is for it to take place.

[24] For reasons we'll get to in chapter 6, I actually think the concept <H_2O> is also opaque, but I ignore this complication for now.

denying that the referents of phenomenal concepts are neurophysiological states. If phenomenal concepts afford us no understanding of what on earth conscious states are, then how on earth could we rule out from the armchair that they are brain states? Without Phenomenal Transparency, the epistemic gap between the physical and the experiential has no metaphysical significance.

Thus I try to show that the charge that physicalism is unable to account for consciousness hangs and falls on Phenomenal Transparency. In the final chapter of the first half of the book I present an argument for Phenomenal Transparency, and on the basis of this I reject physicalism.

1.2.2 Russellian Monism

In 1927, in *The Analysis of Matter*, Bertrand Russell defended a couple of theses that amounted to a novel approach to the mind–body problem. Similar claims were defended by Arthur Eddington in his Gifford lectures of the same year.[25] This approach was forgotten about in the latter half of the twentieth century, perhaps because it didn't fit with the physicalist zeitgeist of the time. However, it has recently been rediscovered, leading to a view—or, better, a school of views—known as "Russellian monism."

There are a number of slight variants on the definition of Russellian monism, but essentially it involves a negative and a positive component:

> *The negative component*: The negative component of Russellian monism consists in the claim that physical science provides only a limited account of the nature of the physical world. This is variously put as the claim that it captures only the *relational, dispositional, extrinsic,* or *structural* properties of matter. Russellian monists argue that there must be some further nature to matter underlying these characteristics—a *non-relational, categorical, intrinsic,* or *non-structural* nature—about which physics remains silent. I call this the "deep nature" of matter.
>
> *The positive component*: The positive component of Russellian monism consists in the claim that the deep nature of matter transparently explains consciousness, in the sense that there is an a priori entailment from facts about the deep nature of matter to facts about consciousness. If you were able to access the deep nature

---

[25] These were published the following year (Eddington 1928).

of my brain, you would in principle be able to deduce the nature of my consciousness. The mystery of consciousness, then, results from our scientific ignorance concerning the deep nature of matter.

Russellian monism is increasingly being seen as an attractive middle way between the extremes of physicalism and dualism, avoiding many of the problems associated with each of these views. Consider the difficulty outlined in the previous section of reconciling mind-brain identities with the transparency of phenomenal concepts. If the concept of pain reveals what pain essentially is and pain just is c-fibers firing, why is it not a priori that pain is c-fibers firing? Many contemporary physicalists try to avoid this worry by simply denying Phenomenal Transparency: it is because phenomenal concepts are opaque—and so do not reveal the physical nature of pain—that the identity <pain=c-fiber firing> is not knowable a priori.

The Russellian monist turns this on its head: it is the *physical* concept, not the phenomenal concept, that is opaque. According to Russellian monism, when we think about c-fiber firing as "c-fiber firing" we characterize it extrinsically, primarily in terms of its functional role in the brain. It is only when we think about c-fiber firing as "the feeling of pain" that we understand its essential nature. For the physicalist pain is essentially c-fiber firing, while for the Russellian monist c-fiber firing is essentially pain.

The Russellian monist, then, is happy to accept that phenomenal concepts are transparent.[26] If am right that the classical challenges to physicalism—expressed in the knowledge and conceivability argument—ultimately reduce to the difficulty of reconciling physicalism with Phenomenal Transparency, then there is good reason to think that the Russellian monist can avoid these difficulties.

Dualism on the other hand has profound problems accounting for mental causation. If—as many philosophers believe—physical reality forms a causally closed system, it is hard to see how a non-physical mind could causally impact on the physical world. But for the Russellian monist (at least in paradigmatic forms) the mind is part of the causally

---

[26] Or at least translucent. I ignore for the moment the subtle distinction between transparent and translucent concepts, which we will get to in chapter 4.

closed physical world, in virtue of being grounded in the deep nature of the physical.

Russellian monism comes in a variety of forms. Broadly speaking there are three dimensions of difference:

Panpsychist versus panprotopsychist—Panpsychist Russellian monists believe that the deep nature of the physical world is experiential. The typical view is that basic material entities have a very simple experiential nature, from which the complex experience of humans and animals is somehow derived. Panprotopsychist Russellian monists in contrast hold that the deep nature of the physical is not itself experiential but somehow intrinsically suited for realizing, or bringing about, experience.

Constitutive versus emergentist—Constitutive Russellian monists believe that human and animal experience is *grounded in*, or *constituted of*, the deep nature of the physical. Emergentist Russellian monists in contrast hold that human and animal experience is *causally brought about and sustained by* the deep nature of the physical.

Smallist versus priority monist—Smallists believe that all fundamental facts are facts concerning micro-level entities and properties; all things exist and are the way they are in virtue of how micro-level entities are. Priority monists in contrast hold that the universe is the one and only fundamental entity; all other things exist and are the way they are in virtue of how the universe is. Russellian monism can be combined with either of these views.

In chapter 6, and in more detail in chapter 9, I raise empirical worries for emergentist forms of Russellian monism. Very roughly, the idea is that if human and animal conscious subjects were fundamental entities, then they would presumably have distinctive causal powers, which differ from the causal powers of basic material entities. It would seem to follow that there would be all sorts of happenings in the brain or body that could not be explained in terms of the kind of causal principles that operate in nature more generally, in both the animate and inanimate realm. The fact that we don't seem to find such events in the brain constitutes an inductive argument against emergentism.

On the other hand, there are significant a priori difficulties facing constitutive forms of Russellian monism. I spend chapters 7 and 8 discussing various forms of the "combination problem" for Russellian monism. In its paradigmatic form, the combination problem is a challenge for small-ist panpsychism that goes as follows: how on earth do we make sense of the idea of little conscious subjects, such as electrons and quarks, combining to make a big conscious subject, such as a human brain? Many related concerns arise when we try to make sense of human conscious subjects as composite objects, and many of these concerns apply to both panpsychist and panprotopsychist forms of Russellian monism.

At the end of chapter 8 I present what I take to be the hardest combination problem, which I call the "subject irreducibility problem." The problem is that conscious subjects seem to be in a certain sense irreducible: it doesn't seem that we can specify what it is for there to be a conscious subject in more fundamental terms. I ultimately argue that the subject irreducibility problem has no solution so long as we are working with smallist models of Russellian monism. In chapter 9, however, I propose a model combining priority monism and panpsychism, which I hope is able to make sense—paradoxical as it may sound—of conscious subjects being both irreducible and non-fundamental.

PART I

AGAINST PHYSICALISM

2

What Is Physicalism?

The first half of this book is spent arguing against *physicalism*, the view that fundamental reality is wholly physical. Physicalism is an extremely popular position in analytic philosophy of mind, and many of the central debates in this area are between physicalists and their opponents. However, there is a great irony here: it is not at all clear upon reflection what exactly physicalism is.

All are agreed that physicalism is the view that fundamental reality is entirely physical: that the physical facts constitute the fundamental nature of the world. But there are two ways in which this initial definition cries out for clarification. Firstly, what is it for a fact to be *physical*? Secondly, what is it for certain facts to entirely constitute *fundamental reality*? I will try in this chapter to answer both of these questions in turn.

Addressing the first question I take to be a largely terminological issue, a matter of working out which use of the word "physical" is best suited for allowing us to have the philosophical discussions we want to have. I won't claim to have given the single best possible definition of physicality, and few if any of the significant conclusions of later chapters are dependent on my favored definition. But this preliminary issue must be cleared up before we can get on to the substantive issues.

Addressing the second question is more substantive, as it takes us to basic issues concerning what metaphysical enquiry is all about. Metaphysicians are not just interested in a big list of all the things that exist: tables (✓), unicorns (X), God (TBC). For one thing putting together such a list would take a very long time. But, more importantly, such a list wouldn't tell us how everything "hangs together"; it wouldn't reveal to us the unity lying behind the plurality of things that exist.

Metaphysicians want to dig deeper, down to the fundamental building blocks of reality. We are primarily interested not in what exists but in what exists *fundamentally*: not in reality but in *fundamental reality*. Fundamental reality is the deep nature of the world, the metaphysical foundations upon which all being depends. In the second half I will articulate a not especially original view as to what this project amounts to.

2.1 The Nature of Physicality

2.1.1 A Priori and A Posteriori Definitions of the Physical

Contemporary debates between physicalists and their opponents have historical connections with debates in the seventeenth and eighteenth centuries between materialists and their opponents. Thomas Hobbes defended the view that fundamental reality was entirely material; in this he was opposed by George Berkeley who thought that fundamental reality was entirely immaterial and by René Descartes who thought that fundamental reality was partly material and partly immaterial.

How these philosophers defined matter was shaped by, and itself shaped, the science of the time. Descartes thought of matter as *extended stuff*: stuff stretched out in three spatial dimensions. John Locke added *solidity* to Descartes' characterization to differentiate corporeal things from souls, which Locke thought might also have a spatial location. This roughly constituted the received understanding of material substance in the early days of the scientific revolution.

The trouble with these definitions is that twentieth-century physics arguably shows that at least some physical stuff lacks these characteristics. Electrons are thought to be "point particles," filling no space at all. So understood, electrons lack extension, and hence by Descartes' definition lack physicality (at least if we take "physical" and "material" to be synonymous, although I will later distinguish them). Modern physics talks about fields and particles—entities not naturally described as "solid"— and macroscopic objects are mostly empty space, which makes their classification as "solid" in any pre-theoretical sense dubious (of course, some objects are "solid" by our modern chemical definition).

If physical stuff isn't characterized by the properties of extension and solidity, which properties do define it? A natural thought is to look to physics to tell us what physical stuff is. It is twentieth-century physics that has rendered the seventeenth-century definition of matter obsolete; perhaps we can use modern physics to plug the hole it has itself created.

There are two ways of doing this. One way would be to abstract from our current physical picture of the world some general characteristics and then stipulate necessary and sufficient conditions for a property to count as "physical." To do this is to give an *a priori definition* of the physical. The worry about such an approach is that, as has proved to be the case with the seventeenth-century definition of matter, as the science moves on, the definition will become outdated. The alternative is simply to define the physical as whatever physicists tell us it is; to do this is to give an *a posteriori definition* of the physical.[1]

Ultimately I will defend an a priori definition of the physical, but before I get to this I will explore the prospects for an a posteriori definition.

2.1.2 Hempel's Dilemma and Physics-Based Responses to It

There is a much discussed problem with a posteriori definitions of the physical, which has become known in the literature as "Hempel's dilemma," due to its origins in the writings of Carl Hempel.[2] The dilemma arises when we ask ourselves whether in our definition of the physical as the subject matter of "physics," we mean current physics with all its flaws, or perfect completed physics of the far-off future. Both options have problems.

The problem with defining the physical in terms of current physics is that current physics is almost certainly false in at least some respects. Our best theory of the very big (i.e., general relativity) is inconsistent with our best theory of the very small (i.e., quantum mechanics). And the history of past physical theories being superseded by later physical theories gives us reason to suppose that current physics will one day be superseded by some more accurate theory of the universe. If physicalism is the view that fundamental reality is made of the kinds of facts current physics talks about, then physicalism is almost certainly false.

There are a number of related difficulties involved in defining the physical facts in terms of future physics. Firstly, there is a worry about *vagueness* (in the non-technical sense of that term). Who knows what weird and whacky entities future physicists will postulate? Without some way of narrowing down what future physics might look like it's not clear what metaphysical views a commitment to "physicalism" is supposed to rule out

---

[1] This terminology is from Ney (2008a).
[2] Hempel 1980.

and hence unclear what view one is signing up to when one claims to be a "physicalist." Some philosophers have expressed a similar worry about *vacuity*. If we just define ideal physics of the future as "the complete final theory of everything," then it looks like a commitment to physicalism rules out nothing, since a theory that failed to include everything would by definition not be ideal physics. So defined physicalism is vacuously true.[3]

A final worry with future physics-based definitions concerns its potentially *counterintuitive implications*. Suppose future physicists postulate fundamental mentality, psychic powers, or even souls. It would then turn out that the truth of physicalism was consistent with the existence of fundamental mentality, which many philosophers find deeply counterintuitive. Physicalism is supposed to be the contemporary analog of seventeenth-century materialism, the arch opponent of dualism and idealism. If physicalism turns out to be consistent with such views, then it seems to lose its point.

There are three options in the light of Hempel's dilemma. We can adopt *currentism*: embrace the first horn of Hempel's dilemma and try to define the physical in terms of current physics. We can adopt *futurism*: embrace the second horn of the dilemma and try to define the physical in terms of future physics, somehow dealing with the worries about *vagueness, vacuity*, and *counterintuitive implications*. Or we can avoid Hempel's dilemma altogether by returning to an a priori rather than an a posteriori definition of the physical.

As far as I know, the only philosopher who has gone for a pure form of currentism is Andrew Melnyk.[4] Melnyk accepts that such a definition entails that physicalism is false. He nonetheless defends physicalism on the grounds that philosophers should aim at the view that is *most probable*. Even if physicalism is false, it may still be more probable than its competitors, such as dualism and idealism. Melnyk's position is ingenious and more difficult to refute than you might think. However, given that one central aim of this book is to argue against physicalism, I will try to avoid beginning with a definition that rules out its truth from the start.

Janice Dowell is perhaps the best-known defender of futurism; for Dowell, the physical facts are whatever completed physics tells us they are.[5] She answers the worries about vagueness and vacuity by putting a

---

[3] For a good survey of philosophical discussion surrounding Hempel's dilemma, see Ney (2008a).
[4] Melnyk 2003.
[5] Dowell 2006.

number of constraints on what counts as physics proper.[6] This is done in two ways. Firstly, physics is defined as our complete and ideal scientific theory of entities existing at *relatively low levels of complexity*. Completed physics then is not just "the complete theory of everything," as was suggested in the concern about vacuity; it is the complete theory of things with relatively few parts. Electrons are currently thought to have no parts and so would clearly be among the subject matter of physics under this definition. Protons are thought to be made up of two up quarks and a down quark, which gives them a bit more complexity, but this number of components is minuscule relative to the enormous number of parts that make up even a single cell (never mind a heart, a brain, or a whole organism).

Already we are starting to get content to the view. This stipulation ensures that the truth of physicalism rules out *emergentism*. Emergentism is the view that fundamental entities emerge at higher levels of complexity.[7] Nineteenth-century British emergentists, for example, were committed to properties or states of affairs at the chemical, biological, and mental levels that were not reducible to, and could not have been predicted from knowledge of, more basic properties and states of affairs.[8] This commitment to properties/states of affairs over and above the properties/states of affairs at low levels of complexity renders emergentism inconsistent with physicalism, given Dowell's definition. For the physicalist, fundamental reality is flat rather than layered.[9]

Dowell puts further flesh on the bone by putting constraints on what kind of theories count as "scientific." A scientific theory for Dowell must have the following four characteristics:

- *Testability*—The inclusion of a set of explanatory hypotheses from which empirically testable implications can be derived.
- *Variety*—Confirmation by the obtaining of a number and variety of the test implications of its explanatory hypotheses.

---

[6] Given these a priori constraints on what physics is, Dowell's definition is not wholly a posteriori.

[7] We shall reach a slightly more nuanced definition of emergentism in chapter 9.

[8] For examples of British emergentism, see Mill (1843), Broad (1925), and Alexander (1920). For a good discussion of British emergentism, see McLaughlin (1992).

[9] A Dowellian physicalist may think reality is a bit layered, if she believes that there are multiple micro-levels with fundamental properties. We could say that for the physicalist reality is fla*tish*.

- *Unity*—The provision of a unified explanation of a variety of empirical generalizations. The theory as a whole provides a unified explanation of the empirical generalizations that are among its testable implications.
- *Holistic*—The theory receives additional empirical support by its fit with what is antecedently known and independently observable.

Having offered these constraints, Dowell then defines a "physical property" as one that is "well-integrated into the most complete and unified explanation possible for the relatively most basic occupants of space-time."[10] This gives further response to the worries about vacuity and vagueness by ruling out certain possibilities. For an entity to be well-integrated into a scientific theory its behavior must be regular and hence predictable. Suppose that there are fundamental spirits that behave on whim and hence are highly unpredictable. Such creatures could not be integrated into our best scientific theory, and hence their nature would not count as physical according to Dowell's definition. The existence of such creatures is inconsistent with physicalism, given Dowell's definition of the view.

What about the *counterintuitive implications* worry? Here Dowell bites the bullet. If physicists of the future end up attributing fundamental mental properties to particles, then the physical facts will involve fundamental mentality: physicalism will entail a form of panpsychism or idealism. How then do we make sense of physicalist's traditional opposition to such views? Dowell thinks that we can avoid this concern by being careful not to conflate two distinct theses: its being highly *improbable* that physicalism will end up being consistent with panpsychism/idealism and its being a priori *incoherent* that physicalism will end up being consistent with panpsychism/idealism. The physicalist can still remain opposed to panpsychism on the grounds that it is vanishingly improbable (according to Dowell) that future physicists will attribute mental properties to particles, and hence the truth of physicalism is highly likely to entail the falsity of panpsychism. It is overkill to insist that the truth of physicalism renders panpsychism not only highly improbable but a priori false.

Dowell's contentment for the definition of physicalism to be consistent with panpsychism has not proved popular. Jessica Wilson offers a physics-based definition of physicalism very similar to Dowell's, although

---

[10] Dowell 2006: 39.

incorporating reference to both present and future physics, but adds the following constraint:

> *NFM Constraint*—The physical facts involve no fundamental mentality.[11]

Given this stipulation, if physicists of the future do end up postulating fundamental mentality, physicalism will thereby be refuted. The NFM Constraint restores physicalism to its position as traditional opponent of idealism, panpsychism, and substance dualism.

Wilson ends up with the following definition of physicalism:

> *The physics-based NFM account*—An entity existing at a world *w* is physical if and only if:
> (i) It is treated, approximately accurately, by current or future (in the limit of inquiry, ideal) versions of fundamental physics at *w*, and
> (ii) It is not fundamentally mental (i.e., does not individually either possess or bestow mentality).

Thus, Wilson's definition is an interesting hybrid of a priori and a posteriori definition: it defers to physics, while retaining the a priori NFM Constraint. Note also that its deferral to physics combines both currentism and futurism.

In what follows I will examine a couple of further constraints on the nature of physics not considered by either Dowell or Wilson, the second of which I will suggest should serve as a constraint on the definition of physicalism. I will then go on to give a general objection to a posteriori definitions of physicalism before finally defending an a priori definition.

2.1.3 Pure Physicalism

One possible constraint not remarked upon by either Dowell or Wilson is the fact that, as discussed in chapter 1, from Galileo onward mathematics has been the language of physics. The maths has changed a great deal, but from Newton to Einstein to the present day there is a deep commonality in the fact that all physical theories are framed in the language of mathematics. In fact, physics is not *entirely* mathematical; it also involves

---

[11] Wilson 2006.

nomic terms, by which I mean terms expressing the concepts of *causation,
natural necessity*, or *laws of nature*. Physics has an entirely *mathematico-
nomic* vocabulary.

This is potentially a serious constraint on physics, answering at least
some of the worries about vagueness and counterintuitive implications.
No matter how weird and whacky fundamental scientific theories of the
future are, arguably no future scientific theory will count as a "physical"
theory if it does not restrict itself to a mathematical and nomic vocabulary. We previously encountered the worry that future physicists might
postulate fundamental mentality or psychic powers. But in so far as
these things have a nature that could not be captured in a mathematical
or nomic terms, it will not be possible to capture them in the language of
physics. Physics as it has existed since the scientific revolution has limited itself to describing the *causal structure* of reality (i.e., that which can
be captured in a mathematico-nomic vocabulary), and we may reasonably take this to be a constitutive constraint on the subject.

What do I mean by talk of what can be "captured" in a mathematical or nomic vocabulary? I do not simply mean what can be *modeled* or
described with mathematical language. In the discussion of transparent
and opaque concepts in chapter 1, I expressed the view that entities, or
at least some of them, have *natures* (or "essences," I will use these words
interchangeably) in the sense that it is a factual matter what the reality
of the entity consists in. The best way to get a grip on this notion, and to
make a case for it, is with reference to examples:

- *The nature/essence of sphericity*: For it to be the case that there is something spherical is for it to be the case that there is something with all
  points on its surface equidistant from its center.
- *The nature/essence of partyhood*: For it to be the case that there is a
  party is for it to be the case that there are people revelling.
- *The nature/essence of water*: For it to be the case that there is water is for
  it be the case that there is something composed of H_2O molecules.[12]

We can call these descriptions "metaphysical analyses" of the entities in
question; descriptions that capture what it is for the entity to be part of
reality. When I say that an entity can be "captured" in a mathematico-

---

[12] Cf. Fine 1994; Rosen 2010. Actually, I don't think this description gives the complete nature
of water, for reasons we will get to in chapter 6, but I will ignore this complexity for the moment.

nomic vocabulary, I mean that a metaphysical analysis of it can be given in that vocabulary; the property of sphericity, or the property of being H_2O, would be examples.

Restricting the physical to that which can be captured in a mathematical and nomic vocabulary is arguably too much of a constraint, as it entails that physicalism is a form of *causal structuralism*: the view that all there is to fundamental reality is causal structure. If physics only describes causal structure and physics gives us a complete description of fundamental reality, it follows that all there is to fundamental reality is causal structure. We shall discuss causal structuralism in detail in chapter 6, but for now suffice to say that this is too austere a metaphysical picture for many philosophers, including many who self-identify as "physicalists."[13] I don't think it's helpful to class all those who find a world of pure causal structure unintelligible as enemies of physicalism. This is especially true if our main interest in defining physicalism is debating the mind–body problem, for many hardened reductionists about consciousness would thereby be counted as "anti-physicalists" simply because they think there's more to reality than pure causal structure.

Nonetheless I do think it's helpful to have a word for the especially pure form of physicalism according to which fundamental reality can be completely captured in the language of physics. Physicalists are philosophers who look to physics for their metaphysics. In the ideal form of this approach, physics has the linguistic resources to completely describe fundamental reality. Let us call physical facts that can be captured in the mathematico-nomic vocabulary of physics "pure physical facts," and physicalism in conjunction with the view that fundamental reality wholly consists of such facts "pure physicalism." It will greatly simplify my arguments against physicalism in the first half of the book to take pure physicalism as my target in the first instance, before going on to show in chapter 6 how those arguments can be applied to physicalism in general.

2.1.4 Naturalism and Value-Laden Causal Explanations

Galileo made our fundamental science mathematical. For the reasons I gave in the last section, I don't think it is helpful to demand that the

---

[13] Lewis (2009) explicitly commits to the falsity of pure physicalism (although not under that label). There is pressure for any Humean to accept that there is a categorical nature to matter that cannot be captured in the mathematico-nomic vocabulary of physical science. We will explore these issues in more detail in chapter 6.

physicalist concur with Galileo in holding that physical reality can be exhaustively described in the language of mathematics. However, there was another crucial way in which Galileo changed the way we do science, and with regards to this second revolutionary change, I do think it reasonable to expect philosophers who call themselves "physicalists" to be on board with it. I am thinking of the Galilean rejection of the teleological explanations of Aristotelian science.

Among other kinds of explanation, Aristotle favored teleological explanations of substances in the natural world. The fact that a plant blossoms could be explained, for Aristotle, in terms of the *telos* of the plant: the set of goals that the plant, by its very nature, aims at. Similarly, the downward movement of the rock could be explained in terms of the telos of the earth the rock is made out of: earth, by its very essence, aims at getting to the center of the universe (which Aristotle believed to be in the center of the Earth).

The notion of a telos is value-laden: what is good for an X is determined by X's telos. The blossoming of the plant—the fulfilling of its telos—constitutes the plant's good. The telos of humanity is *eudaimonia*, which is what constitutes the flourishing human life. Thus, teleological explanations, at least in the Aristotelian system, are value-laden explanations of causal happenings in the natural world.

Teleological explanations are highly controversial, but there is another kind of value-laden explanation that is commonplace: intentional explanations of human agents. All the time we explain the behavior of people in terms of their responsiveness to reasons. When we say that Jimmy refused the job because it would have made him miserable, we are not attributing causal efficacy to a future counterfactual state of affairs: the non-obtaining state of affairs of Jimmy working in a miserable job. Rather, we explain what Jimmy did in terms of his recognition of and responsiveness to a certain reason; Jimmy recognizes that the fact that the job would be miserable counts in favor of his turning it down, and he responds behaviorally in accordance with this reason.

The notion of a reason is constitutively connected to the notion of an ought: what ought to be done is determined by the balance of reasons. Some intentional explanations explain the agent's action in terms of what she *took* to be a reason but was not in fact a reason at all. Consider the following examples from Jonathan Dancy:

> His reason for doing it was that it would increase his pension, but in fact he was quite wrong about that.

The ground on which he acted was that she had lied to him,
though actually she had done nothing of the sort.[14]

In these cases, we get a *motivating* reason—the consideration that the
agent acted for—without a *normative* reason—a consideration that
counted in favor of action. The consideration for which the agent acted
did not in fact obtain and so did not count in favor of the action (as Dancy
points out, motivating reason explanations are not factive). However,
assuming a minimal realism about the normative, there are at least some
cases in which motivating and normative reason go together; in such
cases the agent recognizes and responds to a good reason for action.

It is, I suggest, counter to the spirit of metaphysical naturalism to
take such value-laden explanations to be fundamental. As with the
turn to mathematical theories, the rejection of teleology is a defining
moment in the scientific revolution. While the view that material reality is entirely mathematical is a radical view even among naturalists
and physicalists, the Galilean rejection of value-laden explanations of
the material world has been a widespread and long-standing commitment of naturalistic philosophers. This is particularly clear with respect
to the treatment of intentional explanations of action. Many naturalists deny that intentional explanations may be dispensed with or analyzed into (or superseded by) mechanistic explanations. Nonetheless, it
is assumed that the capacity of an organism to behaviorally respond to
reasons is in some sense constituted by more fundamental goings on,
such that that those more fundamental goings on can be understood
mechanistically.

To make the point vivid, consider the hypothesis that there are angels
with a primitive capacity to respond to reasons. The angel Gabriel sees
that Joan is sick, recognizes that that this gives him a reason to inter-
vene, and miraculously heals her. Gabriel's capacity to respond to reasons
in this manner is not in any sense grounded in some more fundamental
mechanism; he is an incorporeal being with a primitive capacity to act in
response to reasons. Accepting the existence of such a being is, I suggest,
counter to the spirit of naturalism.[15]

---

[14] Dancy 2000: 132.

[15] One might suspect it is the incorporeality of Gabriel that is inconsistent with physicalism.
However, Gabriel is just used for the purpose of vivid illustration; emergentists or libertarians might
suppose that humans have a fundamental faculty to respond to reasons, and this seems to me to be
equally inconsistent with naturalism.

We must distinguish *methodological naturalism*, discussed in chapter 1, from *metaphysical naturalism*, understood as a particular metaphysical theory of reality. Understood in the latter sense, the problems that beset definitions of physicalism reoccur. Just as Dowell and Melnyk offer a posteriori definitions of physicalism, so we might offer an a posteriori definition of naturalism: the natural truths are whatever the natural sciences tell us they are. We will then have to deal with worries about *vagueness, vacuity* and *counterintuitive implications* similar to those previously discussed in the context of defining physicalism. Furthermore, I will presently raise a general difficulty concerning a posteriori definitions of metaphysical positions. Better then to try to come up with an a priori definition of metaphysical naturalism that captures the general view of most philosophers who self-identify as naturalists, so that we can get on with debating whether such philosophers have a view that matches reality.

However we do end up defining naturalism, it ought to involve a commitment to the view that the fundamental causal workings of reality do not involve value. This does not entail that naturalists must deny the reality of value and humans' responsiveness to it, but it does impose on naturalists an obligation to explain the capacity of humans to respond to value in more fundamental terms. This fits with the aspirations of those who call themselves "naturalists" in both meta-ethics and the philosophy of mind. And it chimes with the rejection of value-involving causal explanations in the physical sciences from the scientific revolution onward. This is a metaphysical view suited to those who look to the sciences for their metaphysics, although the definition itself does not defer to the sciences (and thus is an a priori rather than an a posteriori definition).

In line with this, I think it appropriate to consider physicalism as a specific form of metaphysical naturalism. In general the naturalist looks to the natural sciences to find out the fundamental nature of the world. The physicalist looks specifically to our most general and basic science. Emergentism could be thought of as a form of naturalism but one that postulates fundamental laws or entities at higher levels, such as the chemical, biological or mental level. The physicalist need not deny the reality of higher-level laws or entities, but she must deny that they are part of fundamental reality.

Finally we get to my first concern with Dowell and Wilson, which is that neither account rules out value having a role to play in the fundamental causal workings of reality. Dowell's account of a scientific theory places emphasis on regular behavior that is predictable. However, there is no a priori reason why value-involving causal explanations could not yield highly predictable behavior. Suppose that particles have a fundamental telos for constituting living things, a view for which Thomas Nagel has recently expressed sympathy.[16] It could be that the behavior of a particle is highly predictable on the basis of this telos in conjunction with the laws of physics. Nonetheless, contemplating the existence of such laws seems contrary to spirit of physics-based metaphysical enquiry.

Dowell may respond here just as she did to the concern that future physicists will postulate fundamental mentality: physicalists need not reject value-laden causal explanations as inconsistent with their view; they can simply oppose them as highly improbable. However, the rejection of value-laden explanations seems just as plausible a constitutive condition on physics as the four constraints Dowell herself supports. From Galileo onward, physical theories have been framed in the value-neutral language of mathematics and non-normative causation.

It is hard to see how Wilson could evade this concern, as fundamental value seems no less at odds with the spirit of physicalism than fundamental mentality. She claims in defense of her definition that all the entities we intuitively take to be inconsistent with physicalism—free will, intentionality, aesthetic value—are dependent on mentality and hence covered by the NFM Constraint. However, fundamental natural teleology need not be dependent on fundamental mentality and hence is not ruled out by the NFM Constraint.[17] The inconsistency of physicalism with fundamental value-laden laws must be separately stipulated.

This is not a fundamental criticism of either view; a small adjustment could be made to ensure that "the physical," by definition, does not involve value-laden causal goings on. Dowell could incorporate a rejection of value-laden explanations in the definition of science proper as follows:

- *Testability*—The inclusion of a **non-value involving** set of explanatory hypotheses from which empirically testable implications can be derived.

---

[16] Nagel 2012.

[17] For an articulation of the possibility of teleological causation, see Hawthorne and Nolan (2006).

- *Variety*—Confirmation by the obtaining of a number and variety of the test implications of its explanatory hypotheses.
- *Unity*—The provision of a unified explanation of a variety of empirical generalizations. The theory as a whole provides a unified explanation of the empirical generalizations that are among its testable implications.
- *Holistic*—The theory receives additional empirical support by its fit with what is antecedently known and independently observable.

However, I think there is a deeper problem with any physics-based definition of the physical, and it is to this deeper problem I now turn.

2.1.5 Against A Posteriori Definitions of the Physical

One intriguing possibility for avoiding the difficulties associated with Hempel's dilemma, while nonetheless tying physicalism very closely to physics, is given by the "attitudinal" conception of physicalism defended by Alyssa Ney.[18] On this view "physicalism" does not name a metaphysical view of any kind but rather an *attitude* to metaphysical enquiry: a physicalist is someone who, as it were, takes an oath to formulate her ontology solely according to the current posits of physics.[19] When I made my non-negotiable commitment to the Consciousness Constraint in the last chapter, I was in effect taking a different vow: to ensure that my metaphysical view has a place for phenomenal consciousness (in addition to the data of observation and experiment). Even if I came to accept that the ontology postulated by physics happens to suffice for the satisfaction of phenomenal concepts, this fact would not make me an attitudinal physicalist: I would be content with that ontology not simply because it was postulated by physics but because it sufficed for the reality of phenomenal consciousness. To commit to the Consciousness Constraint is to reject attitudinal physicalism.

Therefore, I will continue to think of physicalism as a metaphysical view, as a view about how fundamental reality is independent of how we happen to take it to be. And understood as such, it is prima facie strange to define physicalism with reference to an epistemological

---

[18] Ney 2008b. See also van Fraassen (2002).

[19] Physicalism so understood is analogous to metaphysical naturalism, differing only in that it is focused on physics in particular rather than science in general.

activity of humans, no matter how important we think that activity is to finding out about the world. We are not omniscient beings; we learn about the world through fallible methods, and it is clearly possible that fundamental reality might be different, perhaps in subtle respects, from the picture of reality we get from the best use of those methods. Of particular relevance to our current enquiry, the world might turn out to be different from the picture of reality yielded by ideal physical theory.

My concern is not that physicalism might be false. Few physicalists think that we can be a priori certain of the truth of physicalism, so it is not a problem if the definition of the view is compatible with its falsity (it would be a problem if it weren't). The worry is that ideal physics might get fundamental reality a bit wrong *even if physicalism is true.*

Consider the following example to help focus the issue. Mass is an important property in physics. Suppose there were an epiphenomenal property (i.e., a property with no causal powers) that was always co-located with mass. Call that property "shadow mass." On this supposition, all objects constituted of mass are equally constituted of shadow mass. Physicists are interested in mass because of its dynamical effects: gravitational attraction and resistance to acceleration. But given that shadow mass is epiphenomenal, it's not going to show up even in our best physics. An ideal physics could perfectly predict the behavior of all entities in space and time without ever having need to postulate shadow mass. And if physics never has need to postulate shadow mass, it never will. Nonetheless it could be there. There is no a priori reason to suppose that reality can't outstrip our best theories.

I take it that there could be shadow mass, and we are imagining for the sake of the example that there is. On the physics-based definitions of Dowell and Wilson, shadow mass is not a physical property, as it doesn't show up in current or future physics. Physicalism is therefore false, as there is a non-physical fundamental property. And yet intuitively the existence of shadow mass is not enough to refute physicalism. Philosophers count themselves as physicalists in virtue of their passionate opposition to emergentism, idealism, panpsychism, substance dualism, theism, and belief in demons and poltergeists. Physicalists do not get irked by a property that is no more mental, supernatural, or otherwise extraordinary than mass. Intuitively, in the shadow mass hypothesis, reality is wholly physical; it's just that fallible human physics gets physical reality a tiny bit wrong.

Perhaps some physicalists might feel that the existence of epiphenomenal properties is counter to the spirit of physicalism. But we could easily cook up a different scenario in which reality differs a bit from how ideal physics takes it to be, one not involving epiphenomena. Physicists don't just read off theories from the empirical data; they are guided in theory choice by principles of theoretical virtue. Physicists aim at the simplest, most economical account of the empirical data, and I assume that it is rational for them to do so. But this is not an infallible method: it could turn out that reality itself is not as simple as the simplest interpretation of the empirical data takes it to be, in which case reality will differ from how ideal physics takes it to be. For example, it could turn out that the simplest interpretation of the empirical data postulates four fundamental forces—which entails that ideal physics postulates four fundamental forces—while reality itself involves five fundamental forces.

Wilson predicts something like my concern and offers the following response:

> Some [e.g., Dowell] might respond . . . by accepting that physicalism would be falsified in such a scenario [i.e., one in which fundamental reality deviates from what ideal physics tells us about it]. I prefer rather to put such sceptical possibilities aside, as failing to take the appeal to physics in the proper metaphysical spirit. This appeal is to be understood sufficiently generally that it provides a basis for a contentful, testable appropriately flexible formulation of physicalism. . . . It is not also required that it provide such a basis in the face of every skeptical scenario, whether than involves brains in vats, insuperable cognitive limitations, or entities that are in-principle inaccessible.[20]

Contra Wilson, it doesn't seem to me appropriate to describe the scenario in which ideal physics gets things a bit wrong as "skeptical." A working scientist is entitled to assume that she is not a brain in a vat or the star of the Truman Show, if only because science can't get going unless we rule out such possibilities. But she is not entitled to assume that her science will inevitably get the world exactly right. The possibility that physics may, even in its ideal form, get things a bit wrong is one proper epistemic humility, proper appreciation of human fallibility, requires us to give some credence to.

Given this, Wilson's defense seems to be that her view is usable but either a bit incomplete or a bit wrong. It's a bit incomplete if it has nothing to say about the shadow mass scenario. It's a bit wrong if it rules the truth of physicalism inconsistent with the shadow mass scenario. Why not do better if we can?

Wilson goes on to offer reasons why we may not be able to do better than an a posteriori definition of physicalism: "If the characterization of the foundational entities is to go beyond the bare description of these as existing at relatively low orders of complexity (and as not satisfying the NFM constraint), we have little choice but to appeal to physics . . ."[21] However, in the light of my response to the concern discussed in section 2.1.4, we now have more resources with which to construct an a priori definition of the physical. We can think of metaphysical naturalism as the view that fundamental reality does not involve value-laden causation, and we can think of physicalism as a special form of metaphysical naturalism according to which fundamental reality consists entirely of entities at relatively low levels of complexity.

2.1.6 Definitions of Physicality and Materiality

What about the NFM Constraint? I think at this point we need to confront head on the question of what we're trying to do here. Physicalism isn't some entity out there in the world, which we are trying to discover the essence of. The word "physicalism" is a technical term used by philosophers. In trying to define it, we are either trying to track how philosophers happen to have used this term, which seems to me a project of limited interest, or we are trying to shape a definition that is useful for practitioners of philosophy.

What then are our interests in trying to define physicalism? They seem to me twofold. Firstly, we want to capture a metaphysical view that, inspired by the physical sciences, combines naturalism with opposition to emergence. Secondly, we want to capture one side of the central debates in the mind–body problem: the side that opposes dualism, idealism, and panpsychism; the side that thinks the knowledge argument and the conceivability argument are unsound; the side that thinks we don't need to postulate special entities to explain mentality.

---

[21] Wilson 2006: 73.

Without the NFM Constraint we can only fulfill the first of these needs. Many panpsychists hold that fundamental reality consists only of non-value involving states of affairs at relatively low levels of complexity and yet are on the side of the debate opposite from the one we like to designate with the word "physicalism." In fact, as will become clear in chapter 6 when we encounter Russellian monism, to really capture the two sides of the central debate in the mind–body problem, we need to go beyond Wilson's NFM Constraint and stipulate that physicalism is inconsistent with fundamental mentality and *proto*-mentality (I will offer a definition of proto-mentality in chapter 6).

Therefore, I choose to define physicalism as follows:

> *Physicalism*—Fundamental reality is wholly constituted of facts that (i) concern spatio-temporal entities at relatively low levels of complexity, (ii) do not involve value-laden causation, and (iii) do not involve mentality or proto-mentality.[22]

Accepting this definition of "physicalism" requires us to give a corresponding definition of a "physical fact." In fact, it is useful to have both a broad and a narrow definition:

> *Narrowly physical fact*—F is a narrowly physical fact iff F is a fundamental fact that (i) involves spatio-temporal entities at relatively low levels of complexity, (ii) does not involve value-laden causation, and (iii) does not involve mentality or proto-mentality.

> *Broadly physical facts*—F is a broadly fact iff F is constitutively grounded in a narrowly physical fact(s) (the definition of constitutive grounding is given in the second half of this chapter).[23]

We can further define narrowly physical individuals/properties as the individuals/properties involved in narrowly physical facts, and broadly physical individuals/properties as the individuals/properties involved in broadly physical facts.

---

[22] One could adjust the definition to avoid quantifying over facts. However, I am not concerned in this book with the issue of whether properties or facts are fundamentally real, and so I will continue to quantify over them for the sake of ease of exposition.

[23] The terminology of "broadly" and "narrowly" physical is introduced in Montero (2013).

If we accept my definition of physicalism, then we could not simply define the physical as the subject matter of physics, because the entities to which physics refers may turn out to involve mentality or value-laden causal powers. However, it is useful to have a term for facts concerning individuals and properties at relatively low levels of complexity, regardless of whether they involve mentality or value-laden causation. I will refer to such facts as "material," with the one stipulation that the individuals and properties they concern are mind-independent (so that the existence of matter is by definition inconsistent with idealism).[24] So "matter" is the stuff physics tells us about, and matter is "physical" so long as it doesn't involve fundamental mentality/proto-mentality/value-laden causation.

As in the case of physicality, we can distinguish between a narrow and a broad sense of materiality:

Narrowly material facts—F is a narrowly material state of affairs iff F is a fundamental fact that concerns spatio-temporal entities at relatively low levels of complexity.

Broadly material states of affairs—F is a broadly material fact iff F is constitutively grounded in a narrowly material fact(s).

(Important qualification: In chapter 9 we will consider *priority monism*, the view that all facts are grounded in facts about the universe. As I will explain then, I take priority monism to be anti-emergentist and hence a form of materialism. Forms of priority monism that deny the fundamental reality of [proto]mentality or value-laden causation I take to be forms of physicalism. Hence, at that stage of the book I will extend the definition of materialism and physicalism to allow for priority monist versions. Until that point, for the sake of simplicity, I will work with the micro-level focused definitions just discussed.)

2.2 The Nature of Fundamentality

Now we have a grip on what physicality is, we turn to the question of what it would be for *fundamental reality* to be entirely physical. This calls

[24] I mean "mind-independent" in the sense of not being dependent on being perceived. In a panpsychist world, conscious properties at the micro-level, even though they are mental properties, are "mind-independent" in this sense.

for an account of *fundamentality*, of what it is for certain facts to entirely constitute fundamental reality. There has recently been a return to a very traditional understanding of fundamentality in terms of a distinctively metaphysical notion of *in rem* explanation, or "grounding" as it has become known. In what follows I will explain how I understand grounding, outline a conception of physicalism defined in terms of grounding, and then defend it against alternative accounts of fundamentality.

2.2.1 Constitutive Grounding and the Free Lunch Constraint

I follow the general line in the literature of taking grounding to be a *non-causal explanatory relationship that obtains between facts or other entities*.[25] As with the notion of *essence*, the best way to clarify and make a case for the notion of grounding is with reference to examples. Suppose Rod, Jane and Freddy are dancing, drinking and generally having fun one evening at Jane's. It follows from this supposition that there is a party at Jane's, and moreover that there is a party at Jane's *because* Rod, Jane, and Freddy are dancing, drinking, and so on at Jane's. But the word "because" here does not express a *causal* relationship; the revelling does not causally bring into being the party. Consider a further example. Suppose the rose is scarlet. It follows that the rose is red, and moreover that the rose is red *because* it is scarlet. But the scarlet color of the rose does not *cause* it to be red; the rose does not secrete redness as the liver secretes bile. It seems that in both cases we have a non-causal explanatory relationship, and this we call "grounding."[26]

Is there anything more we can say about the grounding relationship? A striking feature of many grounding relationships is that there is an intuitive sense in which the grounded fact/entity is *nothing over and above* its ground. Focus on the party example. It's not as though there are the people dancing, drinking, and so on, and then there's this extra

[25] There is much debate about what the relata of grounding are. As regards grounding by analysis (see the following discussion), I am attracted to the view (Fine, 2001, 2012) that the logical form of grounding claims are "X because Y," in which X and Y are sentences. On this view, grounding is not, strictly speaking, a relation. However, for ease of exposition I will generally think of grounding by analysis as a relationship between facts. In terms of grounding by subsumption (introduced in chapter 9), I am inclined to think of it as a relation that any kind of worldly entity—individuals, properties, states of affairs—can stand to any other kind of worldly entity. For more discussion of this, and other general issues regarding the nature of grounding, see Trogdon (2013a).

[26] Some key papers on the recent revival of grounding are Fine (2001, 2012), Schaffer (2009a), and Rosen (2010). Proponents of grounding trace the idea back to an older tradition, often citing Aristotle as an influence.

thing—the party—that floats above their heads. There's a very intuitive sense in which the fact that there is a party is *nothing more* than the fact that there are people revelling; a world in which there are people revelling is *already thereby* a world in which there is a party. Or to turn to the color example, it is not as though the rose has two distinct colors: its scarlet color and its red color. There's a very intuitive sense in which the rose's being red is nothing more than its being scarlet; a world in which the rose is scarlet is *already thereby* a world in which the rose is red. I shall call such grounding relationships—in which the grounded fact is nothing over and its ground—"constitutive grounding" relationships.

It is not obvious that all grounding relationships are constitutive grounding relationships. G. E. Moore believed that goodness was a fundamental property in its own right, although one that supervened on the non-normative facts. Perhaps we ought to construe this as a non-constitutive grounding relation, in which the facts about goodness are grounded in but ontologically additional to the non-normative facts. Nonetheless, physicalism is generally understood to be the view that all facts are nothing over and above the physical facts, and hence I will define it in terms of constitutive grounding. (More importantly, as we shall discover in chapter 6, it is only via the postulation of constitutive grounding relationships that physicalism—and indeed Russellian monism, which we will consider in that chapter—has hope of offering a solution to the causal exclusion problem.)

Is there anything more we can say about the "nothing over and above" relationship? I'm inclined to think that we are *obliged* to say something more, and that's because the "nothing over and above" relation has a prima facie paradoxical nature. On the one hand, it seems almost tautological that if x is not *identical* with y, then x is *something over and above* y, from which it would follow that x can be nothing over and above y only if x is identical with y. On the other hand, when we reflect on cases, it is evident that the nothing over and above relation holds between non-identical facts. Recall the party example discussed above: the fact (F1) that there is a party is nothing over and above the fact (F2) that Rod, Jane, and Freddy are revelling. We can see that (F1) and (F2) are distinct facts, as they can obtain independently of each other: if Rod and Freddy leave the party and are replaced by Sally and Solomon, then (F1) will obtain in the absence of (F2).

Thus we have a prima facie paradox: it seems that the nothing over and above relation must be the identity relation, and yet it's clearly not the identity relation. And hence, if we want to indulge in "nothing over and above" talk, we are obliged to clarify the nature of the constitutive grounding relation, in such a way that we have an understanding of how it could possibly be that x is *nothing over and above* y despite the fact that x is *not identical* with y. I call this the "Free Lunch Constraint," after David Armstrong's famous term "ontological free lunch" for an entity that is nothing over and above already postulated facts.[27] In the next section I will outline a conception of constitutive grounding that satisfies this constraint: grounding by analysis.

2.2.2 Grounding by Analysis

In this section I will outline grounding by analysis and suggest that it satisfies the Free Lunch Constraint and thus counts as an adequate form of constitutive grounding. I do not think that grounding by analysis is the *only* form of constitutive grounding; in chapter 9 I will outline an alternative form of constitutive grounding that features large in the metaphysical view I ultimately want to defend. However, grounding by analysis is a widely applicable "all purpose" model of constitutive grounding, and hence in general I will understand physicalism and other views defined in terms of constitutive grounding (e.g., constitutive Russellian monism, which we will be exploring from chapter 6 onward) in terms of it.

In the previous discussion of pure physicalism, I expressed the view that some entities admit of *metaphysical analysis*, in the sense that we can describe *what the reality of the entity consists in*, or, equivalently, *what is essentially required for the entity to be real*. For example, for sphericity to be instantiated, it is essentially required that there is something with all points on its surface equidistant from its center, or for there to be a party, it is essentially required that there are people revelling.

Two things are worth noting about metaphysical analysis. Firstly, the analysis is of the entity itself rather than anything linguistic. Secondly, and perhaps relatedly, the analysis need not be available a priori. We cannot come to know the essential nature of water through a priori reflection.[28]

---

[27] Armstrong 1997: 12.

[28] As we'll find out in chapter 6, I don't think physical science can get us to the essence of water either.

Grounding by analysis involves metaphysical analysis and can be defined as follows:

Fact X is grounded by analysis in fact Y iff:
- X is grounded in Y, and
- Y logically entails what is essentially required for the entities contained in X (including property and kind instances) to be part of reality.

To take a concrete example, the fact (F1) that there is a party is grounded by analysis in the fact (F2) that Rod, Jane, and Freddy are revelling because:

- F1 is grounded in F2, and
- The fact that Rod, Jenny, and Freddy are revelling logically entails what is essentially required for there to be a party (i.e., that there are people revelling).[29]

I submit that grounding by analysis satisfies that Free Lunch Constraint. In cases of grounding by analysis, the grounding fact provides all that is essentially required for the entities contained in the grounded fact to be part of reality; for example, the fact that Rod, Jane, and Freddy are revelling provides all that is essentially required for there to be a party. This gives us a clear sense in which the grounded fact is nothing over and above its ground, even in the absence of identity between the facts or their constituents.

With respect to most of the entities of everyday life, it is a fool's errand to try to specify precisely with necessary and sufficient conditions what their reality consists in. The fact that no philosopher has yet managed to give a counterexample proof definition of what it is for someone to know something, or for one event to be caused by another, has rendered the project of conceptual analysis rather unfashionable. Most of our concepts are rough and ready and highly indeterminate, and the entities they correspond to reflect this. But this does not mean that those entities lack analyses; it just means that what their reality consists in is highly indeterminate, admitting of borderline cases.

---

[29] This account is similar to, and influenced by, that of Dasgupta (2014) and Melnyk (2003), both of which are discussed in what follows.

Indeed, the analysis I have offered of partyhood is, of course, a cheat, as the word "revelling" really just means "whatever is required of people for it to be the case that there to be a party." It is a fun game if you have time on your hands to try to give a counterexample-proof definition of what exactly is required of a situation for it to count as one in which there is revelry. But don't play it if you like games you can win. In some sense we implicitly know what it is for there to be a party; if we didn't, we wouldn't be competent to play the game of judging whether a counterexample resistant definition has been given. But we are unable, or at the very least it is extremely hard, to explicitly articulate the complete definition. This is a curious fact about the human situation that I would like to be able to say more about.

How can grounding by analysis help us make sense of parties, or any other kind of entity, being nothing over and above *fundamental physical facts*? Can we make it plausible that facts about micro-level entities logically entail what is essentially required for a commonsense macro-level entity—a table or a chair, say—to exist?

Given that we are trying to get a grip on the basic definition of physicalism, it would be useful to bracket contentious cases involving consciousness. This is not straightforward, as many common-sense entities have an analysis that involves reference to conscious agents. The reality of parties, of course, requires people, but so too, arguably, does the reality of a tables and chairs. For there to be a table consists in part of its being used as a table or its having been designed to be used as such (something that looks like a table but that appeared by an improbable spontaneous arrangement of particles would not be one).

We can circumnavigate this difficulty by asking for the analysis of a *table-shaped material object*, an entity like a table but defined such that it is not part of its essence that it is treated like a table (so a table-shaped material object could appear by an improbable spontaneous arrangement of particles). What is it for there to be a table-shaped material object? Like most things, a complete analysis is too much to hope for. But I think we can gesture at it, just as we can gesture at what it is for there to be a party.[30]

My thought is that the analysis of table-shaped object can be given in terms of *patterns of penetration resistance among regions of space*. Let us just focus for the sake of simplicity on the synchronic case: on what

---

[30] See Sider (2012: 117–18) for the importance of gesturing at analyses.

it is for there to the table-shaped material object in a particular location L at a particular time. I would say that all that is required is for certain spatial points in L—intuitively, those in a table-shaped region—to resist penetration (to a certain degree). It's hard/impossible to put it precisely, but I think you get what I mean when I say, "If you put a glass on those regions, it won't fall through." And it's plausible that a sufficiently rich description of the micro-level facts located in L would logically entail that each region is, indeed, impenetrable to the required extent. In this way we can, I hope, make sense of the idea that the fundamental physical facts could logically entail what is essentially required for there to be a table-shaped object.[31]

Such analyses in terms of patterns of penetration resistance among regions of space will not do when it comes to natural kinds, the meta-physical analysis of which is tied to the specific nature of their physical components. What it is for something to be water, for example, cannot be analyzed in terms of regions of space resisting penetration; what is important is that those regions of space be filled by a particular kind of physical stuff, namely H_2O molecules. However, it is plausible that chemical or biological kinds are defined in terms of a combination of (A)

---

[31] See Sider (2012: ch. 7, 2013a) and Dorr (2008) for more support for the idea that macroscopic entities might admit of this kind of analysis. See Chalmers (2012) for an extensive defense of a priori connections from micro-level to macro-level truths. Unlike Sider, I am not trying to analyze away unnatural predicates, such as that specifying the pattern of penetration resistance required for there to be a table-shaped object; it is sufficient for the grounding by analysis of tables that such predicates can be analyzed into a (still quite unnatural) relational property that can be instantiated by micro-level entities.

How to extend this analysis to the diachronic case? Some may hold that for the table to move from one place to another requires that its most fundamental parts move with it. But if physicists discovered tomorrow that fundamental particles last for only a very short period of time, that would surely not entail the non-existence of tables. Bracketing again cases involving conscious subjects, it is plausible that the metaphysical analysis of an enduring location-changing macroscopic object can be given in terms of facts concerning patterns of penetration resistance among regions of space. What is it for there to be a table-shaped object O at location L1 at time T1 and for O to be at L2 at T2? It is (very, very roughly) for (A) a table-shaped region at L1 at T1 to resist penetration, for (B) a table-shaped region of the same size at L2 at T2 to resist penetration, and (C) for the gap in space and time between L1 at T1 and L2 at T2 to be bridged by a process involving spatio-temporally contiguous table-shaped regions of space successively resisting penetration. This is, of course, not a precise definition, and I am cheating a bit by quantifying over table-shaped regions, but it serves to gesture at the correct analysis.

In later chapters I will argue that space has a deep nature, which goes beyond what we know about space from physical science. However, given that table-shaped objects can exist in worlds that have a different deep nature to our own, the notion of "spatial regions" employed in the analysis of table-shaped material objects must be given a purely structural analysis. We can think of space as being multiply realized by different deep natures in different possible worlds.

causal role facts and (B) facts about the physical nature of the ultimate constituents involved in the causal role facts (recall that a metaphysical analysis need not be a priori). The latter kind of facts are themselves narrowly physical facts. And the former kind of facts, like facts about table-shaped objects, could in principle be analyzed in terms of facts concerning patterns of penetration resistance among regions of space. In this way—bracketing specific concerns pertaining to the grounding of consciousness—we can make sense of what is essentially required for the reality of chemical and biological kinds being logically entailed by the fundamental physical facts.[32]

2.2.3 A Grounding Account of Physicalism

Now that we have a grip on a usable notion of constitutive grounding, how are we to give a complete definition of physicalism in terms of it? An obvious first attempt would be the following:

> *Strong Physicalism*—Physicalism is the view that all facts that are not narrowly physical facts are constitutively grounded in the narrowly physical facts.[33]

This gives us a clear and straightforward way of understanding the view that fundamental reality is wholly physical: the many and diverse facts that make up reality are all ultimately constitutively grounded in the physical facts. However, Shamik Dasgupta has recently raised problems with Strong Physicalism and urged that it be modified. His concerns arise from his conception of how cases of grounding are to be explained, as we shall now explore.[34]

Suppose that Sarah is currently feeling pain. Strong Physicalism commits the physicalist, as we would expect from a definition of physicalism, to there being some physical fact that grounds the fact that Sarah feels pain. Let us suppose, to continue with the hackneyed and empirically

---

[32] Grounding by analysis is in the first instance a relationship between facts (strictly speaking, I prefer the sentential operator view expressed in footnote 25; for ease of exposition we can think of grounding as a relation between facts). But we can think of the grounding of individuals and token properties as derivative on the grounding by analysis of facts: individual or property token E is grounded in fact F1 just in case E is a constituent of fact F2 and F2 is grounded in F1.

[33] Dasgupta does not use the terminology of "narrowly" and "broadly" physical; he uses the word "physical" to mean what I call "narrowly physical."

[34] Dasgupta 2014.

implausible example favored by philosophers, that that physical fact is the fact that Sarah's c-fibers are firing. Thus we reach the following fact:

> *Pain-Grounding*—The fact that Sarah's c-fibers are firing grounds the fact that Sarah feels pain.

Pain-Grounding is a *grounding fact*, that is, a fact about which facts ground which. In formulating his grounding conception of physicalism, Dasgupta, of course, accepts that the physicalist is obliged to hold that the facts about consciousness are grounded in the physical facts and hence is obliged to accept grounding facts similar to Pain-Grounding. However, he denies Strong Physicalism because he does not think that the physicalist needs to hold that the *grounding facts themselves* (i.e., facts like Pain-Grounding) are wholly grounded in the physical facts.

If Strong Physicalism is true, then Pain-Grounding, like any other fact, is grounded in the physical facts. But Dasgupta argues that Pain-Grounding cannot be satisfactorily explained in terms of the physical alone; rather, it must be explained at least in part in terms of the *nature of pain*. It is truths concerning the nature of pain—that is, what it is for something to feel pain—that explain why it is that the firing of c-fibers grounds pain.[35]

To make this plausible, return to our party example. Just as Pain-Grounding concerns the grounding of pain, so the following fact concerns the grounding of parties:

> *Party-Grounding*: The fact that Rod, Jane, and Freddy are revelling grounds the fact that there is a party.

Why is it the case that the fact that Rod, Jane, and Freddy are revelling grounds the fact that there is a party? Intuitively, this is because of the nature of a party, because of what a party is: a party is the kind of thing

---

[35] Dasgupta also suggests that we might also explain grounding facts in terms of conceptual truths or metaphysical laws but does not outline these proposals in detail. The former alternative would seem to lead to difficulties similar to the difficulties I explore in the following discussion concerning attempts to account for fundamentality in terms of representations of reality rather than in terms of worldly entities. The latter model seems to me not very promising, as metaphysical laws are intuitively the kind of things we want to explain. Dasgupta's discussion starts from a problem Sider (2012) raises with grounding theories of fundamentality, but it would be distracting to explore that here.

that exists when there are people revelling. In this way, the nature of a party "opens itself up" to the possibility of being grounded in specific facts concerning revelling.

On this basis, Dasgupta suggests that Party-Grounding is grounded in the following two facts:

> *Party-Nature*—A party is essentially such that if there are people revelling then there is a party,
>
> *Revelling*—Rod, Jane, and Freddy and revelling.[36]

Note that the entities in the *less fundamental fact*—the fact that there is a party—are doing crucial explanatory work in the explanation of the overall grounding fact. Dasgupta argues, partly through reflection on cases, that we do not get a satisfying explanation of grounding facts from the more fundamental fact alone. For example, it would not be satisfying to answer:

> "Why is it the case that the fact that Rod, Jane, and Freddy are revelling grounds that fact that there is a party?"

with

> "Because Rod, Jane, and Freddy are revelling"

It is only by reference to the nature of parties, to what a party is, that we get a satisfactory explanation of Party-Grounding.[37]

Kit Fine has previously advocated a similar kind of top–down direction in the grounding of grounding facts:

> [W]hat explains the ball's being red or green in virtue of its being red is something about the nature of what it is for the ball to be red or green (and about the nature of disjunction in particular) and not something about the nature of what it is for the ball to

---

[36] Dasgupta's example is in terms of conferences rather than parties, but the substance is the same.

[37] Karen Bennett (2011) and Louis deRosset (2013) try to ground the grounding facts in the fundamental facts. However, I am attracted to grounding by analysis, on account of the fact that it satisfies the Free Lunch Constraint, and grounding by analysis fits the Fine/Dasgupta model (as opposed to the Bennett/deRosset model).

be red. It is the fact to be grounded that "points" to its grounds and not the grounds that point to what they may ground.[38]

It is not that the less fundamental fact "points to" the *specific facts* that ground it; essential truths concerning parties do not involve specific reference to Rod, Jane, and Freddy. Rather the nature of constituents of the less fundamental fact F "point to" some condition that is sufficient for its being the case that F.

Turning to the mental cases, Dasgupta suggests that Pain-Grounding is grounded in the following two facts:

> *Pain-Nature*—Pain is essentially such that for any x, if x's c-fibers are firing, then x feels pain.
>
> *C-Fibers*—Sarah's c-fibers are firing.[39]

Let us call this this view that grounding facts are explained in terms of the nature of constituents of the grounded fact "the grounding via essence" model.[40] There is a tension between the grounding via essence model and Strong Physicalism: Strong Physicalism maintains that all facts are grounded in the fundamental physical facts, while, according to the grounding via essence model, the grounding facts are partly grounded in facts about the nature of higher-level entities and so are not wholly grounded in the fundamental physical facts. Pain-Grounding, for example, is partly grounded in Pain-Nature. The grounding via essence model entails that chains of grounding explanation don't always move in a downward direction. For this reason Dasgupta rejects Strong Physicalism and adopts a definition of physicalism according to which certain facts are "exempt" from needing to be grounded in the physical, even if physicalism is true.

I am not persuaded that the grounding via essence model applies to all cases of grounding. It fits cases of grounding by analysis, in which

---

[38] Fine 2012.

[39] Again, Dasgupta examples are slightly different to mine—involving consciousness rather than pain—but the substance is the same.

[40] Note that I am interpreting the grounding via essence model such that it is the essence of some constituent of the *grounded fact* that explains the overall grounding fact. Certainly in cases of grounding by analysis, constituents of the grounded fact play a crucial role, which is an essential part of the way in which grounding by analysis satisfies the Free Lunch Constraint. Rosen (2010) considers a more permissive model according to which the overall grounding fact is explained either in terms of the grounded fact or in terms of the fact that does the grounding.

the metaphysical analysis of the grounded entities plays a key role in accounting for the overall grounding fact. And as I said previously, I take grounding by analysis to be the most widely applicable "all purpose" model of grounding. However, in chapter 9 I will outline an alternative form of constitutive grounding that works in a quite different way and does not fit the grounding via essence model.[41]

I am also not persuaded that the grounding via essence model, in itself, satisfies the Free Lunch Constraint, because of counterexamples suggested to me by Adam Pautz.[42] We briefly discussed earlier a G. E. Moore style view, according to which goodness is a fundamental property in its own right but that nonetheless the facts about goodness are grounded in the non-normative facts. This would be a case of non-constitutive grounding: the facts about goodness are grounded in, but are ontologically additional to, the non-normative facts. Now the proponent of this view may very well hold that such grounding facts fit the grounding via essence model. They could hold that goodness is essentially such that if an act maximizes well-being, then it is good—even though goodness and well-being are wholly distinct properties—which would explain the fact that facts about well-being ground facts about goodness.

Or, to consider a case closer to our concerns, we might imagine an analogous view of the relationship between the mental and the physical. An emergentist might hold that pain is a fundamental feature of reality but accept Dasgupta's model of the grounding of pain: it is in the nature of pain that if someone has their c-fibers firing, then they feel pain. We can call this view, following Terry Horgan, "Moorean emergentism."[43] We would thus have a case of non-constitutive grounding of the mental in the physical.[44]

The grounding by analysis model seems to me to avoid these concerns. It fits the grounding via essence model but is less permissive. If the fact that action A maximizes well-being logically entails *what it is for goodness to be instantiated*—which can presumably be the case only if all it is for an action to be good is for it to maximize well-being—it follows that the

[41] At least if we understand grounding via essence such that the less fundamental facts explain the overall grounding fact (see footnote 40 for reference to an alternative conception of grounding via essence).

[42] In conversation, but Pautz discusses one such counterexample in Pautz (2015: 34–35).

[43] Horgan 2006.

[44] As I explain in footnote 21 of chapter 6, I am temped by the view these are cases of intelligible causation rather than grounding. If this is so, then the grounding via essence model is badly named.

resulting instantiation of goodness is nothing over and above the fact that A maximizes well-being. Similarly if the fact that Sarah's c-fibers are firing logically entails what it is for pain to be instantiated—which can presumably be the case only if all it is for someone to be in pain is for their c-fibers to be firing—it follows that the resulting instance of pain is nothing over and above the fact that Sarah's c-fibers are firing.

So long as there are cases of grounding that fit the grounding via essence model—and cases of grounding by analysis are such cases—we need a conception of physicalism that allows for them. Strong Physicalism, therefore, must be rejected.

Obviously there must be some limit on which facts physicalism "allows" not to be grounded in the physical; it is inconsistent with physicalism, for example, to deny that the facts about consciousness are grounded in the physical. Dasgupta's view is that physicalism does not require that *facts about natures* are grounded in the physical. This is because, according to Dasgupta, facts about natures are *autonomous* or *not apt to be grounded*; that is, they are not the kind of fact for which the question of grounding arises.

Dasgupta offers an analogy to help clarify and motivate the thesis that facts about natures are autonomous.[45] The analogy is between facts that are not apt for grounding and facts that are not apt for causal explanation. The fact that 2 + 2 = 4 lacks a causal explanation, but not in the sense that the big bang may lack a causal explanation; the fact that 2 + 2 = 4 is not the kind of fact that requires or admits of causal explanation. By analogy there may be a category of fact that neither requires nor admits of grounding explanation, and essential truths are a plausible candidate. According to Dasgupta, the question "What explains the fact that a party is the kind of thing that exists when there are people revelling?" is ill-posed in something like the way "What caused 2 and 2 to equal 4?" is ill-posed. Nobody who knows what a party is should be troubled by this question.

In the light of this, Dasgupta offers the following improvement on Strong Physicalism:

> *Weak Physicalism*—Physicalism is the thesis that all facts that are not narrowly physical facts and that are *substantive* (i.e., apt to be grounded) are constitutively grounded in facts that are either narrowly physical or autonomous.

Even so, the substantive point here would remain, which is that this model does not satisfy the Free Lunch Constraint.

[45] The argument for the autonomy of facts about natures is continued in Dasgupta (2016).

He does not ultimately settle with this definition as, so defined, physicalism is consistent with the existence of God and Platonistic numbers, so long as these things are wholly grounded in autonomous facts about their natures. To avoid this worry, he ends up with the following definition:

> *Moderate Physicalism*—(i) Weak Physicalism is true, and (ii) all autonomous facts help underwrite the kind of grounding explanations required by Weak Physicalism.

Dasgupta's final definition seems to me too strong. The physicalist can surely accept that there are non-physical properties and individuals in other possible worlds, which would seem to require that there are autonomous facts concerning unactualized non-physical natures. And surely such autonomous facts have little to do with grounding explanations in a purely physical world.

We can avoid the worry by stipulating that the physicalist denies that there are any individuals, properties, or events that exist or are instantiated wholly in virtue of autonomous facts, or perhaps more cautiously that the only individuals, properties, or events that exist wholly in virtue of autonomous facts are narrowly physical individuals, properties, or events.[46] We can efficiently ensure this by making the following modification:

> *Reasonably Moderate Physicalism*—Physicalism is the thesis that all facts that are not narrowly physical facts and that are substantive (i.e., apt to be grounded) are wholly constitutively grounded either in narrowly physical facts alone, or in facts that are autonomous *and* in narrowly physical facts.

This modification removes the possibility of a God whose existence is grounded in facts about God's nature, as the existence of such a being would not be grounded in narrowly physical facts.

Thus, the definition of physicalism I will work with throughout this book is as follows:

---

[46] Elsewhere Dasgupta (2016) defends a version of the Principle of Sufficient Reason, which entails that there are entities that exist wholly in virtue of autonomous facts, and takes this to be consistent with physicalism.

Physicalism—All substantive facts that concern entities at greater than atomic levels of complexity and/or that involve mentality/ proto-mentality or value-laden causation are wholly constitutively grounded either in facts that concern entities at atomic or lower levels of complexity and that do not involve mentality/ proto-mentality or value-laden causation, or in such facts in conjunction with autonomous facts.

(As I previously noted, this definition will be slightly modified in chapter 9 to accommodate priority monist forms of physicalism.)

I will not be concerned in this book with *non*-constitutive forms of grounding; hence, from now on I will simply use the word "grounding" with the understanding that it refers to constitutive grounding. And for most of the book I will understand constitutive grounding as grounding by analysis. If we want to adopt a form of constitutive grounding distinct from grounding by analysis, then we must find an alternative way of satisfying the Free Lunch Constraint. I will attempt to do this in chapter 9; until then I will equate constitutive grounding with grounding by analysis, referring to both as simply "grounding."

For the remainder of this chapter I will consider alternative conceptions of physicalism based on alternative accounts of fundamentality.

2.2.4 Alternatives to Grounding Accounts of Fundamentality

2.2.4.1 *Accounts of Fundamentality in Philosophy of Mind*

There has been a strong tradition in philosophy of mind of accounting for the relationship between the mental in the physical in terms of supervenience. There are many technical discussions of how exactly to understand the notion of supervenience, but the rough idea is that for the A-facts to supervene on the B-facts is for the B-facts to *necessarily fix* the A-facts. Plausibly, the economic facts supervene on facts about the actions of economic agents: the facts about people buying, selling, working, making contracts, and so on necessarily determine the facts about the inflation, stock market prices, the value of the Euro, and so on. To a rough approximation: you couldn't have two possible worlds perfectly alike in terms of the behavior of economic agents and yet different in terms of their economic facts.[47]

---

[47] For discussion of the exact nature of supervenience, see Chalmers (1996), Jackson (1998), and Kim (1993b).

However, there is now a broad consensus that we can't define physicalism in terms of a merely modal relationship like supervenience, at least if we want non-(narrowly)physical facts to be *nothing over and above* (narrowly) physical facts.[48] In the "Moorean" examples of non-constitutive grounding via essence relationships previously outlined in section 2.2.3, the grounded facts supervene on facts about their grounds—it is in the essence of pain that if someone's c-fibers are firing, then they are in pain, and facts about essence hold in all possible worlds—and yet ex hypothesi they are ontologically additional to those facts. Mere supervenience does not ensure an ontological free lunch.

Some have suggested that to get physicalism we need to insist that the supervenience relationships between the (narrowly) physical facts and all other facts are *intelligible*, for example, by there being an a priori entailment from the material facts to the mental facts.[49] However, in the previously discussed cases of non-constitutive grounding, there is an intelligible link between from the ground to the grounded, via the essence of constituents of the grounded fact.

While physicalism cannot be completely accounted for in terms of supervenience, it is almost universally agreed that physicalism entails that all facts supervene on the physical facts. If the non-(narrowly)physical facts are nothing over and above the (narrowly) physical facts—if a world in which physical facts obtain is *already thereby* a world in which all other facts obtain—then it's hard to see how the non-physical facts could fail to be necessitated by the physical facts. Hence, I will assume that the supervenience of all facts on the narrowly physical facts is a necessary even though not sufficient condition for physicalism.[50]

Despite the broad consensus that supervenience accounts of physicalism are inadequate, there is little consensus in philosophy of mind as to what should replace it. In what she calls the "powers-based subset strategy," Jessica Wilson explicates the physicalist claim that the mental is nothing over and above the physical in terms of the fact that the causal

---

[48] See, for example, Horgan (1993), Melnyk (2003), and Wilson (2005).

[49] Horgan (1993), Chalmers (1996), and Jackson (1998) hold that supervenience comes with a priori entailment (in a certain qualified sense, which we will discuss in chapter 4), although they never define physicalism in terms of a priori entailment.

[50] Although there is a broad consensus behind the view that physicalism entails that all facts supervene on the physical facts, it is questioned in Montero (2013). Similarly, Leuenberger (2014) and Skiles (2015) argue against the thesis that grounded facts are necessitated by the facts that ground them; deRosset (2010) and Trogdon (2013b) defend this thesis.

powers of the mental are a proper subset of the causal powers of the physical.[51] UK women are a proper subset of UK people, which gives us a clear sense in which the totality of UK women is nothing extra to the totality of UK people. Similarly, if indeed mental causal powers are a subset of physical causal powers, then this gives us a clear sense in which mental causal powers are nothing extra to physical causal powers.

The problem with Wilson's account is that it is too restrictive; it gives us no way of making sense of the nothing over and above relation holding between things that are not powers. While some philosophers take the nature of each and every property to be given by its causal powers—a view I will argue against in chapter 6—most philosophers believe in the existence of *categorical properties*, that is, properties the nature of which cannot be entirely specified in causal terms. Wilson's account offers us no way to make sense of the thesis that higher-level categorical mental properties are nothing over and above lower-level categorical properties. It is also not clear how the view can make sense of the idea that higher-level *objects* are nothing over and above lower-level objects.

Robert Kirk explicates the physicalist conception of the relationship between the mental and the physical in terms of *redescription*: the mental facts are nothing over and above the physical facts iff the mental facts are "pure redescriptions" of the physical facts.[52] And a proposition P is a pure redescription, relative to some base description B, only if the truth of P depends on nothing outside of the reality specified by B. The following would presumably be an example:

Base description: Rod, Jane, and Freddy are revelling.

Pure redescription: There is a party.

Intuitively pure redescriptions are just a different way of carving up the reality specified by the base description.

I feel the intuitions behind Kirk's account. But the problem—put in terms of the example just given—is that the account doesn't tell us anything about *the party itself*. If the redescription <there is a party> is true, then then there is a party out there in reality. What we want is an account of the fact that *the party* is nothing over and above the fact that there

---

[51] Wilson 1999. Sydney Shoemaker (2001, 2007) defends a similar view.
[52] Kirk 2013.

are people revelling. But Kirk tells us nothing about the party itself; he merely tells us something about a proposition that is about the party.

The only way I can think of to extend the account such that it accounts for the nothing over and aboveness of the party itself is to add that the state of affairs of there being a party is grounded in the truth of the proposition <there is a party>. For we could then say that the fact that there is a party is grounded in the truth of <there is a party>, which is a pure redescription of the state of affairs of Rod, Jane, and Freddy revelling (relative to the base description <Rod, Jane, and Freddy are revelling at Jane's>). But this gets things the wrong way round: propositions are representations of reality, and are true in virtue of correctly representing reality. The proposition <there is a party> is true in virtue of there being a party, and not vice versa. And once we accept this, it's hard to see how claims about representations of the party can shed light on the nothing over and aboveness of the party itself (similar difficulties face truthmaker accounts, as discussed in the next section).

Andrew Melnyk accounts for the physicalist conception of the relationship between the physical and the mental in terms of the nature of mental entities rather than mental concepts. The grounding by analysis model I have already outlined is very similar to (and influenced by) Melnyk's view, and I have disagreement with him only in details.

Melnyk's account is focused on the notion of *realization*, which in his 2003 book he defines as follows:

> Token *x realizes* token *y* iff (i) *y* is a token of some functional type, F, such that, necessarily, F is tokened iff there is a token of some other type that meets condition, C; (ii) *x* is a token of some type that in fact meets C; and (iii) the token of F whose existence is logically guaranteed by the holding of condition (ii) *x* is numerically identical with *y*.[53]

Melnyk's use of the words "realization" and "functional" is slightly misleading, as these words are generally used in relation to causally defined properties whereas Melnyk's notion of a "functional type" is tied to the meeting of a condition that may or may not be causal. A functional type is "a higher-order type such that, necessarily, it is tokened iff there is a

---

[53] Melnyk 2003: 21.

token of some or other lower-order type that plays some particular role or—more generally—meets some particular condition."[54]

In this first formulation, it was not explicit that the necessary connection between the token of the functional type and its token realizer obtains in virtue of *an analysis* of the functional type. In the absence of this, it is not clear that Melnyk's realization account of physicalism avoids the troubles faced by supervenience accounts of physicalism. The Moorean emergentist holds that each mental property M is a fundamental property in its own right but one that is tied by its nature to the instantiation of some physical property P, such that M is instantiated iff P is instantiated. On such a view mental properties would be "realized" by physical properties, going by the letter of Melnyk's definition, even though this is not a view according to which mental properties are nothing over and above physical properties.

In a more recent paper Melnyk gives an account of physical realization in which he says that for the mental token to exist "just is" for the realizer to play a certain role; such talk suggests analysis. This more recent account (of what it is for a physical token *p* to physically realize a mental token *m*) is as follows:

1. *M* is a token of a mental state type with a certain *higher-order essence*; that is, *m* is a token of a mental state type *M* such that for a token of *M* to exist *just is* for there to exist a token of some (lower-order) state type such that tokens of that (lower-order) state type play role R_M, the role distinctive of *M*;
2. *p* is a token of physical state type *P* such that, necessarily, given the physical laws, tokens of *P* under physical circumstances *C* play role R_M; and
3. the physical laws hold and physical circumstances *C* obtain.[55]

The resemblance between Melnyk's view and Dasgupta's is striking, which is I think quite revealing about the absence of interaction between philosophy of mind and metaphysics on these foundational questions (N.B. Melnyk's original exposition of this view was published eleven years before Dasgupta's paper was published.)

However, note that this is not a general notion of realization but a notion of *physical* realization. We could of course return to the 2003

---

[54] Ibid., 20.
[55] Melnyk 2014.

definition, altering it to make the connection to analysis explicit. But condition (ii) of the 2003 definition states that the realizer *in fact* meets the condition required for the instantiation of the functional type. This is not sufficient to make the realized token nothing over and above the realizer, for it may be that the realizer token p satisfies the instantiation condition in virtue of contingent facts about p, such as causal powers p has contingently in virtue of the laws of nature (in such a case the mere existence of p will fail to necessitate the realized token). This is why Melnyk ultimately defines physicalism not as the view that all tokens are realized by physical tokens, but as the view that all tokens are *physically realized* by physical tokens (according to a notion of physical realization similar to the one I have just outlined); we are therefore left without an adequate general notion of realization. I have no doubt that this tiny difficulty could be resolved, and I would probably be happy to embrace the resulting theory of fundamentality.

2.2.4.2 Accounts of Fundamentality in Metaphysics

Jonathan Schaffer, although a proponent of grounding, is inclined to think that relationships between levels of reality are mediated by brute metaphysical principles.[56] According to Schaffer, it is perfectly coherent to suppose that fundamental particles never compose composite objects, and without brute composition laws they never would. This kind of view does not satisfy the Free Lunch Constraint: if it takes brute metaphysical laws to get table facts out of particle facts, then the table facts are something over and above the particle facts. Moreover, I think we can do better. Although it is not strictly speaking a contradiction to say "There are people revelling but there is no party," the fact that there are people revelling logically entails all that is essentially required for there to be a party. Similarly, although the particle facts do not logically entail that there are tables, it is plausible that they logically entail all that is required for there to be tables.[57]

One influential alternative to grounding conceptions of fundamentality, developed by John Heil among others, focuses on *truthmaking*.[58] In Heil's view, a great error in twentieth-century metaphysics was the

---

[56] Schaffer forthcoming.

[57] Or at least the particle facts logically entail all that is essentially required for there to be table-shaped objects (see the discussion in section 2.2.2).

[58] Heil 2003, 2012. Cf. Cameron 2008, 2010; Horgan and Potrč 2008.

Quinean orthodoxy of reading off ontology from the entities quantified over in the sentences we take to be true.[59] In this framework, avoiding an ontological commitment to Xs requires avoiding quantifying over Xs, or at least analyzing sentences involving quantification over Xs into sentences not involving quantification over Xs. Contra this Quinean tradition, Heil thinks that ontology should focus, not on the entities quantified over in our truths, but on the entities that serve as *truthmakers* for such truths. By holding, for example, that the truths about tables are made true by states of affairs involving particles being arranged in certain ways—arranged "table-wise" as philosophers tend to say—we avoid an ontological commitment to tables.

I think the truthmaking account faces difficulties similar to those facing Kirk's account of physicalism, which we discussed in the last section. Why should claims about *representations* of tables (e.g., claims about how they are made true) tell us anything about the metaphysical status of tables themselves? Proponents of the truthmaking approach often talk as though non-fundamental entities do not exist, saying, for example, that "in reality" there are no tables, only table-wise arrangements of particles. But if the view is that table-wise arrangements of particles make it true that there are tables, we seem on the face of it to have a contradiction. If it is true that there are tables, then there are tables, which is plainly inconsistent with there being no tables. And if tables do exist, in every sense in which their parts exist, it doesn't make sense to say that we avoid a commitment to them. If they exist, then we're committed to them.[60]

One way to qualify something like the truthmaking approach in order to avoid contradiction is to adopt what we might call "metaphysical elitism." According to the metaphysical elitist, worldly entities are not equals; some are metaphysically privileged, participating in the *metaphysically heavyweight structure of reality*. Theodore Sider is a prominent proponent of this view.[61] On his version, the privileged structure of reality is captured in the "Book of the World": the true and complete description involving only concepts that "carve nature at the joints." All other truths have "metaphysical truth conditions" specified in the metaphysically privileged language (i.e., the language involving only terms that carve

[59] Originating in Quine (1948).
[60] For more problems with truthmaker accounts, see Fine (2012).
[61] Sider 2009, 2012.

nature at the joints) and satisfied by metaphysically privileged truths. Thus contradiction is avoided: it is false in the metaphysically privileged language that "tables exist," but it is true in a common or garden language like English that "tables exist."[62] Tables exist, but they are not part of the *structure of reality*.

Some will be suspicious of the use of primitive notions in metaphysics that don't seem to have any analog outside of metaphysics. As Sider himself confesses:

> I know from bitter experience that philosophers are wary of this primitivism. Many times I have been asked (to murmuring general approval): "What on earth do you *mean* by 'structure'??"[63]

In response to this, Sider tries to make the notion "earn its keep" by demonstrating its theoretical utility. However, Jonathan Schaffer has persuasively argued that Sider fails to do this: Sider invests in a *non-comparative* notion of privilege—concepts either carve nature at the joints or they don't—whereas it is a *comparative* notion of privilege that seems to be needed for the theoretical uses to which Sider wants to put this notion, for example, in accounting for laws of nature and the determinacy of reference.[64]

Moreover, privileged structure seems redundant in meeting the Free Lunch Constraint. Suppose, as Sider does, that the English sentence "There are tables" is true iff there are particles arranged table-wise. When speaking English, we can say all the things we would say if we adopted a grounding account of fundamentality: there are tables, and there are tables *because* there are particles arranged table-wise. And I can see no reason not to take the explanatory relationship expressed by the word "because" in the last sentence to be a grounding relation. One might worry about how a grounding relation could obtain between table facts and particle facts if tables don't really exist. But so long as we are speaking English, tables do "exist."

Even if tables don't "Exist$_H$,"—that is, in the metaphysically heavyweight sense expressed by existence terms that carve nature at the

---

[62] In the metaphysically privileged language, the quantifier carves nature at the joints and hence has a different meaning to the quantifier of an ordinary language like English.

[63] Sider 2012: 9.

[64] Schaffer 2014.

joints—they still "exist$_L$"—that is, in the metaphysically lightweight sense expressed by existence terms in ordinary English. Hence we can talk about essential truths concerning tables, understood as truths concerning what it is for tables to exist$_L$, and secure an ontological free lunch in terms of the grounding by analysis model. Further claims about what is or isn't true in the metaphysically privileged language are surplus to requirements.

I share Sider's intuition that some facts are metaphysically privileged, that the world has a "deep structure." But we can account for this sense of being privileged in terms of constitutive grounding: the privileged facts are those substantive facts that are not constitutively grounded in other substantive facts. This order of explanation seems to me more satisfying that starting off with a primitive notion of "privileged structure" that has no analog outside of metaphysics.[65]

[65] To be honest, I go back and forth on this. In Goff (forthcoming), I try to make it plausible that the notion of privileged existence is present in ordinary language and thought. At any rate, I don't think of the Sider-type view as inconsistent with a grounding conception of fundamentality; it merely adds a further level of analysis.

3

The Knowledge Argument

In the first half of this book I will press a familiar charge: Physicalism is false because it cannot account for consciousness. If physicalism were true, there would be no consciousness. There is consciousness; therefore, physicalism must be false.

There are two much discussed ways of pressing this charge: the *knowledge argument* and the *conceivability argument*. In this short chapter I discuss the first of these arguments. The knowledge argument, as the name suggests, focuses on the relationship between knowledge of physical truths on the one hand and knowledge of truths about conscious experience on the other. It provides a strong case that there is an *epistemic gap* between these two kinds of truth, in the specific sense that one could not deduce any experiential truths about the world from knowledge of the physical truths about the world.

However, physicalism is a metaphysical, not an epistemological thesis. It is the thesis that all of *reality*—including experiential reality—is constitutively grounded in physical reality. It is not the thesis that all *knowledge*—including knowledge of experiential truths—can be derived from knowledge of physical truths. Consequently, although ultimately I think that physicalism can be refuted, I don't think that the knowledge argument, in and of itself, has the resources to do this.

Superficially, my target in chapters 3–5 is not physicalism as such, but what I called in the last chapter *pure physicalism*: physicalism in conjunction with the thesis that fundamental reality can be exhaustively described in the mathematico-causal vocabulary of physics. I do this simply because the arguments of this chapter are more easily stated with pure physicalism rather than physicalism as the target. When in chapter 6 we have got a clear definition of "proto-mentality" and of the distinction between physicalism and Russellian monism, I will show how the case against pure physicalism built in the first half of the book is also a case against physicalism in general.

3.1 Black and White Mary

The knowledge argument against physicalism goes back at least to Leibniz, but its most well-known contemporary formulation is due to Frank Jackson.[1] Jackson's argument is expressed with a story concerning a woman called Mary, who has gone on to become one of the most discussed non-existent characters in philosophy. The story of Mary goes as follows.

Mary is a brilliant neuroscientist who specializes in color vision. In fact, she knows everything the physical sciences can tell us about what goes on in human brains when people see colors. For example, she knows what physical processes arise from the impact of different wavelengths of light on the retina and how these physical processes give rise to various forms of behavior, including verbal reports such as "Ah, what a lovely shade of red." However, for some reason that's never made clear, she's spent her entire life in a black and white room. Despite knowing so much about the science of color vision, she's never actually experienced any colors other than black and white and shades of grey.

At the climax of our story, Mary is liberated from her black and white prison and for the first time sees something red, perhaps a bright red rose lying on the ground outside. According to the proponent of the knowledge argument, when Mary sees red for the first time she learns something new, namely, *what it's like to see red*. Despite her extensive neurophysiological knowledge, Mary's encounter with red gives her a new kind of knowledge. The fact that Mary can learn something new about color experience despite knowing all that the physical sciences can teach about it is supposed to show that there is more going on in color experience than the physical sciences are able to describe. Pure physicalism must, therefore, be false.

[1] Leibniz 1714/2012: section 17; Jackson 1982, 1986. In the same year that Jackson published his argument, Howard Robinson (1982) published a very similar version of the knowledge argument but involving sounds rather than colors.

3.2 Responses to the Knowledge Argument

There are, broadly speaking, three kinds of response to the knowledge argument, each of which concedes a little more to the argument while not quite conceding the falsity of physicalism:

- *The no-compromise response*—Mary learns nothing new when she leaves her black and white room.
- *Non-propositional knowledge responses*—Mary leans something new when she leaves her black and white room, but what she learns is not propositional knowledge but *know-how* or *knowledge by acquaintance*.
- *The new truth/old property response*—Mary learns new propositional truths when she leaves her black and white room, but those truths are simply new ways of thinking about properties and states of affairs she already knew about while in her room.

In what follows I will argue that:

- When fully spelled out, the no compromise response involves some extremely implausible claims and thus is not an adequate response to the knowledge argument.
- While Mary surely does learn some new know-how and some new knowledge by acquaintance when she sees red for the first time, there is strong reason to think that she also gains some new propositional knowledge. Hence, the non-propositional knowledge responses are not adequate responses to the knowledge argument.
- The new truths/old property response constitutes an adequate response to the knowledge argument, at least in the sense that the knowledge argument does not, in itself, have the resources to counter this response.

3.2.1 The No-Compromise Response

In *Consciousness Explained*—commonly referred to by critics as "Consciousness Denied"—Daniel Dennett refuses to accept that there are any grounds for denying that Mary would not be able to work out, from the pure physical facts,[2] what it's like to see red:

---

[2] Dennett does not use my terminology of pure physical facts, but I think it's pretty clear from context that this is what he's talking about.

It is of course true that in any realistic readily imaginable version of the story, Mary would come to learn something, but in any realistic, readily imaginable version she might know a lot, but she would not know everything physical. Simply imagining that Mary knows a lot, and leaving it at that, is not a good way to figure out the implications of her having "all the physical information" any more than imagining she is filthy rich would be a good way to figure out the implications of the hypothesis that she owned everything.[3]

Dennett's response plays on the incomprehensible enormity of knowing *all* the physical truths, down to the tiniest details of each individual field or particle, encouraging the reader to think herself foolish for speculating about what would follow from such an unimaginable cognitive state. However, although this reflects how Jackson sets things up, it's not necessary to hold that Mary knows *all* the physical truths, down to the level of fundamental physics.

Firstly, it is a reasonable assumption that the physical facts relevant to consciousness—at least if physicalism is true—obtain at the neurophysiological level; facts at the level of quarks and electrons will not be relevant. More generally, let us reflect for the moment on what would have to be the case for knowledge of what it's like to see red to be deducible from pure physical truths. Pure physical truths are truths about causal structure: truths that can be specified in the austere mathematico-nomic vocabulary of the physical sciences. Plausibly from such truths about causal structure one can deduce only more truths about causal structure. Thus, if the knowledge of what it's like to see red can be deduced from causal-structural truths, then what it's like to see red must itself be a kind of causal-structural truth. Furthermore, it must be a fairly simple truth concerning the causal role ordinary people associate with red experiences, as ordinary people, including young children, know what it's like to see red.

It seems then that the no-compromise response must be committed to some form of *analytic behaviorism or functionalism*: the view that all truths about mentality, including truths about what it's like to have experiences (assuming there are such truths), concern behavior or behavioral functioning. Truths about pain, for example, are really truths about pain

---

[3] Dennett 1991: 400.

behavior, or inner states that are disposed to instigate pain behavior as the result of bodily damage. If (i) knowledge of what it's like to see red can in principle be deduced from the pure physical facts of the brain and (ii) it is knowledge that is had by children, then it must be knowledge concerning the behavioral-functional role that ordinary people (including children) associate with red experiences. At least, I can see no other way to make sense of the no-compromise response.

Appreciating this reveals that the knowledge argument need not be run with such a far-fetched story as Jackson offers us. If the meaning of "This is what it's like to see red" is given by the behavioral-functional role ordinary people associate with red experiences, then Mary doesn't need to know every last physical detail of what's going on in the brain to come to know that truth. She merely needs to observe, on her black and white television, how people use language relating to red experiences, so that she can get a grip on the causal role ordinary people associate with such experiences. The trouble is that the following is extremely plausible:

> *Extremely Plausible Thesis*—It's not possible to teach a congenitally blind person what it's like to see red by telling them about the causal role ordinary people associate with red experiences.

The Extremely Plausible Thesis entails the falsity of the no-compromise response to the knowledge argument. I am inclined to think that *no* causal structure information can teach you what it's like to see red, but this thesis is more than we need to respond to the no-compromise response.

Perhaps it's wrong to interpret Dennett as someone who thinks there are truths concerning what it's like to see red. Much of what Dennett has written makes it natural to associate him with eliminativism about phenomenal consciousness, and so maybe we should interpret him as thinking that there is nothing that it's like to see red and hence that there's nothing that Mary learns when she sees red. However, I have already said in chapter 1 that I'm taking realism about phenomenal consciousness— as expressed by the Consciousness Constraint outlined in chapter 1—for granted. I do not claim that I know for certain that there is something that it's like to see red. But I take myself to be more justified in believing that there's something that it's like to see red—I contemplate this as I stare at the bright red book cover in front of me—than I am in believing that there is an external world.

3.2.2 Non-Propositional Knowledge Responses

A less extreme response to the knowledge argument concedes that Mary learns something new but holds that this new knowledge falls short of propositional knowledge. This response comes in two forms: *the Ability Hypothesis* and *the Acquaintance Hypothesis*.

According to the Ability Hypothesis, defended by Lawrence Nemirow and David Lewis, the knowledge Mary gains is a distinctive kind of *know-how*: a set of abilities she lacked when she was stuck in the black and white room.[4] These abilities include the capacity to imagine and remember red, and the capacity to categorize external objects as red. Crucially, there is no new information Mary learns when she experiences red: she already knew all the propositional truths about red experiences in her black and white room. Compare: when you learn to wiggle your ears, you don't thereby learn any new facts about the world.

According to the Acquaintance Hypothesis, defended by Earl Conee, Mary gains *knowledge by acquaintance*, where acquaintance "requires the person to be familiar with the known entity in the most direct way that it is possible for a person to be aware of that thing."[5] You could know all sorts of truths about the great Liverpudlian comedian Ken Dodd, but until you've actually met him you don't "know" him, in the sense of knowledge by acquaintance. Similarly, Mary in her black and white room knows all the propositional truths there are to know about red experiences, but she doesn't "know" red experiences, in the sense of knowledge by acquaintance, until she actually has one.[6]

Non-propositional knowledge responses suffer from a problem analogous to the "Frege-Geach problem" for expressivist views in meta-ethics.[7] Talk of what it's like to see red can feature in a truth-preserving argument. For example, when Mary first learns what it's like to see red, she might have had the thought common to many philosophically inclined children that perhaps what it's like for her to see red is different to what

---

[4] Nemirow 1980; Lewis 1988.

[5] Conee 1994: 144.

[6] I am interpreting the Acquaintance Hypothesis as involving a notion of acquaintance such that being acquainted with experiences does not involve gaining any information about the experience. Many anti-physicalists believe in a kind of acquaintance that provides knowledge of the metaphysical nature of experiences, but a commitment to this kind of acquaintance strengthens the knowledge argument rather than constituting a response to it.

[7] Geach 1965.

it's like for others to see red. In entertaining these skeptical wonderings, she might consider the force of the following argument:

1. If this is what it's like for me to see red, then this must be what it's like for every other human being to see red.
2. Geoffrey is a human being.
3. Therefore, this is what it's like for Geoffrey to see red.

Whether or not this argument is sound, it is certainly valid, in the sense that if its premises are true the truth of its conclusion follows. The only way we can make sense of this is by supposing that the phrase "This is what it's like to see red" expresses a truth-evaluable proposition. If so, and if that sentence also expresses what Mary learns when she sees red for the first time, it follows that Mary gains new propositional knowledge rather than mere know-how or knowledge by acquaintance.[8]

There is another less technical concern with the non-propositional knowledge response. It is evident that we can wonder about, or be curious about, what it's like to have certain experiences. I can be desperately curious about what it's like to taste marmite, and my curiosity can be satisfied when I finally taste it, "Ah, so *that's* what it's like." Before leaving her black and white room, Mary might be desperately curious about what it's like to see red and be overjoyed when her curiosity is finally satisfied. We can't make sense of either of these cases without supposing that there is some information about which we are curious, the having of which satisfies the curiosity. But according to the non-propositional knowledge response, there is no information we gain in having experiences.

Of course, one can wonder what it's like to be able to ride a bike, or personally to know Ken Dodd. But plausibly such wonderings do not, strictly speaking, concern the having of an ability or the knowing of a person; rather they concern the *experiences* typically involved in exercising that ability or socializing with the person in question. I want to know what it's like to ride along with the wind in my hair, or to actually feel Ken's wrinkly hand gripping mine. If, as proponents of the non-propositional knowledge response allege, there is no new information one learns when one has an experience for the first time, then we cannot make sense of the having of an experience satisfying a curiosity.

[8] This argument is from Loar (1990/1997).

Both because the sentence "This is what it's like to see red" can be embedded in the premise and conclusion of a truth-preserving argument, and because one can be curious about what it's like to see red, the no-propositional knowledge responses are inadequate.

3.2.3 The New Truth/Old Property Response

Any adequate response to the knowledge argument must concede that Mary gains new propositional knowledge when she sees red for the first time. This is a significant conclusion, for it follows that there is an *epistemic gap* between the pure physical and the experiential:

> *The Epistemic Gap*—For any pure physical truth (i.e., a physical truth specified in a purely mathematico-nomic vocabulary) C and any phenomenal truth (i.e., a truth concerning the instantiation of a conscious state, conceived of in terms of what it's like to have it) Q, it's not the case that C a priori entails Q (i.e., it's not the case that one can rule out <C&~Q> a priori).

From this point onward I will take this epistemic gap between the pure physical and the experiential to have been established. However, as I remarked at the start of this chapter, this significant *epistemological* conclusion is not enough to refute the *metaphysical* doctrine of physicalism. Considering the possibility of the new truth/old property response to the knowledge argument reveals why this is so.

Post-liberation Mary is able to think about red experiences in a way she wasn't able to when she was trapped in the black and white room. She can bring to mind a red experience and think about it in terms of what it's like to have it. You simply can't think about red experiences in this way if you've never before had a red experience.[9] Such concepts, of the kind one deploys when one thinks about a conscious state in terms of

---

[9] It may, of course, be a contingent fact about humans that they get to possess a phenomenal concept of experience E only by having experience E. This does not contradict the crucial point that Mary gains new propositional knowledge, and its implication that Mary gains a new concept. The epistemic gap can be further supported with Martina Nida-Rümelin's (1995, 1998) thought experiment about Marianna. Unlike Mary, Mariana gets to know colors through arbitrarily colored objects. Even though she has phenomenal concepts of various color experiences, she will be unable to work out the relationship between these color experiential states and pure physical states. Hence, even when one has the relevant phenomenal concepts, one cannot move a priori from pure physical truths to experiential truths.

what it's like to have it, have become known as "phenomenal concepts."[10] When Mary sees red for the first time, she gains a phenomenal concept of red experience.

However, from the mere fact that post-liberation Mary has a new concept, a new way of thinking about a feature of reality, it does not follow that the feature of reality she thinks about when she employs that concept is also new. Consider the following analogy. Suppose Mary has a quite ordinary child, Frank. Mary is keen on encouraging Frank to take an interest in astronomy and so points out the Morning Star to him when he is five years old. Frank subsequently thinks a lot about the Morning Star and enjoys spotting in the sky. Now suppose that when he is eight years old Frank hears about Venus and, upon questioning his mother, is told that the Morning Star is Venus. Eight-year-old Frank has picked up a new concept, a new way of thinking something in the world. But he did not thereby learn about some *new thing* in reality: the concept is new, but what it refers to is something Frank already knew about, namely, the Morning Star.

The new truth/old property response to the knowledge argument makes an analogous claim about Mary. Pre-liberation Mary knew about brain state X, the brain state involved in seeing red. Post-liberation she gains a new phenomenal concept, a new way of thinking introspectively about a certain feature of reality. But her new phenomenal concept refers to something she already knew about pre-liberation, namely, brain state X. "What it's like to see red" and "brain state X"—just like "the Morning Star" and "Venus"—refer to one and the same feature of reality.

Thus, Mary gains brand new full-fledged propositional knowledge when she sees red for the first time. But that knowledge consists of a different way of thinking about physical properties she already knew about: she learns that *this thing* (brain state X picked out under a phenomenal concept) is identical with *that thing* (brain state X picked out with a pure physical concept). The knowledge argument refutes physicalism only if Mary learns about new properties when she leaves the room: these would have to be non-physical properties, given that she already knew about all the physical properties in the room. If what Mary

---

[10] The term "phenomenal concept" comes from Chalmers (1996), but use of the term has subsequently become widespread on both sides of the debate.

learns is just new ways of thinking about properties she already knew about, then physicalism is safe.[11]

Some argue that whenever one learns a new way of thinking about something, one thereby discovers a new property of that thing. It might be supposed, for example, that when Frank goes from thinking about the Morning Star as the Morning Star to thinking about the Morning Star as "Venus," he thereby learns a new property of the Morning Star: the property of being the second planet from the Sun. If this is always the case, then in gaining a new concept of red experiences Mary would thereby learn about a new property of red experiences, and the threat to physicalism would return (for, given that Mary didn't know about this property in the black and white room, we are led to the conclusion that that property is non-physical).

However, it is not obviously true that possession of a new concept always comes along with knowledge of a new property. It is possible to possess the concept of Venus without knowing that it's the second planet from the Sun (I had to Google it to make sure). And it's conceptually coherent to suppose that Venus is not a planet at all. We can imagine discovering that in fact Venus is a spaceship created by aliens to spy on us. This hypothesis may not be empirically very plausible but it is not incoherent, from which it follows that it is not a priori that Venus is a planet. It is possible that in picking up the concept "Venus" Frank learns nothing new about the Morning Star; he simply gains a new label for it. Analogously, according to the old fact/new property response, when Mary leaves her room she simply gains a new label for a feature of the world she already knew about.

Some would still want to push the point: there must be *something* new Frank learns about the Morning Star when he learns that it's Venus. There must be *some* positive information associated with the concept "Venus," in terms of which the concept characterizes its referent. Likewise, one might be tempted to think, there must be some positive information associated with the phenomenal concept of red experience, in terms of which the concept characterizes the experience of red. But at this point we can see that the knowledge argument relies on quite substantive claims about the workings of our concepts: that each and every concept picks out its referent by latching onto some property of it, some property

---

[11] This is the most popular response of type-B physicalists, whom we shall discuss in more detail in the next chapter. I will leave referencing them until then.

that is a priori accessible to the concept user. We will be discussing these matters in more detail in the next chapter. For now we can merely note that nothing in the story of black and white Mary justifies this highly contentious meta-semantic assumption.

3.3 Transparency and Opacity: The Moral of the Story

It is useful to think about the knowledge argument in terms of the distinction between transparent concepts and opaque concepts introduced in the first chapter (which is closely connected to the notion of metaphysical analysis discussed in sections 2.1.3 and 2.2.2):

- *Transparent Concept*—A concept C of entity E is transparent just in case C reveals the nature of E (i.e., what it is for E to be part of reality is a priori accessible for someone possessing C, in virtue of possessing C): for example, <sphericity> and <party>.[12]
- *Opaque Concept*—A concept C referring to entity E is opaque just in case C reveals little or nothing of the essence of P, for example, <water> and <gold>.

It is extremely plausible that Mary gains a new concept when she sees red for the first time, a new way of thinking about red experiences. Suppose that that concept is opaque: it reveals nothing about the nature of red experiences. In that case, Mary will gain new propositional knowledge post-liberation, but that new propositional knowledge is no threat to physicalism, as all she has gained is a new way of pointing to something in the world, and what she is pointing at may very well turn out to be one of the physical states she already knew about in the black and white room.

Suppose, in contrast, that Mary's new concept is transparent: it reveals the essence of red experiences. Now pure physicalism looks to be in trouble. For in this case Mary's new knowledge is knowledge of the nature of red experiences, but if pure physicalism is true, she already

---

[12] As I am defining terms, P can be a priori accessible for X even if X is not intelligent enough to access P; intuitively, the thought would be that if X had sufficient rational powers, X would be able to access P. If we are worried about how to define idealized rational powers, we can define transparency as follows: a concept C referring to entity E is transparent just in case there is a possible world in which someone works out the essence of E a priori, in virtue of possessing C, and without any empirical information other than what is required to possess C.

knew the complete nature of red experiences in knowing the pure physical truths, and hence there ought to be nothing more she can learn about their nature.[13]

I will not here dwell too much on this conclusion, as this will be a recurring theme in the first of half of the book: what is really at the heart of the anti-physicalist case is a commitment to *Phenomenal Transparency*, the thesis that phenomenal concepts are transparent. In the context of the knowledge argument, what Mary learns is a worry for the physicalist only if the new phenomenal concept she gains reveals something of the essential nature of color experiences. The problem is that the knowledge argument itself does not have the resources to establish that phenomenal concepts are transparent, without which Mary's knowledge is no threat to physicalism. For this reason the knowledge argument, in and of itself, does not refute physicalism.

---

[13] There are all sorts of further complexities that we will deal with in chapters 4 and 5; for example, I am assuming in this brief argument the falsity of Dual Carving (see section 5.6).

4

The Conceivability Argument

In the last chapter we discussed one of the two "big" arguments against physicalism: the knowledge argument. In this chapter, we discuss the other: the conceivability argument. I will argue against the most well-known contemporary form of the conceivability argument: David Chalmers' two-dimensional conceivability argument. I will then go on to present an alternative conceivability argument: the transparency conceivability argument.

A crucial premise of the transparency conceivability argument is *Phenomenal Transparency*: the thesis that phenomenal concepts are transparent. Thus, the moral of this chapter is similar to the moral of the last chapter: the conceivability argument, just like the threat to physicalism lying behind the knowledge argument, has force only if we can justify Phenomenal Transparency. In the next chapter I will present an argument for Phenomenal Transparency itself. However, once we justify Phenomenal Transparency, a more straightforward anti-physicalist argument presents itself—the transparency argument—which I will also present and defend in the next chapter. Hence, the conceivability argument becomes redundant in the critique of physicalism.

As in the last chapter, my superficial target is *pure physicalism*—physicalism in conjunction with the thesis that fundamental reality can be exhaustively described in the mathematico-nomic vocabulary of physics—rather than physicalism as such. In chapter 6 I show how the case against pure physicalism built in the first half of the book is also a case against physicalism in general.

4.1 Conceivability Arguments

4.1.1 Ghosts and Zombies

A long-standing way of arguing that physicalism cannot account for consciousness is via some kind of conceivability argument. Conceivability arguments involve a *conceivability principle*: a principle asserting some kind of link between conceivability and possibility. The most straightforward form of conceivability principle asserts that anything that is conceivable is possible. Formulated in terms of the conceivable/possible truth of a sentence, we get the following principle:

> *Simple Conceivability Principle (SCP)*—If a sentence is conceivably true, then it's possibly true.

Anti-physicalist conceivability arguments use a conceivability principle to move from something that is plausibly conceivable to a possibility that is plausibly inconsistent with physicalism. The structure of anti-physicalist conceivability arguments, then, is as follows:

1. *Conceivability*—The argument begins with a claim about conceivability.
2. *From conceivability to possibility*—Via the conceivability principle, a move is made from conceivability to possibility.
3. *From possibility to actuality*—It is argued that the possibility that has been demonstrated is inconsistent with the truth of physicalism and hence that physicalism is false.[1]

The inspiration for this style of argument comes from Descartes, who argued in something like the following way:

The Cartesian conceivability argument

Premise 1—I can clearly and distinctly conceive of my mind existing without my brain/body.

Premise 2—Anything I can clearly and distinctly conceive of is possible.

---

[1] I will not be discussing "explanatory gap" arguments (Levine 1983, 2001), as I'm inclined to agree with David Papineau (1998) that identities don't need explaining. Focus on the explanatory gap is a powerful intuitive starting point for the anti-physicalist intuition, but it seems to me to quickly collapse into one of the other arguments.

Conclusion 1—Therefore, it's possible for my mind to exist without my brain/body.

Premise 3—If it's possible for my mind to exist without my brain/body, then my mind cannot be identical with my brain/body.

Conclusion 2—Therefore, my mind is not identical with my brain/body.[2]

One problem with this argument is that even if it is sound, it does not obviously refute physicalism. For the physicalist need not hold that the mind is *identical* with the brain, or that mental states are identical with physical states, so long as facts about the mind and its states are *grounded* in physical facts. The physicalist is obliged to hold that for each mental fact *M* (e.g., the fact that Sarah is feeling anxious), there is some physical fact *P* (e.g., the fact that Sarah is in brain state X), such that *M* is constitutively grounded in *P*. But it is a further step to *identify M* with *P* (e.g., to identify the fact that Sarah is anxious with the fact that she is in brain state X).

Many physicalists hold that mental states are *multiply realizable*; that is, they hold that, for any mental state *M*, there is a wide variety of physical states that could in principle ground *M*. It could be, for example, that the physical state that grounds pain in a human being is very different from the physical state that grounds pain in an octopus. Indeed, although physicalists are obliged to hold that all *actual* mentality is grounded in physical facts, many allow that mentality *could* be grounded in non-physical facts: that there are (non-actual) possible worlds in which there are ghosts and angels whose mental lives are grounded in non-physical goings-on. The physicalist who embraces multiple realization can happily accept the conclusion of the Cartesian conceivability argument.[3]

Hence, in its contemporary guise, most associated with David Chalmers, the conceivability argument against physicalism involves *zombies* (roughly, bodies without minds) rather than *ghosts* (roughly, minds

---

[2] Descartes 1645/1996, sixth meditation.

[3] The conclusion of the Cartesian conceivability argument I have outlined is not that *minds can exist without bodies* but that *my mind is not identical with my body/brain*. A physicalist who is open to the possibility of my consciousness being uploaded onto a computer can accept this conclusion. I don't deny that there may be ways of making the Cartesian argument work (indeed, in Goff 2010a, 2012a, 2014, I defended a form of the Cartesian argument) nor that there are other ways of interpreting Descartes. But it would be distracting to follow these threads in an already complicated chapter.

without bodies).[4] The word "zombie" is a technical term in contemporary philosophy of mind, and so it is important to distinguish "philosophical zombies" from the "zombies" we encounter in Hollywood movies. A philosophical zombie is, by definition, a physical duplicate of a human that lacks consciousness. You stick a knife in a zombie, and it screams and runs away, but it doesn't actually feel pain. When a zombie crosses the road, it looks both ways waiting for the traffic to stop and then carefully crosses the road, and yet it has no visual or auditory experience of the world around it. Zombies behave just like us, because their bodies and brains are physically just like ours, and yet there is nothing that it is like to be a zombie.

As cases of multiple realization show, grounded facts need not necessitate their grounds. However, it is generally accepted that there is a necessitation relation going in the other direction: a grounded fact or entity is necessitated by the obtaining of its ground. If physical fact P constitutively grounds the fact that there is pain, then a world in which P is instantiated is *already thereby* a world in which there is pain. It follows that P could not possibly be instantiated without it being the case that there is pain. We can sum this up with the following broadly accepted principle:

Necessitation: If fact/entity X constitutively grounds Y, then necessarily if X exists/obtains, then Y exists/obtains.[5]

Thus, if all actual facts involving consciousness are grounded in the physical facts, then the physical facts necessitate the reality of consciousness. It follows that there couldn't possibly be a world that is indiscernible from the actual world physically but in which there is no consciousness. But, of course, a world of zombies just is a possible world that is physically identical to the actual world in every respect but in which nothing is conscious. The mere possibility of a zombie world, therefore, is inconsistent with physicalism.

Let us represent the complete pure physical truth about the actual world—that is, the complete physical truth in so far as it can be specified in the mathematico-nomic vocabulary of physics—with the letter "P." "P"

[4] Chalmers 1996, 2009. The term "zombie" with this meaning was coined by Robert Kirk (1974a, 1974b).

[5] The principle is generally put in terms of grounding rather than constitutive grounding. Endorsement of Necessitation is the norm; see, for example, Fine (2012), Rosen (2010), and Trogdon (2013b). There are, however, some who deny it, such as Montero (2013), Leuenberger (2014), and Skiles (2015).

specifies the pure physical properties and relations (i.e., those physical properties and relations that can be captured in the mathematico-nomic vocabulary of physics) of every fundamental physical entity throughout the whole of space and time as well as the fundamental laws governing those entities. We can then form a sentence asserting that the world is a zombie world by conjoining P with the sentence "nothing is conscious." Starting with SCP, we can put the bare bones of the zombie conceivability argument as follows:

The simple zombie conceivability argument

Premise 1—"P and nothing is conscious" is conceivably true.

Premise 2 (SCP)—If a sentence is conceivably true, then it's possibly true.

Conclusion—Therefore, "P and nothing is conscious" is possibly true.

Premise 3—If "P and nothing is conscious" is possibly true, then consciousness is not grounded in the pure physical facts, and hence pure physicalism is false.

Conclusion 2—Therefore, pure physicalism is false.

In fact, we do not need the possibility of a whole world of full-blown zombies to refute physicalism. Pure physicalism is an ambitious thesis: it is the view that *all* properties and states of affairs are grounded in the pure physical facts. If there is even one actually instantiated conscious state that is not grounded in the pure physical facts, pure physicalism is false.

Therefore, taking the letter "Q" to represent an arbitrary conscious state that is actually instantiated, we can give a more general conceivability argument as follows:

The simple conceivability argument

Premise 1—"P and nothing has Q" is conceivably true.

Premise 2 (SCP)—If a sentence is conceivably true, then it's possibly true.

Conclusion 1—Therefore, "P and nothing has Q" is possibly true.

Premise 3—If "P and nothing has Q" is possibly true, then Q is not grounded in the pure physical facts, and hence pure physicalism is false.

Conclusion 2—Therefore, pure physicalism is false.

4.1.2 Clarifying Conceivability

In general, Chalmers thinks of conceivability as *negative ideal conceivability*, and this is also the notion of conceivability I will work with throughout the book. There are two aspects of this notion of conceivability: the "negative" bit and the "ideal" bit.

A sentence S is negatively conceivably true just in case it's not a priori that S is false: we cannot know a priori that "Water is made of ectoplasm" is false, and in this sense its truth is negatively conceivable. In contrast, we can know a priori that the sentence "My Uncle John is a married bachelor" is false, and hence the truth of this sentence is not negatively conceivable.

Chalmers also considers a positive notion of conceivability, which would involve positively imagining a situation in which the relevant sentence is true. In some ways positive conceivability fits better with our intuitive notion of conceivability. When reading Descartes' *Meditations* one finds oneself being persuaded that in some sense one can positively imagine one's mind existing in the absence of one's body.[6] However, positive conceivability is a tricky notion to define as it requires us to get clear on the nature of imagination. In this context, it would be unwise to focus on a notion of imagination closely tied to human mental faculties as we have no reason to think that the limits of human faculties have any bearing on the limits of possibility. Conceivability understood as some kind of rational coherence is more likely to serve as a guide to possibility, and negative conceivability seems to capture this idea.

Similarly, it seems unlikely that the contingent limits of human reason have any bearing on genuine possibility; ideal conceivability abstracts away from such limits. Ideal conceivability contrasts with prima facie conceivability, where sentence S is prima facie (negatively) conceivably true just in case one can't a priori rule out the truth of S upon initial reflection. Square circles are not prima facie conceivable as it is immediately obvious that they can be ruled out a priori. But consider the following sentence: "There are cousins but no siblings." Upon first reflection, one might think that this proposition describes a coherent state of affairs. However, when one thinks about it a bit longer, it is clear that this is a state of affairs that reasoning can rule out, as one's cousin is just the child of one's parent's sibling. Complex mathematical falsehoods (e.g. "$57 \times 89 = 5074$") are

---

[6] I am here using "imagination" in an intuitive sense, in contrast to Descartes' technical sense in which it is tied to sense experience.

more straightforward examples of propositions that can be ruled out a priori but only after a certain amount of reflection. Time travel scenarios in which the past is changed, such as we find in the film *Back to the Future*, may also be incoherent in a subtle way.

A proposition is ideally (negatively) conceivable when *no amount of a priori reasoning* could rule out its truth. The sentence "Water is made of ectoplasm" is thus ideally (negatively) conceivable: I can sit in my armchair thinking about it for as long as I like, but I'm not going to be able to work out that water is not made of ectoplasm.[7] The sentence "There are cousins, but no siblings," and the sentence "$57 \times 89 = 5074$," however, are not ideally negatively conceivable as sufficient reasoning reveals them to be false.

4.2 Type-A and Type-B Physicalism

We can plausibly think of the zombie conceivability argument as the contemporary analog of Descartes' conceivability argument. But between Descartes and David Chalmers there was a fundamental revolution in analytic philosophy, associated with the work of Saul Kripke and Hilary Putnam, which made the defense of any kind of conceivability argument much less straightforward.[8]

Kripke and Putnam persuaded most philosophers in the analytic tradition of the existence of *a posteriori necessities*: sentences that are necessarily true despite not being knowable a priori. One much discussed example is the sentence "Water is H_2O." We cannot find out sitting in the armchair that water is essentially made up of molecules composed of two hydrogen atoms and one oxygen atom: we have to go out and observe the world to discover this. And yet, according to Putnam and Kripke, there is no possible world in which water fails to be H_2O.

Consider the *XYZ world*, a possible world just like ours in every respect except that the colorless, odorless stuff that fills oceans and lakes and falls from the sky has some chemical composition other that H_2O; call it "XYZ." The idea is that XYZ has a different chemical nature to H_2O but has superficially similar macro-level characteristics. Is this a possible world in which

---

[7] If we're worried about how to define idealized rational powers, we can define ideal negative conceivability as follows: proposition P is ideally negatively conceivable just in case there is no possible world in which someone rules out the truth of P a priori, in virtue of understanding P, and without any empirical information other than what is required to understand P.

[8] Kripke 1980; Putnam 1973, 1975.

water is XYZ rather than H_2O? Not according to Kripke and Putnam. Water is the *actual* colorless, odorless stuff that fills oceans and lakes and falls from the sky; it is *this stuff* (I am currently pointing at the water in my glass). But the actual colorless, odorless stuff in oceans and lakes (*this stuff*) is H_2O. The stuff in the XYZ world is merely stuff that superficially resembles water.

If there are a posteriori necessities, then SCP is false. An a posteriori necessity is conceivably false—we cannot know a priori that water is H_2O rather than XYZ—and yet not possibly false—water is H_2O in all possible worlds. Defenders of conceivability arguments must either reject the existence of a posteriori necessities or come up with some more nuanced version of the conceivability principle. In what follows I will go along with the general philosophical consensus that there are a posteriori necessities; this will lead me in later sections to explore the potential of more nuanced conceivability principles.

Before the Kripke–Putnam revolution, physicalists generally took themselves to be obliged to adopt some form of analytic functionalism, that is, the view according to which all mental concepts are functional concepts: concepts that pick out mental states in terms of the *causal role* they play with respect to sensory inputs, behavioral outputs, and other mental states. For the analytic functionalist, to suppose that someone is, say, in pain is just to suppose that she has an inner state that plays the causal role we associate with pain (i.e., causing avoidance behavior as the result of bodily damage, disposing the individual to try to make it stop, etc.). If we can locate in physical reality states that play the relevant causal roles, then we can account for mentality in physical terms.[9]

One can understand why people might have taken this to be the only way to account for mentality once pure physicalism is assumed. If pure physicalism is true, then at a fundamental level our world is pure causal structure (i.e., it can be completely described in a mathematico-nomic vocabulary). But causal structure can ground only more causal structure, and hence a world in which fundamentally there is only causal structure is a world in which there is nothing but causal structure. Therefore, if pure physicalism is true, the only way to analyze mentality in physical terms is to analyze it in causal terms.

---

[9] Ryle 1949; Putnam 1960, 1967; Smart 1959; Lewis 1966, 1970; Armstrong 1968. The situation is slightly more complex than I'm describing. Lewis and Armstrong defended versions of the "identity theory," according to which mental states are identical with physical states. However, they held that the concepts we use to pick out those states are functional. Smart's "topic-neutral" analysis of mental terms can be seen as a kind of halfway house between analytic functionalism and type-B

The problem with this old-school form of physicalism is that it seems to deny the existence *phenomenal concepts*, the distinctive kind of concept we employ when we think about a conscious state in terms of what it's like to have it. We can, of course, think of conscious states *in a third-person way*: I can think of my anxiety in terms of what it's caused by and what it causes me to do. But I can also think of my anxiety *in a first-person way*: in terms of what it's like for me when I have it, in terms of how it feels; and intuitively this is very different kind of concept. The analytic functionalist is obliged either to deny that there are such first-person ways of thinking about our conscious states, or to analyze, somewhat implausibly, first-person ways of thinking about anxiety in terms of third-person ways of thinking about anxiety.

Post the Kripke–Putnam revolution, physicalists slowly started to realize that they had another option. Instead of denying the existence of phenomenal concepts, the physicalist might instead hold that they feature in a posteriori identities with physical or functional concepts. Just as water is a posteriori identical with H_2O, so anxiety is a posteriori identical with brain state X. Just as it is conceivable but not possible that the glass in front of me contains water while at the same time lacking H_2O, so it is conceivable but not possible that the creature in front of me instantiates brain state X without experiencing anxiety. Even if we cannot through armchair reasoning give a priori analyses of facts about consciousness in terms of facts about causal structure, it may nonetheless be possible to empirically identify facts about consciousness with facts about causal structure.[10]

Roughly based around this pre-Kripke–Putnam and post-Kripke–Putnam division of physicalists, Chalmers distinguishes between *type-A physicalists* and *type-B physicalists*.[11] Type-A physicalists take there to be an a priori entailment from the physical truths to all other truths, including the *phenomenal truths* (i.e., the truths about consciousness). That is, if you knew enough about the workings of my body and brain, you could

Physicalism. I will overlook these subtleties as they don't directly bear on the arguments we will be considering.

[10] For examples of this kind of view, see Loar (1990, 2003), Papineau (1993, 2002), Tye (1995), Lycan (1996), Hill (1997), Hill and McLaughlin (1990/1997), Balog (1999, 2012), Block and Stalnaker (1999), Perry (2001), Diaz-Leon (2008, 2010), and Howell (2013). The view is usually credited to Loar, although it was arguably Horgan (1984) who expressed it first. My favorite exposition of the position is Papineau (1998).

[11] Chalmers 2002.

in principle work everything there is to know about my conscious experience; you could work out, for example, whether or not I'm currently feeling anxious. For the type-A physicalist, zombies are inconceivable.

Type-B physicalists, in contrast, deny that the phenomenal truths can be deduced from complete knowledge of the physical truths; no matter how much you knew about my brain states and what they do, you would never be able to deduce whether or not I'm feeling anxious. Despite this epistemological disagreement between type-A and type-B physicalists, as physicalists, both are united in holding that the fact that I am anxious (and, indeed, any other phenomenal fact) is constitutively grounded in the physical facts. And if the phenomenal facts are constitutively grounded in the physical facts, then zombies, whether or not they are conceivable, are impossible.[12]

Since philosophers realized that type-B physicalism was an option, type-A physicalism has not been so popular.[13] Whether or not there is a metaphysical gap between the pure physical facts and the facts about consciousness, it's extremely plausible that there is an *epistemic gap* of the following form:

> *The Epistemic Gap*—For any pure physical truth (i.e., a physical truth specified in a purely mathematico-nomic vocabulary) C and any phenomenal truth (i.e., a truth concerning the instantiation of a conscious state, conceived of in terms of what it's like to have it) Q, it's not the case that C a priori entails Q (i.e., it's not the case that one can rule out <C&~Q> a priori).

In the last chapter I argued that, although the knowledge argument does not refute physicalism, it does provide a fairly conclusive case for this epistemic gap. It follows from the epistemic gap that zombies are conceivable: if the phenomenal truths cannot be deduced from P—the complete pure physical truth about reality—then it will be conceivable that P is true but there is no consciousness. But to demonstrate the falsity of physicalism, we must move from the mere conceivability of zombies

---

[12] Robert Kirk (2008, 2013) defends an interesting hybrid of type-A and type-B physicalism, holding that *the fact that a certain creature is conscious* is entailed by the physical facts but *the content of its consciousness* is not. I argue against Kirk's view in Goff 2007.

[13] Ironically, Frank Jackson (2007) is one of the few remaining proponents of type-A physicalism, having turned his back on poor Mary.

to their genuine possibility. In the next section I will explain David Chalmers' strategy for trying to do this.

4.3 Moving from Conceivability to Possibility

4.3.1 The Two-Dimensional Conceivability Principle

As we have seen, the existence of a posteriori necessities, such as <water is H_2O>, is inconsistent with the Simple Conceivability Principle (SCP). In his full conceivability argument, therefore, Chalmers defends a more nuanced conceivability principle, which I will call the "Two-Dimensional Conceivability Principle," on account of its being defined in terms of his two-dimensional semantic framework, which I will now introduce.[14]

We can think of the two-dimensional framework as a way of modeling what's going on in Kripke's *Naming and Necessity*, the book in which he argues that there are a posteriori necessities. Essentially Kripke's claim is that, with respect to most scientific kinds, we can distinguish between the essence of the kind and its appearance property. For example, the essence of water is *being made up of H_2O molecules*, and the essence of gold is *being made up of atoms of atomic number 79*.[15] The appearance property of a kind, in contrast, is the property we use to pick it out. The appearance property of water is (roughly) *being the colorless, odorless stuff that fills oceans and lakes, and so on*, and the appearance property of gold is *being a heavy, yellowish, metal, and so on*. The two-dimensional framework captures this by distinguishing two aspects of meaning, one of which (the primary intension) corresponds to appearance and one of which (the secondary intension) corresponds to essence.

Chalmers thinks of intensions as functions, from possible worlds to referents in the case of words and from possible worlds to truth-values in the case of sentences.[16] However, we can roughly capture primary and

---

[14] Chalmers 2009.

[15] I am working with Kripke's conception of the essence of water and gold. As we shall see in our discussion of Russellian monism from chapter 6 onward, the concept <H_2O> is arguably opaque. However, I will continue to follow Kripke in talking of the essence of water as *being H_2O* for the sake of simplicity. We can think of "being H_2O" as a placeholder for the essence of water whatever it turns out to be.

[16] Crucially, on Chalmers' framework, the primary intension function can be evaluated a priori, which is why it is appropriate to think of it as capturing an "appearance property." If the property in virtue of which reference is fixed was not a priori accessible to the concept user, then the concept in question would lack a primary intension; such a concept would be "radically opaque," to use the terminology developed in the following discussion.

secondary intensions with descriptions and subordinate sentences, and, for the sake of exegetical ease, this is how I will think of them in what follows.

At the level of words, the primary intension is roughly captured by a description expressing the appearance property of the referent, and the secondary intension is captured by a description of the referent's essence. Thus, the primary intension of "water" is approximated by the description "The colorless, odorless stuff that fills oceans and lakes and falls from the sky, and so on" (from now shortened to "the watery stuff") and the secondary intension of "water" is captured by "H_2O."

For any sentence S, the primary/secondary intension is roughly captured by the subordinate sentence that results when the terms in S are replaced by descriptions that roughly capture the primary/secondary intensions of those terms. Thus, the primary intension of "Water is XYZ" is approximated by the sentence "The watery stuff is XYZ," while the secondary intension of "Water is XYZ" is captured by the sentence "H_2O is XYZ" (Recall that 'XYZ' is used to denote some imaginary chemical property, distinct from H_2O but with superficially similar macro-level characteristics).[17]

The secondary intension of a word reflects the essence of its referent; the secondary intension of a sentence specifies the worlds at which the sentence is true or false. So, for example, knowing that the secondary intension of "Water is XYZ" is captured by the sentence "H_2O is XYZ" makes it apparent that "Water is XYZ" is false at all possible worlds.[18] The primary intension reflects how the meaning of a term or sentence is dependent on facts about the actual world; for example, the term "water" refers to whatever is the watery stuff in the actual world, which is reflected in its primary intension.

Let us begin to move toward the link Chalmers wants to make between conceivability and possibility using this framework. Consider again the XYZ world, the world at which the watery stuff is XYZ. The secondary intension of "Water is XYZ"—that is, "H_2O is XYZ"—is false at the XYZ world. However, the primary intension of "Water is XYZ"—that is, "the watery stuff is XYZ"—is true at the XYZ world. Even though the secondary intension of "Water is XYZ" (and hence the overall sentence) is false at every possible world, there is a genuine possible world at which its primary intension is true.

---

[17] The worlds at which primary intensions are evaluated are *centered*, which captures the role of indexicals in fixing reference. I will overlook this for the sake of simplicity.

[18] I am assuming that the chemical definition of XYZ is inconsistent with the chemical definition of H_2O.

Chalmers takes this to be the case for every sentence that is (ideally negatively) conceivably true: even though it may be false at every possible world, there will be some genuine possible world at which its primary intension is true. Thus, while rejecting SCP on Kripkean grounds, Chalmers takes the following more nuanced principle linking conceivability and possibility to be true:

> 2D-CP—If a sentence is conceivably true, then its primary intension is true at some possible world.

With this principle in place, we can now apply it to the general conceivability argument. Assuming as I am that the pure physical truths do not a priori entail the phenomenal truths, the sentence "P and nothing has Q" is conceivably true. And hence if we accept 2D-CP we can infer that its primary intension is true at some possible world. We have inferred from the conceivability of the pure physical facts without Q to a genuine possibility. But we have yet to show that this possibility is inconsistent with pure physicalism. We have already established that pure physicalism is inconsistent with the possible truth of the whole sentence "P and nothing has Q," but the whole sentence is possibly true only if its secondary intension is possibly true; so far we have only the possible truth of its primary intension.

At this point, Chalmers draws on another aspect of Kripke's work. As previously discussed, Kripke's insight in *Naming and Necessity* is that, with many scientific kinds, the property we use to think about the kind (the appearance property) comes apart from its essence. Water is essentially H_2O, but we think about it in terms of one of its non-essential properties: being the watery stuff. In this sense our thought about water is indirect. However, Kripke goes on to deny that this is the case when it comes to consciousness. We think about a pain in terms of how it feels, but how pain feels is not a non-essential way pain happens to appear to us: pain just is a feeling. In contrast to thought about water, thought about pain is direct. In general, we think about a conscious state in terms of what it's like to be in it; in each case there is no appearance property to be distinguished from the essence of the conscious state. Call this Kripkean thesis that phenomenal concepts do not pick out conscious states in terms of non-essential appearance properties of those states the "Direct Reference Thesis."

The primary intension of a word specifies the appearance property of its referent, the secondary intension its essence. Hence, on the two-dimensional framework, the Direct Reference Thesis comes out as the thesis that terms expressing phenomenal concepts lack distinct primary and secondary intensions. If terms expressing phenomenal concepts lack distinct primary and secondary intensions, then sentences involving those terms lack distinct primary and secondary intensions (unless, of course, they also involve other terms that have distinct primary and secondary intensions). And if the sentence "P and nothing has Q" lacks distinct primary and secondary intensions, and we know its primary intension is possibly true, then we can infer that its secondary intension is possibly true.

We can state Chalmers' version of the conceivability argument as follows:

Two-dimensional conceivability argument

Premise 1—"P and nothing has Q" is conceivably true.

Premise 2 (2D-CP)—If a sentence is conceivably true, then its primary intension is true at some possible world.

Conclusion 1—The primary intension of "P and nothing has Q" is true at some possible world.

Premise 3—It is not the case that "P and nothing has Q" has a primary intension that differs from it secondary intension (Direct Reference Thesis).[19]

Conclusion 2—The secondary intension of "P and nothing has Q" is true at some possible world, and hence physicalism is false.

As Chalmers admits, there is gap in his justification for premise 3. The Direct Reference Thesis has been offered in defense of the claim that terms expressing phenomenal concepts lack distinct primary and secondary intensions. However, the sentence "P and nothing has Q" also contains physical concepts: those used to specify P. We have not yet given reason to think that physical concepts lack distinct primary and secondary intensions, and thus we have incomplete justification for the

---

[19] Chalmers (2009: 153) does argue that that we can run the argument without assuming that phenomenal concepts lack distinct primary and secondary intensions by focusing on the primary

claim that "P and nothing has Q" lacks distinct primary and secondary intensions.

However, if we take this to be an argument against *pure* physicalism, then the problem goes away. This is because pure physical facts can (by definition) be exhaustively captured in a purely mathematico-nomic vocabulary, and causal and formal concepts plausibly do not have distinct primary and secondary intensions. When we think about a causal property in terms of its causal nature, or a mathematical property in terms of its mathematical nature, we pick out the property directly rather than in terms of an accidental appearance property.

This is why matters are simplified if we focus in the first instance on pure physicalism rather than physicalism in general. In the next chapter I will move on to the refutation of physicalism in general, but for the moment I will interpret Chalmers' argument as an attempted refutation of pure physicalism.

4.3.2 Against the Two-Dimensional Conceivability Principle

The two-dimensional framework is built on the assumption that each term has a primary intension that expresses the appearance property of its referent: the property in virtue of which reference is determined and which is a priori accessible to concept user. To put it another way, the concept expressed by each term reveals (i.e., renders a priori accessible) a feature of the referent that uniquely identifies it in the actual world. Where the primary and secondary intensions are identical, the property revealed uniquely identifies the referent in all possible worlds; but, even when primary and secondary intensions are distinct, a substantive feature of the referent is a priori accessible.[20]

---

intensions of phenomenal concepts. However, this move is reliant on the assumption (questioned in the following discussion) that every concept has a primary intension that affords a substantive a priori grasp of some significant property its referent, either its essence or a property that uniquely identifies it in the actual world. Assuming this, even if phenomenal concepts do not afford us a transparent grasp of the essence of consciousness properties themselves, they will afford us a transparent grasp of the properties we use to pick out consciousness properties. Hence, this alternative way of running the argument is also subject to the objection I will make to Chalmers' main argument: that he adopts without sufficient argument a framework that rules out from the get-go the dominant form of type-B physicalism according to which phenomenal concepts are radically opaque.

[20] I am oversimplifying slightly: in fact, Chalmers thinks indexicals are also involved in determining reference, hence the need for the worlds at which primary intensions are evaluated to be centered (cf. footnote 17).

It is crucial to appreciate that the adoption of this framework rules out from the start the dominant form of type-B physicalism. Most type-B physicalists agree with the Kripkean Direct Reference Thesis: that we do not pick out conscious states in terms of non-essential appearance properties. But type-B physicalists also tend to deny that phenomenal concepts reveal essential features of conscious states. The standard type-B line is that phenomenal concepts reveal *no* substantive features of their referents.

We can make this point clearer by returning to the distinction between transparent and opaque concepts discussed in chapters 1 and 3:

- *Transparent Concept*—A concept C referring to entity E is transparent just in case C reveals the nature of E (i.e., what it is for E to be part of reality is a priori accessible for someone possessing C, in virtue of possessing C), for example, <sphericity> and <party>.
- *Opaque Concepts*—A concept C referring to entity E is opaque just in case C reveals little or nothing of the nature of E, for example, <water> and <gold>.

We can further distinguish between two kinds of opaque concept:

- *Mildly Opaque*—A *mildly* opaque concept is one that reveals (under a transparent concept) *significant accidental properties* of its referent, typically those that uniquely identify it in the actual world.[21]
- *Radically Opaque*—A *radically* opaque concept reveals *no significant properties* (neither essential nor accidental) of its referent.[22]

We can think of radically opaque concepts as "blind pointers," allowing the concept user to latch onto an entity without conceiving of it in terms of any of its features.

---

[21] To be more precise, it would be better to say that typically the significant property revealed uniquely identifies the referent in a *centered* possible world considered as actual, where the center picks out the spatio-temporal location of the speaker. This device models the contribution of indexicals in fixing reference. For more on this, see Chalmers (2004).

[22] Putting the word "significant" into the definition of a radically opaque concept adds an element of imprecision. All concepts reveal trivial properties of their referents (e.g., self-identity). And probably all concepts reveal the general ontological category of their referents: in the case of <water> we arguably know a priori that the referent is *uncountable stuff* rather than a countable entity. Perhaps people cleverer than myself might be able to define the notion more precisely, but I don't think it is essential to do this for this category of concept to be useful.

As previously noted, logical or mathematical concepts are plausibly examples of transparent concepts. For example, the essence of sphericity is a priori accessible: if you possess the concept of sphericity and you're clever enough, you can work out that for there to be something spherical is for there to be something with all its surface points equidistant from its center. Most ordinary language natural kind concepts are plausibly examples of mildly opaque concepts: we conceive of water, for example, as the watery stuff. What about radically opaque concepts? How can we possibly think about something without thinking about it in terms of *any* of its properties?

Type-B physicalist David Papineau draws on another aspect of Kripke's work to try to make sense of this: his causal theory of names (it is ironic that both sides of the contemporary mind–body debate draw on Kripke's work).[23] According to the descriptivist theory of names popular before Kripke, names refer in virtue of associated descriptions. It might be supposed, for example, that we pick out Shakespeare as "the person who wrote Romeo and Juliet, Hamlet, Macbeth, and so on." On the descriptivist theory, names are mildly opaque: we conceive of Shakespeare in terms of an accidental property of *being the writer of such and such plays*, which uniquely identifies him in the actual world.

Kripke's objection to such an account is that, for any such description associated with a name, it is coherent to suppose that the individual named does not in fact satisfy that description. It could turn out, as indeed some have claimed, that Shakespeare did not write the plays he is associated with. This makes no sense if "Shakespeare" just means "the person who wrote Romeo and Juliet, Hamlet, Macbeth, and so on." If the descriptivist theory of names is true, then the view that Shakespeare did not write Hamlet would not be historically suspect but incoherent.

After rejecting the descriptivist theory of names on these grounds, Kripke argues for the causal theory of names as its replacement. On this view, there is a complicated causal chain stretching back through history that connects the term "Shakespeare" to Shakespeare himself, and it is in virtue of this causal chain that "Shakespeare" refers to Shakespeare. Plausibly this chain began with Shakespeare's parents baptizing him "William Shakespeare," and the name was then passed on from person to person. The existence of such a chain does not depend on any specific descriptive information being associated with Shakespeare, and hence

---

[23] Papineau 2002, drawing on Kripke (1980).

the term "Shakespeare" does not end up being a priori associated with any substantive property of its referent. Reference is determined "outside of the head" rather than via the understanding of the concept user. On this view, names are radically opaque: it is causal facts that hook up the concept user to Shakespeare, rather than anything the concept user grasps about Shakespeare's accidental or essential nature.

The standard view of contemporary physicalists is that phenomenal concepts are also radically opaque. A phenomenal concept is a certain kind of evolved sub-personal capacity for referring to a certain inner state of the concept user. The reference of this concept is determined either by its evolved function or by certain causal connections between the concept and the inner state it tracks. Reference fixing does not involve the understanding of the concept user, and hence deployment of the concept does not essentially involve any kind of substantive grasp of the referent; we merely have a capacity to "blindly point" at certain inner states. The inner states blindly pointed at turns out to be neurophysiological or functional states of the brain.

Some type-B physicalists are quite explicit about this. Brian McLaughlin says the following:

> Phenomenal concepts are of two sorts: nondescriptive name concepts and type-demonstrative concepts; as such, phenomenal concepts lack any descriptive content. They do not conceptually reveal anything about the essential nature of phenomenal properties: they simply name or demonstrate them.[24]

Type-B physicalist David Papineau goes further in asserting that *all* basic concepts are radically opaque:

> No doubt there are ways of thinking of things that make certain essential properties a priori knowable. But I take such a priori knowledge to derive from (possibly implicit) compositionality in the relevant modes of thinking, and so not to be associated with the most basic ways in which thought makes contact with reality. . . . When it comes to these basic points of contact, I find it hard to take seriously any alternative to the assumption that

---

[24] McLaughlin 2001: 324.

our atomic concepts are related to reality by facts external to our a priori grasp, such as causal or historical facts.... I don't recognise any way in which the mind "captures" something, apart from simply referring to it.[25]

While other type-B physicalists may not be explicit about their commitment to *Radical Phenomenal Opacity*—the thesis that phenomenal concepts are radically opaque—it is often implicit in their favored theories of phenomenal concepts as demonstratives,[26] indexicals,[27] recognitional concepts,[28] or concepts that refer in virtue of facts about teleology or causal connections.[29]

Radical Phenomenal Opacity provides a nice explanation of the conceivable impossibility of zombies. A phenomenal concept of <pain> "blindly points" at brain state X. Pain—the thing referred to by the phenomenal concept <pain>—just is brain state X, and hence pain and brain state X could not possibly exist without each other. But because this is blind pointing, it is not a priori that <pain> denotes brain state X, and so it is conceivable for the concept user that something could have brain state X without feeling pain. Zombies are conceivable but impossible.

Return to the Direct Reference Thesis. Kripke expresses it thus:

> Pain ... is not picked out by one of its accidental properties; rather it is picked out by the property of being pain itself, by its immediate phenomenological quality. Thus pain, unlike heat, is not only rigidly designated by "pain" but the reference of the designator is determined by an essential property of the referent.[30]

What did Kripke mean here? As I read this, Kripke is saying that when we reflect on pain we conceive of it in terms of its essential nature, the view I will defend in chapter 5. But that's not how type-B physicalists interpret Kripke's thesis. In Brian Loar's classic defense of the view that became known as "type-B physicalism," he talks of our "grasping the essence" of

[25] Papineau 2006: 102–6.

[26] Papineau, 1993; Perry 2001.

[27] Tye 1995, chap. 6; Lycan 1996, sect. 3.3.

[28] Loar 1990/1997, 2003; Tye 2000, chap. 2; Carruthers 2000, 2004;, Perry 2001; Levin 2007a, 2007b.

[29] Papineau 2002, 2007.

[30] Kripke 1980: 15–3.

phenomenal qualities. However, on closer examination we find that all he really meant by this is that we don't think about phenomenal qualities in terms of their accidental properties (i.e., that phenomenal concepts are not mildly opaque):

> Phenomenal concepts, as we have seen, do not conceive of their reference via contingent modes of presentation. And so they can be counted as conceiving phenomenal qualities directly. Calling this a grasp of essence seems to me all right, for phenomenal concepts do not conceive their references by way of their accidental properties. . . .[31]

If, as is standard among type-B physicalists,[32] we take the Direct Reference Thesis to be equivalent to the thesis that phenomenal concepts are not mildly opaque, then Radical Phenomenal Opacity entails that thesis: according to Radical Phenomenal Opacity, phenomenal concepts are not mildly opaque but radically opaque. But Radical Phenomenal Opacity also entails the falsity of premise 2 of the two-dimensional conceivability argument, the crucial 2D-CP allowing us to move from conceivability to possibility. If phenomenal concepts lack a primary intension, then "P and nothing has Q" lacks a primary intension, and hence "P and nothing has Q" does not have a primary intension that's true at some possible world, despite its conceivability. 2D-CP has a shot at being true only if each concept has a primary intension, that is, only if there are no radically opaque concepts.

None of this is to say that Radical Phenomenal Opacity is in itself a plausible thesis. It seems to me manifestly an implausible view about phenomenal concepts, and I hope it strikes the reader that way too. Surely when I attend to my pain introspectively, when I think about it in terms of how it feels, I understand *something* about its nature. That's why I care when people feel pain. Judgments of the moral significance of pain are difficult to make sense if pain is just *that thing I know not what*. In knowing how pain feels, I know something of what pain *is*, and it's this understanding that grounds my awareness that pain is, all things being equal, a bad thing. Type-B physicalists often boast that, in contrast to analytic functionalism, their view captures our intuitive view about phenomenal concepts. But the view that

---

[31] Loar 1990/1997: 105.
[32] Loar 1990/1997; Papineau 2002; McLaughlin 2001.

phenomenal concepts are blind pointers seems to me just as revisionary as the view that phenomenal concepts admit of a priori causal analysis.[33]

Nonetheless, if we dislike Radical Phenomenal Opacity, we need to argue against it or at least assert its rejection as an explicit premise in our arguments. It is dialectically inappropriate to just rule it out by the way we set up the discussion, but this is exactly what Chalmers does in framing the argument in terms of the two-dimensional framework. Moreover, Chalmers rules out Radical Phenomenal Opacity by means of a very wide-ranging, highly contentious semantic assumption. The two-dimensional framework assumes that *every single concept* has a primary intension and hence that *no concepts* are radically opaque. It ought to be possible for an anti-physicalist not to stick out her neck so far: rejecting Radical Phenomenal Opacity but remaining agnostic on whether other concepts, such as names perhaps, are radically opaque.

If Chalmers had no argument for adopting a radically-opaque-concept-banning framework, then setting things up in this way would wildly beg the question against the physicalist. As it is, he ultimately defends the two-dimensional framework on the grounds that it allows us to defend a connection between conceivability and possibility, despite the Kripkean exceptions to SCP.[34] However, in the next section I will show how a more straightforward link between conceivability and possibility can be maintained, and one that does not involve the contentious semantic assumption that there are no radically opaque concepts. In the light of this, Chalmers' argument for the adoption of the two-dimensional framework, and consequently the two-dimensional conceivability argument itself, fails.

4.3.3 The Transparency Conceivability Principle

When conceiving of entity e under a transparent concept, one understands (or has a priori access to) the nature of e: one understands what it is for that e to be part of reality (to exist if e is an object, to be instantiated

---

[33] I made this argument in Goff (2011).

[34] Chalmers argues that the link between conceivability and possibility allows us to think of metaphysical modality and epistemic modality as derived for a single set of possible worlds and so to avoid "modal dualism" (see the "Modal Rationalism" section of Chalmers, 2009). The real worry here, I think, is brute modal truths, which the position I end up with at the end of chapter 5 avoids. I explain in more detail in Goff and Papineau (2014) how my position, although perhaps strictly speaking a form of "modal dualism," avoids the brute modal truths Chalmers worries about.

if e is a property, to take place if e is an event, etc.).[35] At the level of whole thoughts, the analog of the transparent concept would be a thought such that in thinking it one understands (or has a priori access to) what it would be for the possible fact being conceived of to obtain.

It is extremely plausible that each property and kind has a unique graspable essence, which distinguishes it from all other properties and kinds. One can understand, for example, what it is for partyhood or sphericity to be instantiated. It is much more contentious whether fundamental particulars have graspable essences. Of course, particular individuals such as electrons fall under kinds, and we can perhaps understand what it is for each of those kinds to be instantiated. But this does not involve understanding what it is for *electron X as opposed to electron Y* to exist. I could presumably know the essences of each of electron x's properties without knowing what it is for *that particular electron*, as opposed to some distinct qualitative duplicate, to exist. This does not seem to be because of cognitive limitations, because of something that, as it were, God understands but we don't. Rather it is natural to suppose that fundamental individuals are *brute one-offs*: the particular existence of some particular fundamental individual is just not the kind of thing that can be understood. It is just a brute fact about electron X that it is the electron it is and not some other electron.[36]

If fundamental individuals are brute one-offs, then the notion of a transparent concept of a fundamental individual gets no purchase. A transparent concept reveals what it is for its referent to exist. If the particular existence of electron X is not the kind of thing that can be understood, then there could not be a transparent concept referring to X itself, as opposed to the properties and kinds that X instantiates. This does not entail that we cannot *refer* specifically to X rather than any other electron; we can perhaps do this by demonstration or in terms of a contingent

[35] Platonists might take properties to be part of reality even if uninstantiated, in which case we could talk about what is required for the property to have concrete reality.

[36] What about non-fundamental individuals? It is plausible that non-fundamental particulars are essentially defined in terms of their origins, and that their origins can be uniquely specified only with respects to the fundamental entities that ground the facts about their origins. If this is correct, then non-fundamental individuals are defined in terms of fundamental individuals, and to this extent their essences will inherit an element of brute-ness from the brute-ness of those fundamental individuals. A term referring to a non-fundamental individual e could be said to be "transparent" in a secondary sense, if it reveals what it is for e to exist in terms of the fundamental entities that define its origin. No doubt the essences of many non-fundamental entities are radically vague, but this is no bar in principle to there being concepts that reveal those radically vague essences.

property that uniquely identifies X in the actual world. But such forms of reference are not transparent.

In so far as we conceive of facts involving individuals that lack unique graspable essences, we do not fully understand what it is for the fact being conceived of to obtain.[37] For example, suppose that Jane lacks a unique graspable essence that distinguishes her from all other women.[38] In this case, one could understand what it is for something to be in pain, but one could not understand what it is for *Jane as opposed to Clare* to be in pain. This is not because there is something about the state of affairs of Jane's being in pain that we can never get at; it is just that Jane, unlike her pain, is not the kind of thing whose concrete existence is comprehensible.

The situation seems, at first, paradoxical: we understand everything that can be understood about the fact that Jane is in pain even though we don't entirely understand the nature of that fact. But the paradox is removed when we again appreciate that there is something about the fact—the particular existence of Jane as opposed to any other woman—that is not the kind of thing that can be understood. Consider the following analogy: we can see everything that can be seen in the room without seeing the electrons in the room, as electrons are not the kind of thing that can be seen. Similarly, we can understand everything that can be understood about a particular fact without understanding everything about that fact, provided there is an aspect of the fact that is not the kind of thing that can be understood.

For these reasons, thoughts involving singular concepts referring to individuals that lack graspable essences can never be entirely transparent. If we want to ensure that we are dealing with fully transparent thoughts, then we can focus on thoughts involving quantification, such as <there are at least two things that feel pain>, rather than thoughts involving singular concepts, such as <Jane feels pain>.[39] We can give sufficient conditions for a transparent thought and a transparent sentence (i.e., a sentence expressing a transparent thought) as follows:

[37] Do things that don't have graspable essences have ungraspable essences? Perhaps one might say that they do in the trivial sense that what it is for fundamental particular X to exist is just *for X to exist*. But I would prefer to stipulate that essences are graspable so that, by definition, we cannot form a transparent concept of something that lacks a graspable essence.

[38] I don't mean to commit to the view that persons lack unique graspable essences. If a person can be defined in terms of her origins, then we can form a concept of a person that is transparent in the secondary sense outlined in footnote 36.

[39] I am assuming that the concepts <existence> and <identity> are transparent.

- A thought is transparent if (i) it involves no singular concepts, and (ii) each of the property or kind denoting concepts involved in it are transparent.
- A sentence is transparent if (i) it involves no singular terms, and (ii) the properties, kinds, and relations expressed by its terms are characterized by those terms under transparent concepts.

Having clarified what transparent thoughts are, I turn now to their relevance to the relationship between conceivability and possibility. When thinking a transparent thought, one thereby grasps what one is conceiving of, metaphysically speaking. In conceiving that there are at least two spheres, I plausibly understand what it is for that fact to obtain. In conceiving that there is water, in contrast, I might not understand what it is for that fact to obtain: finding this out requires empirical knowledge of the chemical composition of the actual watery stuff.[40]

Kripke's examples of a posteriori necessities open up a gap between conceivability and possibility. We can plausibly explain that gap in terms of the opacity of thought. We do not have a priori access to what it is for there to be water that is XYZ: to the nature of the fact that would have to obtain for that thought to be true. As a consequence, we are unable to work out a priori that that fact is impossible and therefore the corresponding thought necessarily false. If we knew that for there to be water that is XYZ is for there to be H_2O that is XYZ, it would be apparent that this fact obtains at no possible world.[41] In other words, it is plausibly our ignorance of the nature of what we are conceiving of that opens up the Kripkean gap between conceivability and possibility.

If the Kripkean gap between conceivability and possibility is to be explained in terms of the opacity of the concepts involved in conceiving, then we need not take there to be such a gap when our thought is wholly transparent. In conceiving that there are two spheres, I understand what it would be for this fact to obtain. The Kripkean examples give me no reason to doubt that in this case I can infer from conceivability to possibility.

We may therefore, consistent with Kripkean a posteriori necessities, propose that conceivability entails possibility *when you grasp what you're*

---

[40] Even then I don't think we'd grasp the essence of water, for reasons we will get to in chapter 6, but I'll overlook this subtlety here.

[41] I am assuming that the chemical definition of XYZ is inconsistent with the chemical definition of H_2O.

conceiving of (metaphysically speaking). We can sum up this view with the following alternative to Chalmers' Two-Dimensional Conceivability Principle:

> *Transparency Conceivability Principle (TCP)*—If a transparent sentence is conceivably true, then it's possibly true.

TCP is logically weaker than 2D-CP. 2D-CP says that *every* conceivably true sentence corresponds to some genuine possibility, while TCP talks only of a certain epistemologically very special group of sentences: the transparent ones. 2D-CP entails TCP—at least on the plausible assumption that a transparent sentence is a sentence with identical primary and secondary intensions—as both principles entail that every transparent sentence will be true at some possible world. TCP does not, however, imply 2D-CP: TCP has nothing to say about non-transparent sentences and hence does not entail the things 2D-CP says about such sentences.

So 2D-CP goes beyond TCP in claiming that every conceivably true sentence corresponds to a genuine possibility. But it is able to say this only because of the implicit ban on radically opaque concepts. If there is a conceivably true sentence S containing a radically opaque concept R, then R does not have a primary intension (as radically opaque concepts do not have primary intensions) and hence (in virtue of containing R) S does not have a complete primary intension, and hence S does not have a primary intension that is true at some possible world. Chalmers' argument for his radically-opaque-concept-banning framework is that it allows us to maintain a link between conceivability and possibility despite Kripkean a posteriori necessities. However, TCP does the same thing without banning radically opaque concepts, and hence Chalmers has failed to provide us with a justification for a general ban on radically opaque terms and concepts.[42]

We have not yet positively argued that there is *any* link between conceivability and possibility. The point here is that the fact that we can link conceivability to possibility via TCP rather than the weaker 2D-CP undermines Chalmers' defense of 2D-CP. Also undermined is the fairly common argument that the Kripke–Putnam examples of a posteriori necessity conclusively demonstrate that *no* inference can be made from conceivability to possibility. 2D-CP and TCP allow for inferences from

---

[42] I make this criticism of Chalmers in Goff and Papineau (2014).

conceivability to possibility but are consistent with the Kripke–Putnam counterexamples to SCP.

Suppose we accept TCP. We could then use it to run the following form of the conceivability argument:

Transparency conceivability argument

Premise 1—"P and nothing has Q" is conceivably true.

Premise 2 (TCP)—If a transparent sentence is conceivably true, then it's possibly true.

Premise 3—"P and nothing has Q" is transparent.

Conclusion—"P and nothing has Q" is possibly true, and so pure physicalism is false.

The transparency conceivability argument is dialectically superior to the two-dimensional conceivability argument in that it doesn't rely on a semantic framework that presupposes that the dominant form of type-B physicalism is false. However, while there is a broad consensus on both sides of the debate that premise 3 of the two-dimensional conceivability argument is true, premise 3 of the transparency conceivability argument is likely to be much more contentious. Let us examine this in more detail, setting to the side for the moment the question of whether TCP itself is true.

Whether or not "P and nothing has Q" is transparent depends on whether or not the concepts involved in "P and nothing has Q" are transparent, which obviously depends on whether pure physical concepts are transparent and on whether phenomenal concepts are transparent. It is extremely plausible that pure physical concepts are transparent. To know the causal role of a causal role property, or the mathematical description of a mathematical property, is to know its essence. The much more controversial question is: are phenomenal concepts transparent?

Chalmers argues that phenomenal concepts are transparent on the basis of the Kripkean Direct Reference Thesis: the thesis that phenomenal concepts are not mildly opaque. If, as the two-dimensional framework assumes, (i) all concepts are either transparent or mildly opaque and (ii) phenomenal concepts are not mildly opaque, then it follows that phenomenal concepts are transparent. Hence, within the two-dimensional framework, the Direct Reference Thesis entails Phenomenal Transparency (the thesis that phenomenal concepts are transparent).

However, we have already seen that there is another option available to the physicalist: she can suppose that phenomenal concepts are radically rather than mildly opaque. The two-dimensional framework rules out this option from the outset, but without a good argument for adopting the two-dimensional framework, this has little dialectical force.

We may also question the implicit assumption hitherto made that the categories of "transparent" and "opaque" are exhaustive. Perhaps some property/kind concepts reveal *something but not everything* of what is for their referents to have instances. It's plausible to think the concept <being a sphere the same mass as the Earth> is an example of such a concept. One aspect of what it is for there to be a sphere the same mass of the Earth—there being something that is spherical—is transparently understood by the concept user; a full understanding of what it is for there to be a sphere the same mass as the Earth can be known only through empirical investigation to find out the mass of the Earth.

Including such concepts, we can make our threefold categorization of concepts fourfold:

Transparent—A concept referring to entity *e* is transparent just in case it reveals the essence of *e*.

Translucent—A concept referring to *e* is translucent just in case it reveals some significant aspect of the essence of *e*, but not the complete essence.

Mildly Opaque—A concept referring to *e* is mildly opaque just in case it is not transparent or translucent, but it transparently reveals (i.e., reveals under transparent concepts) significant accidental properties of *e*, typically properties that uniquely identify *e* in the actual world.[43]

Radically opaque—A concept referring to *e* is radically opaque just in case it does not transparently reveal any significant properties (either essential or accidental) of *e*.

The type-B physicalist can straightforwardly avoid the transparency conceivability argument by defending Radical Phenomenal Opacity, the

---

[43] As noted in footnote 21, it would probably be better to say that the property revealed uniquely identifies the referent in a *centered* possible world considered as actual, where the center picks out the spatio-temporal location of the speaker. This device models the contribution of indexicals in fixing reference. For more on this, see Chalmers (2004).

thesis that phenomenal concepts are radically opaque. Indeed if we have
no a priori insight into the essential nature of phenomenal properties,
then it's hard to see what philosophical grounds we could have for denying that they are pure physical properties.

It is less clear whether the physicalist can avoid the transparency conceivability argument by defending *Phenomenal Translucency*, the thesis
that phenomenal concepts are translucent. If a property denoting concept C is translucent, then there is some aspect of its referent—call it
"A"—that is transparently revealed to the concept user. An aspect of
a property is itself a property. It follows that C affords its possessor a
transparent concept of a property, namely, A. To return to the previous
example of <being a sphere the same mass as the Earth>, the possessor of
this concept transparently understands what it is for there to be a sphere,
and thereby possesses a transparent concept of sphericity.

Thus, if phenomenal concepts are translucent, the anti-physicalist
can try to run the transparency conceivability argument not in terms
of an arbitrary (actually referring) phenomenal concept <Q> itself, but
in terms of the transparent concept involved in <Q>, call it <Q*>. For if
the physical facts ground and hence necessitate all the facts, then they
ground and hence necessitate the fact that Q* is instantiated. Just as the
possibility of P without the instantiation of Q is inconsistent with physicalism, so is the possibility of P without the instantiation of Q*. We can
put this modified version of the transparency conceivability argument as
follows:

The specialized transparency conceivability argument

Premise 1—"P and nothing has Q*" is conceivably true.

Premise 2 (TCP)—If a transparent sentence is conceivably true, then
it's possibly true.

Premise 3—"P and nothing has Q*" is transparent.

Conclusion—"P and nothing has Q*" is possibly true, and so (pure)
physicalism is false.

Whether or not premise 1 of the specialized transparency conceivability
argument is true, however, will depend on the specific manner in which
the translucency of phenomenal concepts is cashed out. It may perhaps
be that phenomenal concepts reveal merely causal structural features

of conscious states—causal structural features that may turn out to be instantiated in the physical structure of human brains and hence implied by P. Physicalist Robert Schroer, for example, has an account of phenomenal concepts according to which they reveal the internal structure of phenomenal qualities, a view I will discuss in more detail in the next chapter. Suppose that Q is identical with some neurophysiological property a priori entailed by P that has structure S as part of its essential nature. Suppose further that S is the aspect of Q revealed by <Q>; that is, "S" and "Q*" are analytically equivalent. It follows that "P and nothing has Q*" is not conceivably true, as P involves a term that is analytically equivalent with Q*. In this case, the first premise of the specialized transparency conceivability argument is false and the argument fails.

For the specialized transparency conceivability argument to work, the aspects of conscious states to which we have a priori access must be ones that are *not* a priori entailed by the physical facts, and hence ones that it is conceivable that zombies lack. Correspondingly, if the physicalist wants to resist the specialized transparency conceivability argument (without denying TCP—we will consider that option later), then she must give an account of phenomenal concepts such that they are either opaque or reveal only properties that are a priori entailed by the physical facts. Defending Phenomenal Translucency with this restriction is not straightforward.

We might usefully distinguish, then, between *Hard Phenomenal Translucency*, according to which phenomenal concepts reveal essential features of phenomenal qualities that are *not* a priori entailed by the physical facts, and *Soft Phenomenal Translucency*, according to which phenomenal concepts only reveal essential features of phenomenal qualities that *are* a priori entailed by the physical facts. If the physicalist can make sense of Soft Phenomenal Translucency, as Schroer tries to do, she can resist the specialized transparency conceivability argument.

In summary, TCP gives us a simple principle linking conceivability and possibility that (i) is not subject to Kripkean counterexample and (ii) does not beg the question against the physicalist by ruling out radically opaque or translucent concepts. 2D-CP is stronger than TCP, and if we can justify its adoption, the refutation of physicalism is more straightforward: it is entailed by the Direct Reference Thesis. However, 2D-CP is supposedly justified by the alleged need to link conceivability to possibility; given that the weaker TCP also links conceivability to possibility, we have no justification for going beyond TCP and adopting 2D-CP.

Framing the conceivability argument in terms of TCP rather than 2D-CP allows the physicalist a means of resistance that doesn't require breaking the link between conceivability and possibility: she can defend Radical Phenomenal Opacity or Soft Phenomenal Translucency. To complete the argument, the anti-physicalist must not only defend TCP itself, but must also defend Phenomenal Transparency or Hard Phenomenal Translucency. In the next chapter I will defend Phenomenal Transparency, before going on to consider the plausibility of TCP itself.

5

Revelation and the Transparency Argument

I don't believe that the considerations of conceivability discussed in the last chapter get to the heart of the anti-physicalist intuition in relation to consciousness. The chain of reasoning from (a) the conceivability of certain scenarios, to (b) the possibility of those scenarios, to (c) the actual falsity of physicalism is a fairly fancy form of argumentation. There is a more immediate and widespread conviction that *that*—a feeling of pain—is not the same thing as *that*—a brain state. If this conviction is rational, rather than simply something we are inclined to believe for psychological reasons, then it must result from an understanding of the nature of those properties. It must be that (a) we grasp what it is for someone to feel pain, and (b) we grasp what it is (at least in general) for someone to instantiate a certain (pure) physical state, and hence (c) it is apparent to our understanding that these are not the same thing.

This is indeed what I think is going on at the heart of the conviction that feelings can't possibly be brain states. In this chapter I will defend this conviction, and articulate it as an argument against physicalism.[1]

As in the last two chapters, my immediate target is *pure physicalism*: physicalism in conjunction with the thesis that fundamental reality can be exhaustively described in the mathematico-nomic vocabulary of physics. In chapter 6 I will extend the argument such that it targets physicalism in its general form.

---

[1] I proposed versions of this argument in Goff (2011, 2015b). See also Nida-Rümelin (2007) and the argument outlined, although not endorsed, in Lewis (1995).

5.1 Revelation and Transparency

I believe that we are in a unique epistemic situation with respect to our conscious states. A normal human being is able to attend to one of the conscious states she is currently instantiating and form a *direct phenomenal concept* of that state: a phenomenal concept of a conscious state the content of which is wholly based on attending to that state.[2] In having a direct phenomenal concept, the token conscious state being attended to is *directly presented* to the concept user, in such a way that (i) the complete nature of the type to which it belongs is apparent to the concept user, and (ii) the concept user knows with certainty (or something close to it) that the token conscious state exists (as a token of that type). To take a concrete example, when I attend to a specific pain and form a direct phenomenal concept of it, that token pain is directly presented to me, and because it is "right there" for me, (i) I know exactly what it is for someone to feel that way, and (ii) I know with certainty (or something close to it) that I myself feel that way. Call this hypothesis "Revelation."[3]

We should note that Revelation is not the same as Phenomenal Transparency, although the former entails a qualified form of the latter. Phenomenal Transparency is the thesis that phenomenal concepts reveal the essence of the states they denote. According to Revelation, when a person attends to a token conscious state under a direct phenomenal concept, the complete nature of the type to which it belongs is apparent to her; this entails *Direct Phenomenal Transparency*: the thesis that direct phenomenal concepts are transparent.

However, the entailment does not go the other way. Revelation involves the nature of the property instance being *directly presented* to one; it is *because* the concept application involves direct presentation that the nature of the property type is known (and the property token known with certainty to exist). But one could hold that phenomenal concepts are transparent, while denying that this is because applications of the concept involve a direct presentation of a token of the referent. Presumably analytic functionalists have this view: conscious states are causal/functional properties, and paradigmatic concepts of them pick them out as

---

[2] The notion of a direct phenomenal concept comes from Chalmers 2003.

[3] The word "revelation" was first used by Mark Johnston (1992) to describe Galen Strawson's (1989) view that the nature of color is wholly given in color experience. The term later became used in the mind-body debate to refer to the view that the nature of experience is given in experience (e.g., Stoljar 2006). Note that I am using it here in a slightly more specific sense.

such.[4] More generally, logical and mathematical concepts are transparent, and yet applications of such concepts do not involve direct presentations of logical and mathematical properties (or at least not obviously so).

Some will be content to take Revelation as a bedrock assumption, a thesis that is evident enough not to need independent support. This does not mean taking the thesis itself to be certain; it just means that it is to be believed, or at least that it is reasonable to believe it, in the absence of strong evidence or argument to the contrary. I would like to invite the reader to spend a few minutes reflecting on the thesis and deciding for herself whether it seems evident enough to be taken as bedrock. William James declared that metaphysics is nothing other than an unusually obstinate attempt to think clearly.[5] I think that's an exaggeration, but it's perhaps underrated in contemporary analytic metaphysics how power-fully persuasive calm and careful meditation on a doctrine can be.[6] I offer the following (clearly biased) presentation of the thesis in question as a focus for the reader's calm and careful meditation:

> Surely, you know exactly what your pain is—what it is for some-one to feel pained in precisely that way—just by attending to pain and thinking about in terms of how it feels. There is noth-ing in any way hidden from you about the reality of how you're feeling; nor is it possible that you're not really feeling that way. And that's because the feeling is "right there" for you, in such a way that its reality cannot be doubted.

Please don't read on until you have taken a few minutes to consider this.

---

[4] Perhaps we should interpret analytic functionalists as not believing in phenomenal concepts. But if there were an analytic functionalist who wholeheartedly accepted the existence of phenom-enal concepts, then it seems that such a person would take phenomenal concepts to be transparent.

[5] James 1890/1981.

[6] I have often found contemporary metaphysicians giving the instantaneous reply "I don't have that intuition," as though consulting one's intuitions took no longer than consulting Google.

If as the result of this meditation you are content to take Revelation as bedrock, premise 3 of the transparency conceivability argument is already secure, so long as we take "Q" to express a direct phenomenal concept (although we are yet to consider the truth of premise 2), because Revelation entails Direct Phenomenal Transparency.

Transparency conceivability argument

Premise 1—"P and nothing has Q" is conceivably true.

Premise 2 (TCP)—If a transparent sentence is conceivably true, then it's possibly true.

Premise 3—"P and nothing has Q" is transparent.[7]

Conclusion—"P and nothing has Q" is possibly true, and so pure physicalism is false.

Readers who don't need to be further persuaded of the truth of Revelation may skip to section 5.6. However, I suspect that many readers did not come out of meditation persuaded of the evident truth of Revelation. Therefore, in what follows I will try to build a case for it in terms of more obvious premises.

5.2 The Case for Revelation

I will begin building the case for Revelation with the observation that introspection reveals substantive knowledge concerning our conscious states. Perhaps the most straightforward examples are within color experience: I can know through introspection that what it's like to see red is similar to what it's like to see orange. It is also plausible that we know through introspective reflection that pain is *ceteris paribus* a bad thing: knowing what it's like to feel pain reveals to me what a terrible thing it is to be in pain. Another plausible example: attention to my conscious states make me aware of their representational properties; for example, attention to my current visual experience of a tomato reveals it to be an experience as of a red, round thing at a certain distance from me. To avoid getting into more controversy than is necessary, I'll focus on

---

[7] As we noted a number of times in the last chapter, it is highly plausible that pure physical concepts are transparent. To conceive of a causal property in terms of its causal nature, or a mathematical property in terms of its mathematical nature, is to conceive of that property in terms of its essential nature.

introspective knowledge of the resemblances between our sensory states, which is perhaps the most uncontentious case of this kind of knowledge.

The mere fact that we have substantive information through introspection does not entail Revelation. The physicalist will no doubt simply postulate a faculty of introspection analogous to our perceptual faculties: a kind of "inner sense" through which we learn about our consciousness. The strange thing about introspection, though, is that it yields beliefs that are as certain as our beliefs concerning mathematics and logic.

Suppose you are at an exhibition of contemporary abstract art, staring at a work entitled "Red and Orange Splodges." The work consists of a huge, homogenous patch of orange paint—which fills most of the left half of your visual field, and a huge homogenous patch of red paint—which fills most of the right half of your visual field. Contrast the following two judgments:

- The *perceptual judgment* that there are in front of you—out there in the mind-independent world—two similar splodges of paint.
- The *introspective judgment*, based on attending to your experience, that you are currently having two similar experiences.

It is very easy to entertain sceptical doubts about the perceptual judgment. Perhaps I am having a particularly vivid—although admittedly rather dull—dream of being in an art gallery looking at splodges of paint, when in fact I am tucked up in bed with my eyes closed. Perhaps I am in the Matrix, being made to experience a virtual art gallery, when in fact the evil computers have long since destroyed real world galleries. The introspective judgment, in contrast, is much harder to doubt. Even supposing I am asleep or in the Matrix, it's hard to dissuade myself of the evident truth that what it's like for me to experience *that*—the left-hand splodge—is similar to what it's like for me to experience *that*—the right-hand splodge.

One might take it that this merely reflects something psychological about human beings, or perhaps about human beings educated in a certain philosophical tradition. On this view we just happen to find it very hard to doubt certain of our introspective judgments, just as we find it hard to believe that we don't have libertarian free will or that the universe has no purpose. However, I want to suggest that this difference between perceptual and introspective judgments reflects not merely a psychological fact about us but a deep and important fact about our epistemic situation. It is the foundational Cartesian truth, and it stands as good today as it did when Descartes first declared it: facts about one's own experience are known with much greater certainty than facts about the external world.[8]

What is certainty? It is important to distinguish between the *psychological fact* that we have a certain amount of confidence in a given proposition, and the *epistemic fact* concerning the degree of confidence one is *entitled* to feel in that proposition (taking into account, for example, one's evidence). A person might be wildly confident that climate change is caused by the moon, while in fact—because she lacks any evidence—that person *ought* to have little or no confidence in that proposition. We can say that such a person has a high degree of "psychological confidence," but that that psychological confidence is not "rational confidence." When a person has a rationally permissible degree of confidence in a given proposition, we can say that that person has "rational confidence" in that proposition.

We are entitled to be much more confident of basic truths of maths and logic than we are of the basic truths of perception. That is, I can achieve much higher levels of rational confidence that $1 + 1 = 2$ than I can that there is a table in front of me. This is reflected in the fact that it is much easier to entertain sceptical doubt about the latter fact than the former. I submit that many of our introspective judgments about our conscious experience are such that the degree of confidence we are entitled to hold in them is roughly the same as the degree of confidence we are entitled to hold in our basic mathematical judgments. I am entitled to be as confident that *this experience*—the experience of the orange splodge—is similar to *that experience*—the experience of the red splodge—as I am that $2 + 2 = 4$. I will express this claim by saying that certain introspective judgments are "super-justified."

I am not saying that either mathematical or introspective beliefs are *rationally certain*, that is, such that we are entitled to believe them with a credence of 1. Perhaps all beliefs are such that we ought to entertain *some* degree of doubt; perhaps the evil demon is making it seem evident that $2 + 2 = 4$, when in fact $2 + 2 = 5$. And, of course, within the class of mathematical beliefs, and within the class of introspective beliefs, the degree of permissible confidence will vary; complex calculations, or introspective judgments made without concentrating, will incur a much greater

---

[8] Augustine (426/1998) had previously defended a similar view. See Ben-Yami (2015) for an interesting discussion of Augustine and Descartes on this issue.

possibility of error. This is all consistent with the claim that in general the degree of confidence it is permissible to have with regards to mathematical and introspective beliefs is much higher than the degree of confidence it is permissible to have with regards to perceptual beliefs, and that the degree of confidence it is permissible to have with regards to introspective and mathematical beliefs is roughly similar. We can call this thesis "Super-Justification."

There will, of course, be philosophers who will deny Super-Justification, insisting that what I have described are merely psychological facts about human beings, or perhaps human beings infected by a Cartesian philosophical heritage. It could be claimed that, although mathematical truths are known with much greater certainty than empirical truths, empirical and introspective truths are in the same epistemic boat. Or it could even be denied that mathematical truths are known with greater certainty than empirical beliefs. Perhaps the fact that we find it much harder to entertain sceptical doubts concerning <2 + 2 = 4> simply reflects a psychological fact about us.

At this point we have reached bedrock. The thesis that introspective truths are super-justified—in the sense that (i) they are known with a degree of rational confidence roughly similar to that of mathematical and logical beliefs, and that (ii) this is significantly higher than the rational confidence associated with perceptual beliefs—seems to me as evident as any philosophical starting point. Super-Justification is the rock upon which I shall build my argument.

Although it seems evident, if it is true that introspective judgments are super-justified, this is a startling fact about the human situation. It is one thing to know with great certainty facts about the Platonic realm—that 2 + 2 = 4 or that square circles are impossible—but how is it that I can know with a similar degree of certainty a fact about the concrete, contingent world—for example, that a particular experience I am currently having resembles some other particular experience I am currently having?

I submit that the best explanation of Super-Justification is Revelation. Return to the experience of red and orange splodges. According to Revelation, when I attend to the token conscious state representing the red and orange splodges, that state is directly presented to me in such a way that (i) the complete nature of the type of which it is a token is apparent to me, and (ii) its reality (as a thing with that nature) is known to me with something close to rational certainty. In grasping the nature of each aspect of the experience—the aspect representing the red splodge and the aspect representing the orange splodge—I grasp that they have similar natures. And given that I have great rational confidence in the reality of each aspect, each having the nature that is directly presented to me, I thereby know with an extremely high degree of rational confidence that they resemble. Revelation explains Super-Justification.[9]

This explanation might seem somewhat ad hoc and unilluminating. Of course, if you postulate a relationship to consciousness such that "its reality is known with something close to certainty," it entails that the reality of consciousness cannot be rationally doubted—just as the postulation of a "dormitive power" in sleeping pills entails that they put you to sleep—but one might suspect that no genuine explanation has been given here. However, the crucial point is that Revelation isn't a philosopher's invention that is cooked up to try to explain Super-Justification; if it were, then the proposed explanation would indeed be rather unsatisfying. I submit that Revelation captures how our relationship with consciousness *seems to be* upon reflection. It does seem that my pain is directly presented to me in such a way that its nature is known and its reality certain.

My argument is not: *it seems to be the case that x*, therefore x. What I am presenting is an argument for the best explanation of Super-Justification (which is a bedrock premise). But the fact that Revelation reflects how things seem to be, rather than being a philosophical concoction put together for the purpose of explaining Super-Justification, removes the worry of ad hocery. The structure of the argument is as follows:

> By supposing that things are as they seem to be, we get a good explanation of Super-Justification;
>
> Therefore, things are as they seem to be.

Compare: There seems to be an external world, and supposing that things are as they seem to be in this respect explains the structure and regularity of our experience; therefore, there is an external world. Unless and until deniers of Revelation can give us an alternative explanation of Super-Justification, we have strong reason to accept Revelation as the best explanation of Super-Justification.[10]

[9] To pre-empt a fiddly objection, I am not saying that the thesis of Revelation logically entails Super-Justification; I am just saying that it provides a satisfactory explanation of it.

[10] I am implicitly assuming here that Super-Justification is a striking fact about the human epistemic situation and, as such, something we require an explanation of.

Naïve realists will deny that Revelation captures how things seem to be.[11] According to this view, the properties we are immediately aware of in experience are properties of the *external world*—colors on the surfaces of objects, for example. Experiential properties, considered as introspectable intrinsic features of experience, are a philosophical invention. As the name of the view implies, proponents of naïve realism argue that their view captures how things *seem to be*; it is the naïve view of the common woman.

Of course, it is in some sense true that naïve realism reflects how things seem to be *upon first reflection*. But I would also say that it doesn't take much philosophical reflection to dissuade oneself of that viewpoint. When one goes through the process of Cartesian doubt—doubting the external world and then realizing that one cannot doubt the reality of one's own experience—one immediately realizes that the properties one is aware of in experience are possibly separable, or at the very least conceivably separable, from the properties of the objects of experience. Naïve realists may claim that the process of Cartesian doubt leads us into confusion, but then the onus is on them to make a case for this. Although naïve realism is how things seem to be before one does any philosophy, it is plausible that Revelation captures how things seem to be after a little basic philosophical reflection.

Of course, this brief discussion of naïve realism does not constitute anything like an adequate response to it, and I appreciate that the view constitutes a strong challenge not only to this argument but also to the very foundations of the view I defend in this book. But one cannot respond to all challenges in a single book, and on this topic I will have to defer to the criticisms of others.[12] My aim here is simply to clarify the sense in which Revelation captures how things seem to be, in order to avoid the charge that my proposed explanation of Super-Justification is ad hoc.

Although it is for me an epistemic building block, it seems unlikely that Revelation is a brute truth about the world. Plausibly, Revelation is grounded in some more fundamental relationship that conscious subjects bear to their conscious states. Independently of the issues we have been considering in this chapter, many philosophers have defended the idea that instantiating a conscious state involves bearing a certain kind

[11] Martin 1997.
[12] See, for example, Robinson (1985, 1994).

of non-mediated, non-conceptual, pre-reflective awareness relation to that state. Following philosophical custom, we can call that relationship "acquaintance." A creature cannot experience pain, for believers in acquaintance, without being acquainted with their pain and, in that basic sense, aware of it.[13]

Given a commitment to acquaintance, it is natural to explain Revelation in terms of acquaintance. Hamsters are acquainted with their conscious states but lack the cognitive sophistication that would enable them to attend to those states. For creatures able to attend to their conscious states, the non-conceptual awareness of acquaintance is transformed into a conceptual understanding of the nature of those states: Acquaintance + Attention = Revelation.[14]

This is, of course, only a cursory account of the relationship between acquaintance and revelation; others have attempted to spell out the details in more depth.[15] I mention acquaintance simply to pre-empt a concern that I am taking Revelation to be a rather strange kind of brute truth. My positive case for Revelation is not dependent on a commitment to acquaintance. Rather, it is dependent on the need to explain Super-Justification.

5.3   Can the Physicalist Account for Super-Justification?

Is there any way for a physicalist to account for Super-Justification? Some phenomenal concept strategists have defended a *constitutional account* of direct phenomenal concepts, according to which direct phenomenal concepts refer to phenomenal qualities in virtue of being partly constituted by those qualities. When I am in agony and I deploy a phenomenal concept to think about my agony, that concept, and the thought it is involved in, are literally constituted by the feeling of agony itself.[16]

We can understand this view by analogy with quotation marks. When we put quotation marks around a word, we create something that refers to a word by containing that word as a part. For example, the term "dog"

---

[13] Russell (1910) argued that we are acquainted in this sense with our sense data.

[14] The word "acquaintance" is used in lots of different ways. Explaining Revelation would require a quite specific kind of acquaintance relation, of the kind outlined in Chalmers (2003).

[15] See Chalmers (2003) for a detailed account of acquaintance and its relationship with phenomenal concepts.

[16] Papineau 2002; Block 2006; Balog 2012.

refers to a certain three-letter word of the English language, and it does so by containing that word within itself. We can think of phenomenal concept as "quoting" the phenomenal qualities they refer to, on the constitutional account. This model is not—at least not obviously—inconsistent with physicalism: the phenomenal quality "quoted" may be a pure physical property, even though it is not revealed as such to the concept user.

Proponents of the constitutional account claim that it is an advantage of their view that it can account for the infallibility of certain phenomenal judgments. Given that a direct phenomenal concept of pain involves within its constitution the feeling of pain it refers to, a subject cannot judge that she is in pain by employing a direct phenomenal concept of pain without actually being in pain: she must be feeling pain for that pain to constitute the direct phenomenal concept. Such a judgment, therefore, cannot fail to be true.[17]

Even if this view can secure infallibility, it does not immediately follow that it can secure Super-Justification. The fact that one of my beliefs cannot fail to be true is a *non-normative* fact, which has no obvious implications for *normative* facts about what I am entitled to believe and the strength with which I am entitled to hold those beliefs. Super-Justification, as the name suggests, is a thesis about justification, not infallibility. But even if the constitutional view can ensure the super-justification of some introspective judgments, it can be applied only to a very narrow class of such judgments—too narrow as it turns out.

The constitutional account of infallibility/Super-Justification only applies to introspective judgments of the following form: I am currently having *this experience*, where a direct phenomenal concept is used to pick out *this experience*. There is no way of using the constitutional model to make sense of the super-justification of our knowledge of resemblances between experiences, or between aspects of a single experience, such as the case previously discussed of the super-justified judgment that my experience of the red splodge resembles my experience of the orange splodge.

There is a quite different physicalist account of phenomenal concepts, which might be thought better able to handle these cases. I have in mind *semi-descriptivist views*, according to which phenomenal concepts are a kind of hybrid concept formed of descriptive and radically opaque elements. Such views have been defended by Janet Levin and Robert Schroer. The advantage of taking phenomenal concepts to involve

---

[17] This account of infallibility is defended by Papineau (2002) and Balog (2012).

descriptive elements is that these descriptive elements can potentially account for the *substantive information* conveyed by phenomenal concepts concerning their referents. As Schroer puts it, the hope is that the involvement of these descriptive elements can account for the "beef" of phenomenal concepts.[18]

Levin's view mingles elements of analytic functionalism and type-B physicalism. The reference of a phenomenal concept is determined in two distinct ways. On the one hand, a phenomenal concept picks out a conscious state by characterizing it in causal-functional terms and/or in terms of the similarities and differences between phenomenal qualities. On the other hand, a phenomenal concept picks out a state by being causally connected to that state in the right kind of way. This makes reference a little precarious, as both of these reference-fixing routes must be successful for the phenomenal concept to refer. If the phenomenal concept fails to be causally connected in the right way to anything, or if the thing the phenomenal concept is causally connected to doesn't have the relevant causal-functional/similarity properties, then reference fails.

Schroer thinks that phenomenal concepts are descriptive concepts that pick out conscious states in terms of their mode of composition from more basic phenomenal elements. The concept "phenomenal orange 7," for example, characterizes its referent as being composed of phenomenal red hue and phenomenal yellow hue, as well as some specific degree of phenomenal saturation and phenomenal lightness. But the sub-concepts referring to the phenomenal elements are radically opaque: reference to phenomenal elements is determined by causal facts outside of what is a priori accessible. For Schroer, the phenomenal elements turn out to refer to physical properties, and hence the conscious state out of which the phenomenal elements are composed turns out to be a composite physical state. Zombies are nonetheless conceivable as there is no a priori information in the sub-concepts that would allow us to know that they refer to physical properties.

Both of these views are able to account for the super-justification of the following judgment: phenomenal red resembles phenomenal orange. On Schroer's view, it is stipulated by the description that determines the reference of the concept <phenomenal orange> that the state denoted

---

[18] Levin 2002; Schroer 2010. Diaz-Leon (forthcoming) offers an account of this knowledge grounded in the dispositions of concept users to draw certain inferences. I find it hard to see how this view could account for Super-Justification. I hope to address this view in more detail in future work.

involves phenomenal red hue, and it is stipulated by the description that determines reference of the concept <phenomenal red> that the state denoted involves phenomenal red hue. In virtue of this, it is a priori that phenomenal red and phenomenal orange share a common element and thus resemble, in something like the way it is a priori that "French women"—so described—resemble "African women"—so described—in being women. On Levin's view, it is built directly into the descriptive content of the concept <phenomenal red> that its referent resembles phenomenal orange, rendering it incoherent that anything correctly called "phenomenal red" fails to resemble anything correctly called "phenomenal orange." In either case, <phenomenal red resembles phenomenal orange> becomes a kind of analytic truth, and hence known with comparable certainty to the truths of logic and mathematics.

The limitations of these semi-descriptivist views become apparent when we turn our attention from phenomenal resemblance judgments that are abstracted from any specific experience, to phenomenal resemblance judgments that concern conscious states *actually instantiated by the judger at the time of judgment*. In the art gallery example, my super-justified judgment does not concern merely the fact that anything that is a red experience resembles anything that is an orange experience; rather, it concerns the fact that *this*—a conscious state I demonstrate in my experience—resembles *this*—another conscious state I demonstrate in my experience.

Semi-descriptivist views are unable to make sense of the super-justification of these judgments. Suppose that through introspection I am aware of a conscious state that presents itself as falling under the concept <phenomenal orange>. Assuming that that quality is phenomenal orange, it is a priori that it resembles phenomenal red. But how do I know that that quality I am aware of *is* phenomenal orange? Neither Schroer nor Levin fill in the details, but presumably there must be some reliable sub-personal mechanism that gathers information about the quality and ensures that I deploy the correct phenomenal concept, that is, <phenomenal orange> rather than <phenomenal green>, <pain>, or <anxiety>.

This puts introspective beliefs about which phenomenal qualities I am currently instantiating in the same epistemological boat as ordinary perceptual beliefs: reliant on the proper functioning of an information-gathering mechanism. My belief that there is a table in front of me is reliant for its truth on the proper functioning of my senses. Similarly, for Schroer and Levin, my judgment that I am experiencing phenomenal orange (as opposed to phenomenal green, pain, or anxiety) must be dependent on the proper functioning of some information-gathering mechanism involved in introspection. Levin and Schroer cannot make sense of my judgment <I am currently experiencing phenomenal red and phenomenal orange> being super-justified, and hence—given the way in which the super-justification of my phenomenal resemblance judgments (on their view) depends on my correctly characterizing the relevant conscious states—they cannot account for the fact that my judgment <the two states I am currently demonstrating resemble> is super-justified.[19]

One option the physicalist might want to explore is that phenomenal properties are a kind of *response-dependent property*, such that all it is for me to have experience *e* is for me to judge that I am having experience *e*.[20] This option would secure infallibility—I can't be wrong that I'm experiencing *e* if all it is for me to experience *e* is for me to judge that I'm experiencing *e*—but at the cost of a much less realist view about experience. Physicalists tend to want to identify conscious states with fully real physical properties of the brain, properties that are expressed by neurophysiological predicates, rather than reduce them to mere shadows of our judgments.

Moreover, if this approach is to rule out the epistemic possibility (for the subject) of her phenomenal judgments being false, then the response-dependent nature of conscious states must be apparent to the subject instantiating them. If I denote my conscious states with opaque concepts, then, even if as a matter of fact my conscious states are response-dependent properties, it will not be apparent to me that my conscious states are response-dependent properties, and hence it will be epistemically possible for me (even though in fact impossible) that my phenomenal judgments are false. Hence Super-Justification can be accounted for in terms of response-dependent phenomenal properties

---

[19] I am not claiming that the judgement <I am currently experiencing phenomenal red and phenomenal orange> is super-justified. The point is that for Levin and Schroer to account for the fact that the judgement <the two states I am currently demonstrating resemble> is super-justified, they would need to make sense of the judgement <I am currently experiencing phenomenal red and phenomenal orange> being super-justified.

[20] Katalin Balog suggested something like this response to me in conversation, although with respect to phenomenal resemblance, and it resembles the view of Shoemaker (1981, 1982). See Lee (2016) for a good discussion of Shoemaker's view.

only if phenomenal concepts are transparent, and this is all that is required to secure the crucial premise of the transparency conceivability argument.[21]

5.4 Full and Partial Revelation

One might question whether revelation of the *complete essence* of phenomenal red and phenomenal orange is required to account for Super-Justification. Following Galen Strawson, we can distinguish Full Revelation from Partial Revelation:

> *Full Revelation*—In having a direct phenomenal concept of token conscious state C, C is directly presented to the concept user, in such a way that (i) the complete nature of the type to which C belongs is apparent to the concept user, and (ii) the concept user knows with rational certainty (or something close to it) that C exists.

> *Partial Revelation*—In having a direct phenomenal concept of conscious state C, some aspect A of C is directly presented to the concept user, in such a way that (i) the complete nature of the type to which A belongs is apparent to the concept user, and (ii) the concept user knows with rational certainty (or something close to it) that A exists.[22]

Just as it is important to distinguish Revelation from Phenomenal Transparency, so it is important to distinguish Partial Revelation from mere Phenomenal Translucency; in both cases the former entails the latter, but not vice versa. The views of Levin and Schroer previously outlined involve Phenomenal Translucency: phenomenal concepts reveal part of the essential nature of the states they denote. But they do not entail Partial Revelation, because for Levin and Schroer translucency is secured in virtue of the semi-descriptive nature of phenomenal concepts, rather than in virtue of phenomenal concepts involving a *direct presentation* as previously characterized.

---

[21] Trogdon (2016) is a recent response to arguments from Revelation, which I hope to respond to in future work.

[22] Strawson 2006b: 252. This is not exactly how Strawson defines these terms.

Once clearly defined, it is apparent that Partial Revelation would not account for Super-Justification. When I form a direct phenomenal concept of conscious state C, what I am super-justified about is that *I instantiate C*; Partial Revelation, however, entails only Super-Justification of the proposition *I instantiate A*, where A is some aspect of C. Perhaps instead we might try to explain Super-Justification in terms of the following thesis:

> *Quasi-Revelation*—In having a direct phenomenal concept of conscious state C, C is directly presented to the concept user, in such a way that (i) there is some aspect A of C such that the complete nature of the type to which A belongs is apparent to the concept user, and (ii) the concept user knows with rational certainty (or something close to it) that C exists.

By definition, Quasi-Revelation would entail (more or less) Super-Justification. But Quasi-Revelation is a cooked-up notion that bears no resemblance to the revelatory relationship we seem (upon reflection) to stand in to our conscious states. The relationship postulated in Full Revelation has two epistemic implications—(i) the knowledge of its nature, and (ii) the certainty that it is instantiated (with that nature)—which are unified around the notion of direct presentation. It is because my pain is directly presented to me—is "right there" for me—that its nature is apparent to me, and it is because my pain is directly presented to me—is "right there" for me—that I am certain of its existence. If (i) it is the fact that I am directly presented with a (token of a) property that makes its nature apparent to me, and (ii) (a token of) pain is directly presented to me, then the complete nature of pain ought to be thereby made apparent to me. It makes no intuitive sense for a direct presentation of *the entire token of pain* to reveal merely the nature of *some aspect* of that token. And because it bears no relationship to how things seem to be, Quasi-Revelation does not constitute a good explanation of Super-Justification; it is simply the ad hoc proposal that there is some relation R such that R accounts for Super-Justification.[23]

---

[23] One might propose that we have a fully revelatory relationship of *phenomenal resemblance relations* but not their relata. Such a proposal would fail to account for the super-justification of our judgements that conscious states themselves are instantiated. Maybe the physicalist could suppose that this element of Super-Justification can be secured in some other way, perhaps via the constitution view. But a further problem is that phenomenal resemblance relations are internal relations, grounded in the nature of the relata, and direct phenomenal concepts reveal this to us. It is apparent

Moreover, a physicalist is unlikely to want to commit to any of the Revelation theses (Full/Partial/Quasi), because it's hard to see how any of them could be accounted for in physical terms. Physicalist theories of reference tend to involve causal connections between concept and referent, or perhaps descriptive information concerning the referent. It's hard to see how a revelatory relationship between a concept user and a property, a relationship in which the essence of a property is directly revealed to the understanding of the concept user, could be entirely accounted for in physical terms.[24] Katalin Balog, who offers an extensive articulation and defense of the type-B constitutional view, at times sounds as though she is committing to Revelation. She uses the word "acquaintance," and says that introspecting our conscious states affords us a "direct, unmediated, substantial insight into their nature."[25] However, she also says that "this kind of direct insight ... does not reveal anything about the metaphysical nature of phenomenality."[26] So whatever Balog means by "substantial," it does not involve knowing the essential nature of experience.

5.5 The Conceivability Argument and the Transparency Argument

I take myself at this point to have established Full Revelation, on the grounds that a commitment to Full Revelation is the best explanation of Super-Justification (my bedrock commitment), and hence to have secured the truth of premise 3 of the transparency conceivability argument:

to us (with super-justification) that phenomenal red is such that of necessity it resembles phenomenal orange. Revelatory access to the phenomenal resemblance relation alone could not account for this. A final proposal: phenomenal orange is a complex property composed of aspects A1 and A2; the phenomenal concept <phenomenal orange> refers by constitution to the full complex property, which accounts for our certainty that the full property is instantiated, but also involves revelatory access to A1, which somehow accounts for our knowledge that phenomenal orange resembles phenomenal red. To avoid the specialized transparency argument discussed at the end of the last chapter, it would have to be argued that A1 is a purely causal-structural property. Even if this could be done, the view entails that <phenomenal orange> involves two distinct modes of presentation referring to conceivably separable properties, which in itself seems quite implausible.

[24] As I have discovered in conversation, it is something like this kind of consideration that persuaded Joe Levine to reject physicalism, rather than any form of modal argument.

[25] Balog 2012: 33.

[26] Balog 2012: 24.

Transparency conceivability argument

Premise 1—"P and nothing has Q" is conceivably true.

Premise 2 (TCP)—If a transparent sentence is conceivably true, then it's possibly true.

Premise 3—"P and nothing has Q" is transparent.

Conclusion—"P and nothing has Q" is possibly true, and so pure physicalism is false.

But what about premise 2, the crucial principle allowing us to move from conceivability to possibility? In the last chapter we encountered three principles connecting conceivability to possibility: SCP, 2D-CP, and TCP. I argued by a process of elimination that TCP is the one to go for. There are plausible counterexamples to SCP: the Kripkean a posteriori necessities. And 2D-CP is a kind of TCP+, where the aspects that go beyond TCP have not been sufficiently defended. But why think that there must be any such connection between conceivability and possibility? On the face of it, what is conceivable is an epistemic matter, and what is possible is a metaphysical matter. Why should the former have implications for the latter?

It is important to make vivid what is involved in denying even the weak link between conceivability and possibility asserted by TCP. A counterexample to TCP would be a *strong impossibility*: a thought T that cannot possibly be true, despite the fact that (A) a complete understanding of the essence of T's truthmaker (i.e., the fact that would have to obtain for T to be true), in conjunction with (B) idealized rational capacities, would not allow one to work out that T cannot possibly be true. Suppose that T is the thought *that there is a million-sided object*. Imagine an omnipotent and perfectly rational being trying to bring about a million-sided object. She has a complete understanding of what it would be for there to be such an object, spends an infinite amount of time examining the notion from all sides, and can find no contradiction or incoherence in it. Hence she confidently tries to create such an object and finds . . . she is unable. It's just a brute fact that such an object is impossible—impossible in a way that can never be rendered intelligible, even to God. Intuitively, something seems to have gone wrong when coherence and possibility are so radically divorced from each other.

There are also good theoretical reasons for accepting TCP, as it fits well with what to my mind is the most plausible proposal philosophers have thus far dreamed up for accounting for the metaphysics of possibility and necessity: explain truths concerning possibility/necessity in terms of truths concerning essences.[27] If the modal status of proposition P is determined by the essences of the entities P refers to, then it is natural to think that complete knowledge of those essences will allow one to work out (given sufficient power of reason) P's modal status. This is pretty much equivalent to TCP. It is beyond the scope of this book to launch a complete defense of this approach to modality, but the fact that TCP fits well with a plausible theory of modal truth gives us reason to take it seriously.

For these reasons, I think a strong case can be made for TCP. It is crucial to note, however, that once we have committed to Direct Phenomenal Transparency it is not clear that we need to justify a move from conceivability to possibility to reject pure physicalism, or type-A physicalism for that matter. For according to either of these views, my conscious states are causal-structural states. If (i) phenomenal concepts reveal the complete nature of the conscious states they refer to, and (ii) conscious states are pure physical states, then phenomenal concepts should reveal their referents to be pure physical states. But this would entail that there is no epistemic gap between the pure physical and the experiential, contrary to what we established in chapter 3.

Thus, we can wield the following argument against pure/type-A physicalism:

The transparency argument against pure/type-A physicalism

Premise 1—If Direct Phenomenal Transparency and either pure physicalism or type-A physicalism are true, then phenomenal concepts reveal their referents to be pure physical states.

Premise 2—If phenomenal concepts reveal their referents to be pure physical states, then there is no epistemic gap between the pure physical and the experiential.

Premise 3—There is an epistemic gap between the pure physical and the experiential.

Conclusion 1—Therefore, either Direct Phenomenal Transparency is false, or pure physicalism and type-A physicalism are false.

Premise 3 (Revelation)—Direct Phenomenal Transparency is true.

Conclusion 2—Pure physicalism and type-A physicalism are false.[28]

---

[27] Fine 1994; Lowe 2012.

[28] If Hard Phenomenal Translucency could be justified on the basis of some form of Partial Revelation, this would yield a specialized version of the transparency argument analogous to the specialized version of the transparency conceivability argument (discussed in section 4.3.3). However, at this point I am assuming Full Revelation rather than Partial Revelation.

I think that this kind of argument is what is really at the heart of the intuition that physicalism cannot account for consciousness. The deep conviction that pain is not a physical property is not grounded in a chain of reasoning starting from the conceivability of c-fibers firing without pain, and then moving to the real possibility of c-fibers firing without pain, and then moving to the fact that c-fibers firing and pain are not identical. It is rather grounded in the conviction that *we know what pain is* through feeling pain, and hence that if pain were c-fibers firing, we'd know about it. But we don't, so it isn't. I directly grasp the qualitative nature of pain when I attend to it, and it is thereby apparent to me that what I am attending to is more than mere causal structure.

5.6 The Dual Carving Objection

Dual Carving is the thesis that there are multiple ways of grasping the essence of some properties or kinds. More precisely, for at least one property/kind K, there are at least two conceptually distinct transparent concepts of K. That is, there are transparent concepts C1 and C2 of K, such that one could not move a priori from knowing that K is instantiated thought of under C1, to knowing that K is instantiated thought of under C2, or vice versa.

The falsity of Dual Carving is an implicit assumption in the transparency argument. The key move in the argument is that if (i) direct phenomenal concepts reveal the essence of their referents, and (ii) their referents are essentially pure physical states, then direct phenomenal concepts would reveal their referents to be pure physical states. However, if Dual Carving is possible, it could be that thinking of pain under a phenomenal concept on the one hand, and thinking about pain under a pure physical concept on the other, are just two equally good but conceptually distinct ways of grasping the essence of pain.

Since I raised the issue of Dual Carving in a 2011 paper, there have been two attempts to give instances of it.[29] In my 2011 paper I suggested that <bachelor> was an example of a transparent concept, and went on to say that "it is difficult to make sense of the thought that the notion of a bachelor . . . could be understood in two conceptually distinct ways."[30] This was

[29] In my 2011 paper I referred to the negation of Dual Carving with the blatantly biased title "The Thesis of Dubious Intelligibility."

[30] Goff 2011: 198.

supposed to be prima facie evidence for the implausibility of Dual Carving. However, Esa Diaz-Leon has pointed out there are in fact a number of conceptually distinct ways of understanding the property of bachelorhood:

- (A): For x to be a bachelor is for x to be an unmarried man.
- (B): For x to be a bachelor is for x to be an unmarried male Homo sapiens.
- (C): For x to be a bachelor is for x to be an unmarried Homo sapiens with XY chromosomes.
- (D): For x to be a bachelor is for x to be an unmarried male member of such and such clade (insert here a correct description of the clade that corresponds to the species Homo sapiens, according to the cladistic account of species).

What I think we learn from this is that I was just plain wrong that <bachelor> is a transparent concept, given that <male> is not a transparent concept. Indeed, if we suppose, as Diaz-Leon does, that the essence of biological species is partly historical, then the essence of a species will not be entirely graspable, and consequently it will probably not be possible to form a transparent concept of an unmarried male Homo sapiens.[31]

Hence, I am now inclined to think not only that <bachelor> is not a transparent concept, but that there could not be a fully transparent concept of the property of being a bachelor, on account of the fact that there could not be a fully transparent concept of the species Homo sapiens.[32] If this is correct, then Diaz-Leon's examples do not provide us with an instance of Dual Carving.

To be fair, Diaz-Leon claims only that A–D give us examples of multiple "transparent/translucent" ways of referring to a single property, which is aimed at refuting my claim in the 2011 paper that the physicalist cannot even hold that phenomenal concepts are translucent:[33]

---

[31] This is because fundamental individuals lack graspable essences, and the historical origin of the species will be defined in terms of such ungraspable fundamental entities. This is discussed in more detail in section 4.3.3, in particular in footnote 36 of that section. In line with what I say there, it may be possible in principle (although practically impossible) to form a concept of a species that is "transparent" in the secondary sense that it reveals the definition of the species' origins in terms of fundamental entities.

[32] Although perhaps there could be concept of the species Homo sapiens that is transparent in the secondary sense discussed in footnote 36 of section 4.3.3.

[33] Diaz-Leon 2014: 10.

If the phenomenal concept of pain is translucent, then it reveals an aspect of that property. But, crucially, an aspect of a wholly physical state is itself a physical state. Therefore, if the phenomenal concept of pain were translucent, it would reveal that how pain feels involves a physical state. But this is precisely what the a posteriori physicalist [i.e., the type-B physicalist] denies. A posteriori physicalism is inconsistent with the claim that phenomenal concepts are translucent.[34]

I agree that A–D are plausibly examples of translucent concepts, and I now accept that this argument fails. Indeed, this has already been shown in earlier discussions. The accounts of phenomenal concepts by Schroer and Levin that we previously explored (section 5.3) each entail that phenomenal concepts reveal purely structural features of conscious states, structural features that may well be a priori entailed by the physical facts. This kind of translucency—what I earlier called "soft translucency"—is not a threat to physicalism. I think such accounts are inadequate, as I tried to show, but I concede that dismissing the translucency option for the physicalist is not as easy as I had previously thought.[35]

The second attempt to provide an instance of Dual Carving is due to John Henry Taylor.[36] Taylor suggests that a certain fairly popular view on the metaphysics of properties entails Dual Carving, namely the *powerful qualities view*, associated with C. B. Martin and John Heil.[37] According to Martin and Heil, causal powers are neither bare dispositions nor grounded in qualitative nature; rather, causal powers are *identical* with the qualitative properties of objects. An example often given in support of this thesis is *sphericity*. We may consider sphericity as a kind of quality: the quality an object has when all of its surface points are equidistant from its center. But we may also consider sphericity in terms of the dispositions it endows to an object: the disposition to roll, or to imprint a spherical shape when pressed into plasticine.

Taylor's appeal to the powerful qualities view is multifaceted. Not only does he take it to provide an instance of Dual Carving, but it also

---

[34] Goff 2011: 197.

[35] In more recent work, Diaz-Leon (forthcoming) has offered a more developed account of phenomenal concepts as translucent. I discuss this view briefly in footnote 18, and hope to address it in more detail in future work.

[36] Taylor 2013.

[37] Martin 2007. Also see Armstrong et al. (1996), Martin and Heil (1998), Heil (2003, 2012), and Strawson (2008).

suggests a novel way of defending type-B functionalism. We can identify phenomenal states with functional states, but rather than embracing the standard rather implausible type-B physicalist line that phenomenal concepts tell us nothing about the nature of those states (or, heaven forbid, embracing analytic functionalism), we can simply say that functional concepts refer to mental states under a dispositional mode of presentation, while phenomenal concepts refer to *those very same states* under a qualitative mode of presentation.

The problem with Taylor's suggestion is that the very examples that the proponents of the powerful qualities view raise in support of their view also make it plausible that powerful qualities are not an instance of Dual Carving. Indeed it is this very fact that gives the view whatever plausibility it has. Martin and Heil try to persuade us that qualities are identical with dispositions by persuading us that there are *intelligible connections* between dispositional and qualitative nature. There seems to be an intelligible connection, for example, between the categorical property of sphericity and the disposition to roll (or to make a spherical impression when pressed into plasticine), which makes us question received philosophical wisdom that we have here two properties. If the connection between sphericity-understood-qualitatively and sphericity-understood-dispositionally struck us as brute, then consideration of the case would lend no support whatsoever to the powerful qualities view. Either the powerful qualities view does not entail Dual Carving, or we have no reason to believe it.

There seem to me to be no clear instances of Dual Carving. But is there any reason to suppose that there couldn't be? The basic problem with Dual Carving is that, like the denial of TCP, it commits us to the world being radically unintelligible. If we deny TCP, then there are modal facts that are unintelligible even to God. And if our world admits of Dual Carving, no amount of reasoning can reveal to us that the numerous ways of carving up the world "hang together" (i.e., are just different ways of understanding the same reality). An omnipotent and infinitely rational being could bring into existence a wholly pure physical reality and be surprised that that same reality can also be described in experiential terms. Indeed, Dual Carving implies the falsity of TCP: if Dual Carving is true, there are unintelligible necessary connections between distinct carvings. Thus, even though the transparency argument does not involve a link from conceivability to possibility, the resistance to strong impossibilities that justifies such a link goes hand in hand with resistance to Dual Carving.

Dual Carving physicalism, as we might call it, is much more radical than type-B physicalism as it is typically understood. The natural way to understand the type-B position is that the physical truths fail to entail the phenomenal truths only because phenomenal concepts are opaque (or softly translucent). The neurophysiological or functional essence of the properties denoted by phenomenal concepts could in principle be intelligibly derived from the fundamental physical facts. In this sense there are no unintelligible connections in reality itself; the epistemic gap is wholly the result of our mental concepts failing to transparently reveal the reality they denote. The type-B physicalist need not deny that the world would be in any respect unintelligible to a being for whom all truths were transparent.

I take the deep intuitive strangeness of Dual Carving (upon careful reflection) to be a strong reason to reject it, just as the deep intuitive strangeness of strong impossibilities is a strong reason to accept TCP. However, it is important to note in this context that my demand for intelligibility in rejecting Dual Carving is much weaker than the "Canberra plan" demand of Frank Jackson and David Chalmers that all truths be a priori deducible from the fundamental truths.[38] I am quite happy to allow that all sorts of truths may be opaque and hence not deducible from the fundamental truths. It is only the small and very special category of transparent truths that I claim are deducible from the fundamental truths; and those truths are deducible only because they reveal what is required from reality for their truth: a transparent thought reveals what it would be, metaphysically speaking, for the fact upon which its truth depends to obtain. If phenomenal truths are not in this category, then we have no grounds for expecting them to be a priori entailed by the fundamental facts.

As opposed to the across the board intelligible connections that the Canberra plan is committed to, my bedrock thesis here is a kind of *minimal rationalism*, a conviction that reality is minimally intelligible in the following sense:

Minimal Rationalism (1st formulation)—For any non-fundamental truth T, a *transparent rendering* of T is a priori entailed by a *transparent rendering* of the fundamental truths,

---

[38] Jackson 1998; Chalmers 2012.

where a "transparent rendering" is defined as follows:

> *A transparent rendering*: A transparent rendering of description
> D is a description that is indiscernible from D, except that each
> term expressing a non-transparent concept is replaced with a
> term expressing a transparent concept of the same entity.

A transparent rendering leaves unchanged facts about reference and extension. It merely, as it were, opens the curtains on each concept, revealing the nature of the entity referred to.

The principle of Minimal Rationalism I have just outlined has limited application. As discussed in section 4.3.3, it is plausible that fundamental individuals lack graspable essences. And for any entity that lacks a graspable essence, it will not be possible to think of that entity under a transparent concept, and hence in so far as a description involves terms referring to entities that lack graspable essences, it will not be possible to swap those terms for co-referring transparent concepts. If the fundamental facts involve entities without graspable essences, it will not be possible to transparently render those facts.

However, assuming that every property and kind has a graspable essence, we can give a more useful formulation of Minimal Rationalism in terms of *non-singular truths* (i.e., truths that don't involve singular terms):[39]

> *Minimal Rationalism (2nd formulation)*—For any non-fundamental
> non-singular truth T, a *transparent rendering* of T is a priori
> entailed by a *transparent rendering* of the fundamental non-
> singular truths.[40]

---

[39] We can further stipulate that non-singular truths do not involve predicates expressing properties that are analyzed in terms of particular individuals (e.g., "being on the left of John").

[40] Does the lack of a priori entailment between descriptions involving singular terms entail that reality is unintelligible? As far as I can see, not in any problematic sense. So long as the essences of non-fundamental individuals are defined in terms of the essences of fundamental individuals (see footnote 36 of chapter 4), we can make sense of their being grounded by analysis in facts about fundamental individuals. Slight qualification: to ensure that the fundamental facts *logically entail* what is required for each non-fundamental entity to be party of reality, we would need to ensure that the terms referring to fundamental entities in the metaphysical analysis of non-fundamental entities are a priori equivalent to the terms referring to those same fundamental entities in the fundamental truths.

At best, the adoption of Dual Carving looks like a particularly desperate way for the physicalist to account for consciousness. It smacks of cheating. After all, with respect to any kind of truths that are troublesome to naturalize or account for, we could pull this kind of move:

1. Suppose we are naturalists worried that the normative force of genuine reasons cannot be captured in a naturalistic vocabulary. No worries, just identify reasons with natural properties but hold that there are two conceptually distinct ways of grasping the essence of those properties: one normative and one natural. We might even indulge in real fire and brimstone moral properties, such as sin and evil, but identify these properties with common or garden natural properties with which they bear no intelligible relationship.[41]
2. Suppose I believe in a world of categorical properties, the nature of which can be completely captured in non-causal terms, but I'm worried that without real powers the continuing regularity of the world is just a massive cosmic coincidence.[42] No worries, just identify the categorical properties with pure causal powers, even though there is no intelligible connection between conceiving of a property as categorical and conceiving of it as a pure causal power.
3. Suppose you really want to believe in the spirit of the woodland, who cares for the trees and wishes them well. No worries, simply hold that the chemical nature of the bark can be truly described in these terms.[43]

Dual Carving seems to involve giving up any kind of constraint in metaphysics. Each of these positions feels like a fiddle: smuggling in ontology without paying a fair price for it. Tax avoiders stick to the exact letter of the law while blatantly flouting its spirit. Dual carvers are the ontological equivalent: sticking to the exact letter of Occam's razor but disrespecting its spirit.

Perhaps the proponents of Dual Carving might counter this worry by imposing some kind of theoretical cost on a commitment to multiple

---

[41] I am not ruling out the view that ethical properties are identical with natural properties. My point is just that the naturalist needs to do some work to make such identities intelligible, as is done, for example, in Frank Jackson's 1998 defense of ethical naturalism.

[42] This sort of worry is defended in Strawson (1986, 1987, 1991) and Chalmers (2012: 336–40). We will return to it in chapter 9.

[43] As far as I know no one in the literature has defended this specific identity.

fundamental carvings: a cost to ideology rather than ontology. But in this case, if the "monistic" view that fundamental reality admits of both physical and mental carvings ends up being just as theoretically costly as standard forms of dualism, it is far from clear that it is appropriately classed as a form of physicalism.

At any rate, if the physicalist wants to try to make sense of Dual Carving, the onus is on her to make sense of this strange idea and to argue that physicalism remains attractive with such a commitment. Until that is done, I maintain the falsity of Dual Carving, from which follows the truth of premise 1 of the transparency argument.

This completes my case against pure physicalism.

PART II

RUSSELLIAN MONISM: AN ALTERNATIVE

6

The Elegant Solution

6.1 Impure Physicalism and Russellian Monism

6.1.1 The Austerity Problem

Pure physicalism is physicalism in conjunction with the view that fundamental reality can in principle be captured in the vocabulary of physical science. In the first half of this book I argued that this view cannot account for consciousness. I want to begin the second half by exploring a problem for pure physicalism that has nothing to do with consciousness and hence would arise even for an eliminativist about experience.

Pure physicalism fits with a certain popular picture of what physics since the scientific revolution has all been about: a continuous story of progress in understanding the essential nature of space, time, and matter. Of course there is a long way to go; physicists have so far been unable to unify our best theory of the very big (i.e., general relativity) with our best theory of the very small (i.e., quantum mechanics). But at some point, it is supposed, these wrinkles will be ironed out and physicists will proudly present the public with the Grand Unified Theory of everything. There may be a dispute among the religious and the secular, but this is generally construed not as a dispute about whether physicists are adequately equipped to capture the material realm, but about whether as well as the material realm studied by physicists there is also an immaterial realm revealed by faith.

However, there is a problem with pure physicalism, even when we set aside the question of whether there is anything "beyond" the physical realm and even before we get to worries about whether pure physicalism can account for consciousness. As we discussed in chapters 1 and 2, from Galileo onwards physics has worked with a very austere vocabulary: its predicates express only mathematical and nomic concepts. In chapter 1 I argued that proper respect for science does not require supposing that fundamental reality can be completely captured with such an austere vocabulary. In the first half of this chapter, I will argue (independently of considerations pertaining to consciousness) that there *must* be more to fundamental reality than can be captured with physics' austere vocabulary.

Think about what physics tells us about an electron. Physics tells us that an electron has negative charge. What does physics have to tell us about negative charge? Rough and ready answer: things with negative charge repel other things with negative charge and attract other things with positive charge. Physics tells us that an electron has a certain amount of mass. What does physics have to tell us about mass? Rough and ready answer: things with mass attract other things with mass and resist acceleration. All the properties physics ascribes to fundamental particles are characterized in terms of behavioral dispositions. Physics tells us nothing about what an electron *is* beyond what it *does*.

More generally, physics provides us with mathematical models that capture the *causal structure* of the universe: reality in so far as it can be captured in a purely mathematico-nomic vocabulary. This is very useful information; it enables us to manipulate nature in all sorts of extraordinary ways, leading to extraordinary technology. But mathematical models abstract away from the concrete reality of their subject matter. A mathematical model in economics, for example, abstracts away from the concrete features of real world consumers, such as the nature of their labor and the specific things they buy and sell. Intuitively, wherever there is mathematico-causal structure, there must be some *underlying concrete reality* realizing that structure. Physics leaves us completely in the dark about the underlying concrete reality of the physical universe.

On the heterodox "big picture" I proposed in section 1.1.3, the scientific revolution marks the point when "natural philosophy" stopped trying to give a complete description of fundamental reality and instead focused on formulating useful mathematical models of its causal structure. This limited project has been incredibly successful, yielding a technological revolution that has transformed society beyond recognition. Somewhere along the line this impressive record has created in the public mind the conviction that physics is providing us with a complete account of the fundamental nature of the universe. But physics is successful precisely because it is aiming and succeeding at a much less ambitious task.

In the next two sections I will try to demonstrate that this hetero-dox view is obligatory. I will argue that the language of physics is simply not up to the job of adequately characterizing the fundamental nature of matter.

6.1.2 Against Causal Structuralism

How should philosophers respond to the recognition that physics only tells us about causal structure? One response is the following: "If physics only gives us causal structure, then causal structure is all there is." This is the response of the causal structuralist, for whom the complete essen-tial nature of a fundamental property is given by its causal profile: by how the property disposes its bearers to affect and to be affected. For the causal structuralist each and every fundamental property is a *pure causal power*. Behaviorists or functionalists believe that the nature of a mental state can be completely captured in causal terms. Causal struc-turalists generalize this model to the whole of reality, resulting in a kind of *metaphysical behaviorism*. Things are not so much *beings* as *doings*. Pure physicalism is a form of this view.[1]

However, there are good reasons to think that a concrete world con-taining nothing other than pure causal structure is unintelligible. One difficulty that has been pressed by a number of philosophers is that it is hard to see how we can capture the nature of any causal power without referring to properties that are not causal powers.[2] This is because the nature of a causal power is given with reference to its *manifestation,* that is, the property it gives rise to. For example, the manifestation of *fragil-ity* is *breaking*; the manifestation of *flammability* is *catching fire.* Arguably the manifestation of a causal power is a *categorical property,* that is, a property whose nature cannot be captured with only formal or causal predicates. If this is the case, then we cannot fully describe the nature of a power with only formal and causal language. Let us call this the "speci-fication problem."

The obvious response for the causal structuralist is to deny that the manifestation of a causal power is a categorical property. Why can't the manifestation of a given causal power be another causal power?

---

[1] Bird 2007a; Ellis 2001, 2002; Molnar 2003; Mumford 2004.
[2] Campbell 1976; Robinson 1982; Blackburn 1990; Armstrong 1997; Heil 2003; Lowe 2006.

The problem is that if the manifestation of causal power F is itself a causal power—call it "G"—then we can only understand the nature of G by understanding *its* manifestation—call it "H." If H is also a causal power, then we can understand its nature only by understanding *its* manifestation—call it "I"—and so on ad infinitum. Unless at some point we find a manifestation that is not itself a causal power, we will never reach an adequate specification of the nature of F.

We can make the specification problem vivid by imagining interrogating a causal structuralist about the nature of some property F:

- "Right causal structuralist, I want straight answers: What's the essence of F?"
- "Easy, F is a causal power to give rise to G."
- "Fair enough, but if the essence of F is given in terms of G, then to understand the essence of F, I need to understand the essence of G. So what's the essence of G??"
- "No sweat. G is a causal power to give rise to H."
- "Ok . . . if the essence of G is given in terms of H, then to understand the essence of G, I need to understand the essence of H. So what's the essence of H???"
- "H is a causal power to give rise to I. . . ."

Until we reach a specification of a manifestation not given in causal terms the explanatory buck will continue to be passed, and we will never reach an adequate definition of the original causal power.

G. K. Chesterton said, "We cannot all live by taking in each other's washing." Bertrand Russell played on this idea in his articulation of this worry for the causal structuralist:

> There are many possible ways of turning some things hitherto regarded as "real" into mere laws concerning the other things. Obviously there must be a limit to this process, or else all the things in the world will merely be each other's washing.[3]

The standard causal structuralist response to the specification problem is to hold that the essence of a causal power is given by its pattern of causal

---

[3] Russell 1927: 325.

relationships. Consider a world containing three causal powers, F, G, and H, such that:

- Fs are disposed to give rise to Gs.
- Gs are disposed to give rise to Hs.
- Nothing is disposed to give rise to Fs.

We know the nature of F, according to this response, when we know the pattern of causal relationships this property bears to the other two properties co-instantiated with it, that is, when we know that:

- There is some property that F is disposed to give rise to.
- The property F is disposed to give rise to is itself disposed to give rise to some other property.[4]
- There is no property that is disposed to give rise to F.

According to the causal structuralist, all it is for something to be F is for it to bear those causal relationships with two other properties.[5]

It is certainly true that a causal power stands in a pattern of causal relationships to other properties, and perhaps we can uniquely pick out any actual causal power in terms of its pattern of causal relationships. However, to describe such a pattern is not to specify the essence of a causal power. To have a causal power is to be disposed to bring about some change in the world, to make a difference. When I ask what a causal power is, I want to know what change it brings about in the world: what property it gives rise to. And I learn what change F brings about in the world when I understand the nature of its manifestation G. But so long as we are restricted to causal predicates, an explanation of G's nature is continuously deferred and never given.

This may sound like it's begging the question. Surely the causal structuralist can just repeat her claim that the essence of a causal power *is* given by the pattern of causal relations. But by definition a causal power is something that gives rise to a certain property, and hence to understand what a causal power is, we need to understand the nature of the property it gives rise to. And as we have seen, with only causal or formal

---

[4] Perhaps to give a complete characterization of the causal relations we should add that there is no further property that that third property is disposed to give rise to.

[5] Hawthorne 2001; Bird 2007b.

predicates the account of that nature can never be given. Describing at a certain level of abstraction the pattern made by the property given rise to, the property it gives rise to, and the property it gives rise to, and so on, does not tell us what the initial causal power *does,* and if you can't tell us what a causal power *does,* then you can't tell us what that causal power *is.*

Even setting aside the specification problem, there is a basic intuition that causal powers are too *metaphysically thin* to constitute the complete nature of fundamental concrete objects. A causal power concerns how its bearer points toward other entities and toward its own non-actual but potential manifestation in reaction to those entities. But, intuitively, fundamental objects must also have a *manifest nature:* a nature that does not consist in such shadowy pointing, but consists in how the object is *in and of itself.* This view is commonly expressed with the analogy that a world of pure powers is like a world in which things are continuously packing their bags for a journey that is never taken: objects continuously change their potentialities, but those potentialities never result in anything *actual.*[6]

This argument relies on the intuition that dispositions are not themselves real enough to constitute the actual nature of objects. Brandishing such brute intuitions may not help to persuade committed causal structuralists. Hugh Mellor wittily compares such metaphysical intuitions to reactionary social attitudes of days gone by: "Dispositions [i.e., causal powers] are as shameful in many eyes as pregnant spinsters used to be— ideally to be explained away, or entitled by a shotgun wedding to take the name of some decently real categorical property."[7] But for those metaphysicians who, after careful reflection, find the notion of a fundamental object of pure potency about as intelligible as the notion of an individual with no properties at all, it is entirely reasonable to look elsewhere for a picture of reality. This is the position I find myself in.

Pure physicalism is a kind of causal structuralism. Hence, if the previous considerations persuade us that causal structuralism is incoherent, then we have another reason to reject pure physicalism, a reason that has nothing at all to do with consciousness.[8]

---

[6] Armstrong (1997: 80) took this expression from Professor A. Boyce Gibson, who applied it to ordinary language philosophers.

[7] Mellor 1974: 157, reported in Bird (2007b).

[8] The powerful qualities view—that is, the thesis the causal powers are identical with the categorical properties of objects (Martin 2007, in Armstrong et al. 1996; Martin and Heil 1998; Heil 2003, 2012; Strawson 2008)—is one way of avoiding these difficulties for causal structuralism. I am

6.1.3 Introducing Impure Physicalism

There is an alternative for the physicalist squeamish about causal structuralism, but it means dropping pure physicalism. Instead of taking physical concepts to be transparent concepts revealing the essence of physical properties, we rather take them to be mildly opaque concepts revealing the appearance properties of fundamental physical properties. In other words, we apply the Kripke model of natural kinds like water, outlined in chapter 4, to fundamental physical kinds. Recall that, according to Kripke, we pick out water as *the colorless, odorless stuff that fills oceans and lakes and falls from the sky*, while water's essential nature as H_2O lies behind this superficial appearance. If we want to apply this model to physical properties, we would hold that, although we pick out mass in terms of its dynamical effects (gravitational attraction and resisting acceleration), mass has a categorical essential nature lying behind this superficial appearance. By adopting this Kripkean approach, the impure physicalist can avoid the conclusion that mass is a purely causal property, and hence avoid a world in which things are "merely each other's washing."[9]

Call this form of physicalism "impure physicalism." The impure physicalist gives up on the bold view that completed physics will one day give us the complete metaphysical truth. However, she can still maintain the hope that completed physics will be *referentially adequate*: it could be that all and only physical entities are fundamental entities, even if there is more to the nature of those entities than physics makes known to us.

Does this still count as physicalism? It seems unwise to demand that the physicalist accept such a contentious view as causal structuralism, and most of those who self-describe as physicalists do not. Even if we think that fundamental properties cannot be fully characterized in the vocabulary of physics, one might still take it that they do not involve mentality or value-laden causation, and that they are instantiated by entities at relatively low levels of complexity. In this case, impure physicalism

happy with the view that categorical properties are "powerful" in the sense that things behave as they do because of their categorical properties, but I think this is better expressed as the view that dispositional properties are grounded in categorical properties. I have difficulty making sense of the idea that the disposition itself is identical with a categorical property, but nothing much will hang on this.

[9] Lewis (2009) defends impure physicalism, and Jackson (1998) expresses sympathy. Arguably, physicalism in conjunction with Humeanism about causation entails impure physicalism.

still counts as physicalism according to the definition I developed in chapter 2.

(It is important to recall at this point that in section 2.1.6 I distinguished between "physical" and "material" facts. Material facts are facts concerning entities at relatively low levels of complexity, and facts grounded in facts concerning entities at relatively low levels of complexity. Physical facts are material facts that don't involve fundamental mentality/proto-mentality or value-laden causation; I will finally define "proto-mentality" in the following discussion. We should also keep in mind the distinction I made in the same place between "narrowly material/physical" facts, which are facts that concern entities at low levels of complexity, and broadly material/physical facts, which are facts that are grounded in narrowly material/physical facts.)

6.1.4 Introducing Russellian Monism

In the 1920s the realization that there may/must be more to the material world than is revealed by physics suggested to Bertrand Russell and Arthur Eddington (working independently) a novel solution to the mind–body problem: perhaps the hidden nature of the material world might somehow explain mentality.[10] The essence of the mind–body problem is that we have two kinds of stuff that don't seem to fit together, that don't seem to belong to the same world. Historically dominant solutions have either twisted the mental out of all recognition to try to squeeze it into the material, or twisted the material out of all recognition to try to squeeze it into an essentially mental world. The Russell/Eddington approach was to put the problem down to our limited understanding of matter, at least in so far as that understanding comes from physical science. We human beings are limited in perception to conceiving of matter in terms of its extrinsic properties—in terms of what it does—and it is for this reason that we cannot understand matter's capacity for mentality. When, as it were, God looks down at the material world and conceives of it in terms of its essential nature, there is no ill-fit between matter and mind.

This attractive approach did not fit with the zeitgeist of the latter half of the twentieth century and does not appear in received histories of

---

[10] Russell 1927; Eddington 1928.

twentieth-century analytic philosophy of mind.[11] In the twenty-first century, it is enjoying a rebirth, with discussion focused on a Russell inspired view that has become known as "Russellian monism."[12] Unlike substance dualism, Russellian monism is a monistic view according to which the explanatorily basic properties of the world are those referred to by fundamental physics.[13] Beyond this we can think of it as having a negative and a positive aspect to its definition:

- *The negative aspect of Russellian monism*—Russellian monists agree with impure physicalists that material properties have a non-structural categorical nature that goes beyond the mathematico-nomic nature captured by physics. For both impure physicalists and Russellian monists, then, we can distinguish between the mathematico-nomic properties in terms of which physics characterizes material properties—these are the pure physical properties—and the "hidden" categorical features of material properties that lie behind their pure physical nature—call these the "deep nature" of matter, or "deep material properties."
- *The positive aspect of Russellian monism*—Unlike impure physicalists, Russellian monists think that the deep nature of matter plays a certain special role in the explanation of consciousness. While consciousness *cannot* be explained in terms of pure physical properties, it *can* be explained in terms of the deep nature of matter. (We can make this positive claim more precise by saying that for the Russellian monist: the complete pure physical truth does not a priori entail the complete phenomenal truth, but the complete truth about the deep nature of matter does a priori entail the complete phenomenal truth.)[14]

---

[11] In these received histories problems with dualism led to behaviorism, problems with behaviorism led to identity theory, problems with identity theory led to functionalism, and problems with functionalism led to dualism. Perhaps it's time to start over. . . .

[12] See, for example, Pereboom (2011) and Alter and Nagasawa (2015). There were some forms of the view, although not under that name, defended in the twentieth and early twenty-first century (e.g., Feigl 1967; Maxwell 1979; Lockwood 1989; Chalmers 1996; Griffin 1998; Strawson 1994; Stoljar 2001; Strawson 2003). Russellian monism is not taken to be precisely the same as the view Russell held. For discussion of the relationship between Russellian monism and view Russell actually held see the essays by Wishon and Stubenberg in Alter and Nagasawa (2015).

[13] The emergentist Russellian monist—addressed in the following discussion—thinks that certain macro-level properties and individuals are fundamental. Nonetheless, she still holds that the properties referred to by physics are explanatorily basic in the sense that they explain the emergence of the fundamental macro-level properties and individuals.

[14] More precisely, for the Russellian monist the complete *non-singular* truth about the deep nature of matter a priori entails the complete *non-singular* phenomenal truth. In my view, even if Russellian

According to the Russellian monist, the reason we find it hard to accept that matter can explain consciousness—the reason it seems that zombies are conceivable—is that we conceive of matter in terms of its extrinsic dispositional nature. If I could magically perceive the deep nature of the fundamental particles making up your brain, it would cease to be conceivable that something with your material nature could lack consciousness: a zombie version of you would cease to be conceivable. The essence of the mind–body problem for the Russellian monist is rooted in our scientific ignorance about the deep nature of the material world.

Russellian monism comes in two basic forms. Panpsychist Russellian monists take deep narrowly material facts to be themselves phenomenal facts, that is, to involve the instantiation of consciousness. On this view, the fundamental constituents of the material world have a consciousness-involving essence, a crude experiential nature that underlies and explains the experiential nature of people and animals.[15] Panprotopsychist Russellian monists take deep narrowly material facts to involve protophenomenal properties: properties that are not themselves phenomenal properties but that are crucial ingredients in facts that *explain* consciousness, in the sense that transparent specifications of such facts a priori entail the phenomenal truths (where that a priori entailment is not wholly in virtue of the pure physical truths thereby entailed). In either case, deep material properties play a crucial role in explaining consciousness.

Given that we are exploring views in which consciousness is to be found in places we don't normally expect to find it (e.g., in fundamental matter), it would be good to have a word for the forms of consciousness we ordinarily believe in: the forms of consciousness we pre-theoretically associate with humans and animals. I call this "o-consciousness" ("o" for "ordinary" or "organism"); o-consciousness is just the consciousness we believe in in everyday life, before we start doing philosophy. Relatedly, I will use the terms "o-subject" and "o-phenomenal fact" to refer to conscious subjects and consciousness facts that we have a pre-theoretical commitment to.[16]

---

monism is true, the deep nature of the physical will not a priori entail indexical phenomenal truths, such as that *this person* is feeling anxious. I will ignore this qualification until section 6.1.6.

[15] I won't be discussing panpsychism in the history of philosophy. See Skrbina (2007) for discussion of panpsychism in the history of Western philosophy.

[16] I take it that Russellian monism is compatible with the powerful qualities view: the thesis the causal powers are identical with the categorical properties of objects Martin 2007, in Armstrong et al. 1996; Martin and Heil 1998; Heil 2003, 2012; Strawson 2008. On such a view physics doesn't reveal the deep nature of matter *qua* categorical, and it is the deep nature of matter *qua*

6.1.5 The Distinction between Russellian Monism and Physicalism

Should we count Russellian monism as a form of physicalism? Most Russellian monists agree with physicalists that all and only narrowly material properties are fundamental properties.[17] They think there is more to nature of those properties than can be captured by physics, but then so does the impure physicalist. On the other hand, the Russellian monist thinks that the fundamental properties involve mentality or proto-mentality, which is at odds with the definition of physicalism developed in chapter 2. Some philosophers feel passionately that Russellian monism certainly is a form of physicalism; others are equally passionate that it is not. David Chalmers describes the situation well: "While the view arguably fits the letter of materialism, it shares the spirit of anti-materialism."[18]

I don't think there is any fact of the matter here; both "physicalism" and "Russellian monism" are technical terms that we can define as we like to suit our purposes. However, in line with the definition of "physicalism" I developed in chapter 2, I prefer not to think of Russellian monism as a form of physicalism. This way we get a clear(ish) divide between those philosophers who do and those who don't think we must make distinctive metaphysical commitments to account for consciousness. Here are the crucial differences between Russellian monism on the one hand, and type-B and type-A forms of impure physicalism on the other:

The distinction between Russellian monism and impure type-B physicalism

The impure type-B physicalist believes in deep material properties. If she is an identity theorist, she may take deep material properties to be essential constituents of conscious states. But she doesn't believe that our lack of grasp of deep material properties accounts for the mind–body problem. For the impure type-B physicalist, even if I could magically perceive the deep nature of the material world, I wouldn't thereby get a transparent

categorical that explains o-consciousness. I have some reservations about the powerful qualities view, briefly expressed in footnote 8, but I think the arguments and views of part II of this book could be equally well understood in a powerful qualities framework.

[17] Emergentist Russellian monists do not agree with physicalists on this point.

[18] Chalmers 2002: 265.

explanation of consciousness; even with a God-like grasp of the nature of your brain, a zombie version of you would still be conceivable. The impure type-B physicalist is more likely to explain the mind–body problem in terms of the opacity of *phenomenal concepts*: it is because phenomenal concepts don't reveal the physical/functional nature of conscious states that we struggle to see how consciousness could be material.

In contrast, the Russellian monist thinks that the deep narrowly material truth a priori entails the o-phenomenal truth, and that it is our lack of grasp of deep material properties that accounts for our difficulty understanding consciousness as material. If human beings were able to perceive the deep nature of matter, it would never have occurred to us that there is a difficulty reconciling matter with mind.

The distinction between Russellian monist and impure type-A physicalism

The type-A physicalist thinks that the complete pure physical truth a priori entails the complete o-phenomenal truth. An *impure* type-A physicalist thinks that the totality of pure physical facts do not exhaust reality: they are merely the appearance properties we use to pick out facts involving deep material properties. However, like all physicalists, type-A physicalists do not think that deep material properties play any special role in explaining consciousness. The complete deep narrowly material truth a priori entails the complete o-phenomenal truth, but only because it a priori entails the complete pure physical truth. In contrast, the Russellian monist thinks that pure physical truths alone do not a priori entail phenomenal truths.[19]

We have, then, three different kinds of view, all of which are monistic and all of which believe in the deep nature of matter:

- *Impure type-A physicalism*—The complete pure physical truth does not exhaustively characterize fundamental reality; nonetheless, the complete pure physical truth a priori entails the complete o-phenomenal truth.

[19] The definition of Russellian monism offered by Alter and Nagasawa (2015) is problematic because it counts type-A impure physicalists as Russellian monists, as I point out in Goff (2015a).

- *Russellian monism*—The complete pure physical truth does not a priori entail the complete o-phenomenal truth, but the complete deep narrowly material truth does a priori entail the complete o-phenomenal truth.
- *Impure type-B physicalism*—Neither the complete pure physical truth nor the complete deep material truth a priori entails the complete o-phenomenal truth; nonetheless, the totality of deep narrowly physical facts grounds the totality of o-phenomenal facts.

6.1.6 The Transparency Argument against Physicalism

Now that we have clearly distinguished between Russellian monism and type-B physicalism, we are in a position to see how the case against physicalism built up in the first half of the book works against type-B physicalism. In chapter 5, I used the following form of the transparency argument to reject pure physicalism and type-A physicalism:

The transparency argument against pure/type-A physicalism

Premise 1—If Direct Phenomenal Transparency and either pure physicalism or type-A physicalism are true, then phenomenal concepts reveal their referents to be pure physical states.

Premise 2—If phenomenal concepts reveal their referents to be pure physical states, then there is no epistemic gap between the pure physical and the experiential.

Premise 3—There is an epistemic gap between the pure physical and the experiential.

Conclusion 1—Therefore, either Direct Phenomenal Transparency is false, or pure physicalism and type-A physicalism are false.

Premise 3 (Revelation)—Direct Phenomenal Transparency is true.
Conclusion 2—Pure physicalism and type-A physicalism are false.

The impure type-B physicalist does not accept that fundamental reality is wholly constituted of pure physical facts; rather, it is constituted of deep material properties organized into pure physical structures. Furthermore, she may deny that conscious states are pure physical states, taking them to essentially involve deep physical nature. This argument is therefore ineffective against the impure type-B physicalist.

However, if we assume the Minimal Rationalism I defended in the last chapter, we can show that Direct Phenomenal Transparency is inconsistent with type-B physicalism. Let us remind ourselves of what Minimal Rationalism is:

> *Minimal Rationalism (2nd formulation)*—For any non-fundamental non-singular truth T, a transparent rendering of T is a priori entailed by a transparent rendering of the fundamental non-singular truths.

A "transparent rendering" is defined as follows:

> *A transparent rendering*: A transparent rendering of description D is a description that is indiscernible from D, except that each term expressing a non-transparent concept is replaced with a term expressing a transparent concept of the same entity.

According to physicalism the fundamental truths are narrowly material truths. Thus we reach the following:

> If physicalism is true, then a transparent rendering of the complete (non-singular) narrowly material truth a priori entails a transparent rendering of the complete (non-singular) phenomenal truth.

Remember that for the type-B physicalist narrowly material properties are not phenomenal or protophenomenal, and hence it is not the case that transparent renderings of narrowly material truths a priori entail phenomenal truths. Thus, impure type-B physicalism entails the following:

> If type-B physicalism is true, then a transparent rendering of the complete (non-singular) deep narrowly material qualitative truth does not a priori entail the complete (non-singular) phenomenal truth.

But Direct Phenomenal Transparency entails that there is no distinction between the complete (non-singular) phenomenal truth (conceived of under direct phenomenal concepts) and a transparent rendering of the complete (non-singular) phenomenal truth.

We can therefore offer the following transparency argument against type-B physicalism (taking the phenomenal truths to be conceived of under direct phenomenal concepts):

The transparency argument against type-B physicalism

Premise 1—Type-B physicalism is true. [Assumed for reductio]

Premise 2—If type-B physicalism is true, then a transparent rendering of the complete (non-singular) deep narrowly material truth does not a priori entail the complete (non-singular) phenomenal truth.

Premise 3—If type-B physicalism is true, then a transparent rendering of the complete deep (non-singular) narrowly material truth a priori entails a transparent rendering of the complete (non-singular) phenomenal truth (from Minimal Rationalism and the definition of physicalism).

Premise 4 (Direct Phenomenal Transparency)—The complete (non-singular) phenomenal truth is identical with a transparent rendering of the complete (non-singular) phenomenal truth.

Conclusion 1—Therefore, the (the complete [non-singular] deep narrowly material truth a priori entails the complete [non-singular] phenomenal truth) & ~ (the complete [non-singular] deep narrowly material truth a priori entails the complete [non-singular] phenomenal truth).

Conclusion 2—Type-B physicalism is false.

Now that we have refuted physicalism, I turn to exploring Russellian monism as an alternative way of finding a place for consciousness.

6.2 Varieties of Russellian Monism

6.2.1 Constitutive and Emergentist Forms of Russellian Monism

Russellian monists think that the deep nature of matter explains consciousness, that is, that the deep material truth a priori entails the o-phenomenal truth. In line with the Minimal Rationalism I defended in chapter 5, I am inclined to think that if fact X constitutively grounds fact Y, then a transparently rendered proposition expressing X a priori entails a transparently rendered proposition expressing Y.[20] However, I don't believe this conditional runs in the other direction; that is, I don't

---

[20] This claim is consonant with, although not quite entailed by, my principle of Minimal Rationalism.

believe that if a transparently rendered proposition expressing X a priori entails a transparently rendered proposition expressing Y, then X constitutively grounds Y.

Some examples should serve to make the point. We can move a priori from *God's willing that there be light* to *there being light*, and furthermore (in the imagined scenario in which both obtain) the latter state of affairs obtains *because* the former obtains; in this sense, the state of affairs of there being light is intelligibly produced by the state of affairs of God willing that there be light. Nonetheless, there being light is not *constitutively grounded* in God's willing that there be light. Recall that by definition if X constitutively grounds Y, then Y is nothing over and above X. But in willing that there be light God creates new being, and hence the fact that there is light is something over and above—and hence not constitutively grounded in—the fact that God wills that there be light. To take a non-theological example: causal structuralism in conjunction with determinism entails that we can move a priori from facts about the past to facts about the future (if causal structuralism is true, then knowing which properties an individual instantiates entails knowing its causal dispositions), and yet clearly facts about the future are something over and above—and hence not constitutively grounded in—facts about the past.

We can distinguish, therefore, between two forms of intelligible production: *constitutive grounding*, in which the produced is nothing over and above the producer, and *intelligible causation*, in which the produced is something over and above the producer. The fact that there are eleven drunk teenagers revelling in a room intelligibly produces the fact that there is a party; the product is nothing over and above the producer, and we have a case of constitutive grounding. Assuming causal structuralism and determinism, the fact that a lump of sugar is dropped in a cup of tea intelligibly produces the fact that there is sugary tea; the product is something over and above the producer, and we have a case of intelligible causation.

The cases of intelligible causation considered thus far have been cases of diachronic causation (i.e., the causation happens across time). However, there could also be synchronic intelligible causation, for example, cases in which a fundamental lower-level property intelligibly causally sustains a fundamental higher-level property. This would be a case of *intelligible emergence*: fundamental lower-level properties bringing into being fundamental higher-level properties in such a way that one could, in principle, move a priori from the instantiation of the lower-level property to the instantiation of the higher-level property.[21]

In the light of this, we can distinguish two forms of Russellian monism. The *constitutive Russellian monist* believes that the deep narrowly material facts *constitutively ground* the o-phenomenal facts and hence that the o-phenomenal facts are nothing over and above the deep narrowly material facts. The *emergentist Russellian monist* believes that deep narrowly material facts *intelligibly cause* the o-phenomenal facts and hence that the o-phenomenal facts are something over and above the deep narrowly material facts.[22]

Perhaps the most natural way of thinking about emergentist Russellian monism is as a kind of layered view of nature involving upwards synchronic causation, the kind of intelligible emergence previously discussed. The micro-level subjects (or proto-subjects: i.e., bearers of protophenomenal properties) in the brain causally bring into being the o-conscious subject; micro-level subjects and o-subject then co-exist, with the former causally sustaining the existence of the latter. At death, or perhaps during dreamless sleep, the micro-level subjects cease to be arranged in an o-subject sustaining way, and the o-subject consequently ceases to exist. Call this the "layered" form of emergentist Russellian monism.[23]

Traditionally emergentism has been thought of as involving brute rather than intelligible causation. However, assuming the coherence of intelligible forms of causation opens up the possibility of intelligible emergentism. Indeed, given its definitional commitment to an a priori entailment from the deep material truths to the o-phenomenal truths, intelligible emergentism is the only form of emergentism consistent with Russellian monism.

There is an alternative to the layered conception of emergentism, defended by William Seager and Hedda Hassel Mørch.[24] On this view, an o-subject comes to be as the result of micro-(proto)subjects *fusing*

---

[21] It is tempting to analyze the distinction between grounding and causation in terms of whether or not the product is something over and above the producer. However, this would require denying that there could be cases of *non-constitutive* grounding; the "Moorean emergentism" considered in chapter 1 would turn out to be a case of intelligible causation (we would perhaps have to deny the coherence of the Moorean metaethical view). I am attracted to this view, but I haven't thought it through enough to defend it here.

[22] This distinction between "constitutive Russellian monism" and "emergentist Russellian monism" comes from Chalmers (2015).

[23] Rosenberg (2004) and Brüntrup (2016) defend layered emergentism.

[24] Seager 2016; Mørch 2014.

together to form a single entity, giving up their individual existences in the process. Micro and o-(proto)subjects do not co-exist: the o-subject—identical with the brain of the conscious organism—is a perfectly unified entity, lacking fundamental parts of any kind.[25]

How could it be plausibly held that a human brain lacks fundamental parts? The brain has rich structure: it has different properties associated with what we think of as its different regions; the brain is not just a single homogenous blob. How can any of this be made consistent with the thesis that the brain is a mereologically simple entity? One way to make sense of this is with reference to Josh Parsons' work on *distributional properties*. Distributional properties are properties that concern how a region of space is "filled in"; examples of distributional properties are *being polka dotted* or *being striped*.[26]

It is natural to think of distributional properties of an object as grounded in the properties of its parts; for example, the carpet has the distributional property of *being polka dotted* because of the colors of its various bits. However, Parsons suggests that it is at least coherent to suppose that fundamental distributional properties might be had by objects that lack parts. There could have been a fundamental particle which had the brute property of *having a polka dotted distribution of mass*, despite having no parts to ground that property.[27]

If this all makes sense, then it is coherent to suppose that post-fusion a mereologically simple object is formed that nonetheless has rich structure in virtue of instantiating complex distributional properties. What we think of as different parts of the post-fusion brain are actually different aspects of the distributional properties instantiated by the fundamental brain. One could, of course, remove a bit of someone's brain, but only by causing the fused whole to dis-unify into many distinct entities, some of which are then removed. Call this view "non-layered emergentist Russellian monism," or "fusionism" for short.

Even if coherent sense can be made of the brain's lacking parts, one might nonetheless object to the view on the grounds that it is wildly counter to common sense. But the fusionist could allow that the brain

---

[25] In fact, Seager and Hassel propose panpsychist forms of this view, but we can easily imagine a panprotopsychist version.

[26] Parsons 2004.

[27] I myself have doubts concerning the coherence of extended simples. But I certainly think that the notion of an extended fundamental particle with dependent parts is coherent. We shall return to these issues in chapter 9.

has *non-fundamental* parts, grounded in the distributional properties of the fundamental whole. On such a view, facts about the whole brain and its distributional properties ground facts about the brain's parts. It is quite common to suppose that macroscopic parts of the brain are non-fundamental, grounded in facts about micro-level parts; the fusionist just offers an alternative ground for these non-fundamental parts. And while common sense may insist that micro-level parts of the brain exist, it does not have firm feelings on their ontological status.[28]

In contrast to both forms of emergentism, the constitutive Russellian monist denies the fundamentality of o-phenomenal facts. The constitutive Russellian monist picture of the universe is structurally very similar to that of the physicalist: both take fundamental reality to be wholly constituted of facts concerning individuals and properties at low levels of complexity.[29] The constitutive Russellian monist differs from the physicalist only in her insistence that low-level entities must be conscious or proto-conscious to account for the existence of o-consciousness.

6.2.2 The Causal Exclusion Problem

The structural similarity with physicalism allows the constitutive Russellian monism to avoid a much discussed difficulty, associated with Jaegwon Kim, known as the causal exclusion problem.[30] This problem arises from the difficulty of reconciling two theses many philosophers find attractive:

Micro-level causal closure—Any caused material event has a sufficient micro-level cause. This is roughly equivalent to thesis that completed physics will in principle be able to causally explain any caused event.[31]

---

[28] It is natural to take this form of grounding to be *grounding by subsumption*, which we will discuss in chapter 9, rather than *grounding by analysis*, which we discussed in chapter 2.

[29] Unless they adopt cosmopsychism, the view we will explore in chapter 9. The cosmopsychist's picture of the world is structurally similar to that of the priority monist physicalist.

[30] Kim 1989, 1993a, 1998, 2005. An early version of the point is due to Malcolm (1968).

[31] Two qualifications: (A) Causal explanation may be non-deterministic, in which case we can say that the chances of material happenings are fully determined by prior micro-level events (see appendix of Papineau 2002), and (B) Micro-level causal closure does not ensure that micro-level events *directly* cause macro-phenomenal events; more plausibly if micro-level event MICRO causes macro-level event MACRO, then it does so indirectly by causing the micro-level event in which MACRO is grounded. Some might prefer to characterize the principle in terms of "causal explanation" rather than "causation."

Causal efficacy of o-consciousness—O-phenomenal facts have causal effects in the material world; for example, my pain causes my screaming and running away.

Assume the truth of both of these theses. Now consider some material event E caused by an o-phenomenal fact; for example, my screaming and running away caused by my feeling pain. Given causal closure, E must have a sufficient micro-level cause M; but E is also caused by the fact that I am in pain. Hence, E seems to have too many causes: M and the fact that I am in pain.

On the face of it, accepting both of the theses just outlined seems to lead to *systematic over-determination*: every single material event caused by an o-phenomenal fact has two sufficient causes. While there may be fluky one-off situations in which events are over-determined—Sarah's death is over-determined when she happens to be shot and struck by lightning at the same time—it would be deeply theoretically unattractive to suppose that every single event that results from o-consciousness is over-determined in this way. However, many philosophers are reluctant to deny either of the theses that in conjunction seem to push us in this direction.

The physicalist arguably avoids this worry by holding that o-conscious facts are constitutively grounded in micro-level facts. Consider the following case of an event with two causes:

- My sleepless night was caused by the fact that there is a party upstairs.
- My sleepless night was caused by the fact that there are people dancing and drinking upstairs.

In some sense my sleepless night has two causes:

- The fact that there is a party upstairs.
- The fact that people are dancing and drinking upstairs.

However, this is not a worrying case of over-determination as the fact that there is party upstairs is nothing over and above the fact that there are people dancing and drinking upstairs.

One more example:

- The baseball smashed the window.
- Particles arranged baseball-wise acting in concert smashed the window.

In some sense the smashing of the window has two causes:

- The fact that the baseball impacted on it.
- The fact that particles arranged baseball-wise impacted on it.

But again, this is not a worrying case of over-determination so long as the fact that there is a baseball impacted on the window is nothing over and above the fact that the particles arranged baseball-wise impacted on the window.

Call such cases of over-determination, in which one of the causes is nothing over and above the other, cases of "superficial over-determination." The case of the woman's death being caused by both a bullet and a bolt of lightning is not a case of superficial over-determination, as the two causes are grounded in distinct facts neither of which is grounded in the other. Call such cases "deep over-determination."

The physicalist avoids the causal exclusion problem, as on her view the cases of over-determination of behavior implied by micro-level causal closure are really cases of superficial over-determination. Return to the case we started with:

- The fact that I am in pain caused me to scream and run away.
- Micro-level fact M caused me to scream and run away.

The physicalist is likely to hold that my pain is grounded in M. Perhaps M is a micro-level event underlying the neurophysiological state with which my pain is identical. Or perhaps my pain is a functional state realized by a neurophysiological state, which is in turn grounded in M. In either case, my pain is nothing over and above the fundamental physical goings on that cause my behavior and hence worries about over-determination evaporate.

The constitutive Russellian monist, given the structural similarities between her view and physicalism, is able to give the same solution. The only difference would be that, as the constitutive Russellian monist tells the story, M is a micro-level event involving consciousness or proto-consciousness:

- The fact that I am in pain caused me to scream and run away.
- M (=the fact that certain micro-level entities with certain [proto]phenomenal states are related in such and such a way) caused my screaming and running away.

According to a standard form of constitutive Russellian monism, the fact that I am in pain is grounded in—is nothing over and above—some fact concerning certain of my fundamental material parts and their (proto) phenomenal properties. If we identify that fundamental fact with the micro-level cause of my pain behavior, then the over-determination of my pain behavior turns out to be superficial and unproblematic.[32]

This advantage is not shared by layered emergentist Russellian monism, as on this view o-phenomenal facts are something over and above the micro-level (proto)phenomenal facts that produce them; the relationship between the micro-level (proto)phenomenal and the o-phenomenal is intelligible causation rather than grounding. The o-phenomenal fact of my feeling pain co-exists with the (proto)consciousness-involving micro-level fact that sustains it, each being a fundamental fact in its own right. If the two facts are both sufficient causes of my screaming and running away, then this is clearly an instance of deep, and so problematic, over-determination (assuming micro-level causal closure).[33]

The situation is slightly more complicated for the fusionist. There is no over-determination, as post-fusion there are no longer any fundamental micro-level events taking place in the conscious brain; there is just the fundamental macro-level brain. Hence, unlike layered emergentism, there aren't two fundamental levels to potentially deeply over-determine behavior. But fusionism appears to be inconsistent with micro-level causal closure in a more direct way: if there is no micro-level cause of my screaming and running away (as the fundamental brain caused the action), then micro-level causal closure is false.

Fusionist Hedda Hassel Mørch has explored ways of getting around this.[34] As we noted earlier, the fusionist may hold that the brain has non-fundamental parts, grounded in the fundamental brain and its distributional properties. It is thus an option to hold that there is a sufficient cause of my screaming and running away among these non-fundamental micro-level goings-on. We would then get a case of superficial over-determination, this time because the micro-level cause is grounded in the macro-level cause rather than vice-versa.

---

[32] A similar argument is made in Chalmers (2015).

[33] Worries about over-determination would also be removed if the two causes were on a single causal chain, but this does not seem to be the case here.

[34] Mørch 2014.

Mørch concedes, however, that this response is not straightforward. Although not breaking the letter of micro-level causal closure, fusionism seems inconsistent with its spirit. The proponent of micro-level causal closure doesn't just think that for every event there happens to be some sufficient cause at the micro-level. The conviction in the background is that facts at the micro-level are "running the show"; that is, they are the ultimate causal source of the evolution of the universe. We will examine in chapter 9 whether there is any justification for this conviction, but for now we can note that fusionism is inconsistent with it: post-fusion it is the macro-level brain rather than anything at the micro-level that is running the show. Pre-fusion micro-level parts are running the show; post-fusion the macro-level brain is running the show.

We should further note that the post-fusion micro-level parts are not numerically identical with the pre-fusion micro-level parts, as the former—being grounded in facts about the newly created fundamental macro-level brain—only come into existence at the moment of fusion. The fusionist might insist that the post-fusion micro-level parts behave according to exactly the same laws as did the pre-fusion micro-level parts; in this way they would preserve the letter but not the spirit of micro-level causal closure. However, it is deeply strange that these new post-fusion entities should continue to behave exactly as the numerically distinct pre-fusion micro-level entities behaved, as though no change had taken place.

What takes place when an o-conscious entity comes into existence, according to the fusionist, is a radical change in nature. A huge number of micro-level entities pass out of existence and are replaced by a fundamental macro-level entity; we go from a situation in which trillions of things at the micro-level are in the driving seat to a situation in which a single macro-level entity is in the driving seat. It would be weird if that change in driver didn't show up empirically, if the brand new macro-level entity continues to make the micro-level run just as it did when it ran itself. We would be left with the sense that nature was conspiring to hide this radical change from us.[35]

---

[35] The essence of the concern I am raising here for fusionism is from Mørch (2014). A similar charge of nature "conspiring" to hide certain facts from us is often made against "neo-Lorentzian" alternatives to special relativity (Balashov and Janssen 2003); in this case, nature is "conspiring" to make it seem as though the speed of light is constant in all frames of reference.

There is strong pressure then for the emergentist, of either the layered or non-layered variety, to deny either *causal efficacy of o-consciousness* or *causal closure of the micro-level*. The win-win solution to the causal exclusion problem that is available to the constitutive Russellian monist is not available to the emergentist Russellian monist. This is widely seen to be a significant *prima facie* advantage to constitutive versions of Russellian monism. How great an advantage this really is depends on how great the evidence is that the micro-level is causally closed. This will be explored in chapter 9.

We can see, then, that constitutive Russellian monism is a very attractive position. Physicalism pushes us to choose from a set of prima facie unattractive options:

- *Phenomenal opacity*—The thesis that phenomenal concepts are opaque.
- *Analytic functionalism*—All mental concepts admit of causal analysis, which seems to entail that phenomenal concepts don't exist.
- *Dual Carving*—There are two conceptually distinct ways of understanding the essences of certain fundamental material properties.

Dualism or emergentism also has its own prima facie unattractive options:

- *Epiphenomenalism*—O-consciousness has no causal efficacy.
- Denial of micro-level causal closure. (At least, many philosophers think of this option as unattractive; we will discuss in chapter 9 whether it really is.)

Constitutive Russellian monism elegantly avoids all of this pain. The necessitation of the o-phenomenal by the micro-level is perfectly intelligible; it is merely the opaque grasp of matter afforded by the physical sciences that bars us from appreciating this. And because o-phenomenology is constitutively grounded in micro-level facts, we can happily accept its causal efficacy without denying micro-level causal closure. The constitutive Russellian monist can have her cake and eat it too.

6.2.3 Panqualityism

There is a form of Russellian monism—dubbed "panqualityism" by Herbert Feigl and prominently defended in recent times by Sam Coleman—that doesn't easily fit into the categories previously discussed.[36] If fusionism comes pretty close to substance dualism (like Descartes, the fusionist thinks the mind is fundamental and indivisible—it's just that the brain is too!), then panqualityism comes pretty close to physicalism. In fact, pan-qualityism is perhaps best seen as a kind of hybrid of Russellian monism and type-A physicalism. The type-A physicalist explains consciousness in terms of the pure physical properties of matter. The Russellian monist explains consciousness in terms of the deep nature of matter. The pan-qualityist analyzes consciousness into two different aspects; one of these aspects is explained by the pure physical properties of matter, while the other is explained by the deep nature of matter.

The two aspects the panqualityist analyzes consciousness into are *qualitivity* and *subjectivity*. Qualitivity is the quality-involving nature of consciousness. Intuitively, consciousness involves qualities: the redness involved in our experience of red, the sweet smell one experiences when smelling flowers, the spiciness of the taste of paprika. As discussed in chapter 1, the scientific revolution arguably begins with Galileo taking these qualities out of the material world. However, Galileo didn't elim-inate these qualities; he put them inside the mind. Similarly, the pan-qualityist doesn't think we can get rid of these qualities as their reality is evident in our experience; she follows Galileo in putting them inside the mind, which she takes to be identical with the brain. The redness in your experience, the spiciness in your conscious experience of paprika, the sweet smell in your experience of flowers—for the panqualityist, all of these qualities characterize the matter of your brain. Matter is, as it were, multicolored. It is precisely because a pure physical description of your brain doesn't capture these qualities that pure physicalism cannot be true.

Subjectivity, the second aspect of consciousness, is a matter of these qual-ities being *for the subject*. When I'm looking at something red, the redness is *for me* in the sense that it characterizes my experience: it's part of what it's like to be me.[37] It is with respect to this second aspect of consciousness that the panqualityist is effectively a type-A physicalist. Pure physical structure alone can't account for qualities, but once we have qualities organized in

---

[36] Feigl (1960) credits it to a conversation with Stephen C. Pepper. Versions of the view were held by William James (1904), Ernst Mach (1886), Bertrand Russell (1921), and Peter Unger (1999). Coleman elaborates and defends the view in Coleman (2012, 2014, 2015, 2016).

[37] Something like this distinction between subjectivity and qualitivity is made in Kriegel (2008: 45–57) but not in the service of a defense of panqualityism.

the right kind of pure physical structures, we thereby get subjectivity: we get qualities that are *for a subject*. Facts involving qualities arranged in pure physical structures ground facts about subjective experience. The panqualityist may, for example, define consciousness as *awareness of qualities*, where the relevant notion of awareness admits of functionalist analysis. For me to have a conscious experience of red is for me to be aware of a red quality in my brain; for me to be aware of a red quality in my brain is for that red quality to stand in the right kind of causal arrangement with other bits of my brain.

The resulting view is not type-A physicalism, as the pure physical truths alone cannot account for consciousness: you need the qualities. Nor is it type-B physicalism, as the fundamental material truths— qualities and pure physical structures—a priori entail the phenomenal truths. But it's not straightforwardly a form of panprotopsychism either. For panprotopsychists, the mystery of consciousness is rooted in our ignorance of the deep nature of matter. For panqualityists, this is half right: the qualitative aspect of consciousness is mysterious because of our ignorance of the qualitative aspect of matter, but the subjective aspect of consciousness can be explained away in standard physicalistic terms. To distinguish panqualityism from the undiluted physicalist views we have already rejected, I shall think of panqualityism as a form of constitutive Russellian monism—for one thing, it is arguably the view of Russell himself![38]—but one distinct from either panpsychism or panprotopsychism.[39]

There is a sense in which panqualityism is closer to panpsychism than panprotopsychism: for both panpsychists and panqualityists, the deep nature of matter consists of qualities akin to those we find in our experience. Presumably the qualities we find in o-experience are not precisely the same as those instantiated in fundamental matter, but they are of the same general type. The difference is that for the panqualityist the qualities that we find in experience can exist unexperienced, and they do so exist in fundamental matter. Before the highly developed point

---

[38] Russell 1927. There is controversy about how exactly to interpret Russell's view and its relationship to contemporary Russellian monism; see the essays of Wishon and Stubenberg in Alter and Nagasawa (2015).

[39] Tom McClelland (2013) defends a not unrelated view. He also distinguishes between qualitivity and subjectivity and proposes a type-A physicalist-style account of the former and a Russellian-style account of the latter. However, McClelland favors a kind of *noumenalism* (see next chapter) about the deep nature of matter.

in evolution when qualities come to be arranged in the right functional structures, they existed unexperienced.

This can be seen to lead to conceptual difficulties for the view. Can we make sense of the qualities in our experiences existing unexperienced? Consider a pain in your leg. Could that very quality exist unfelt? Arguably, the qualities in our experience just are, in their essential nature, experience-characterizing properties. The quality I find when I attend to the pain in my leg is *what it's like to feel pain (of a certain kind)*. How could *what it's like to feel pain* be instantiated without anyone feeling pain?

Moreover, even if we can make sense of the qualities in our experience existing unexperienced, it's not clear that merely putting them into certain causal structures will render them experienced. As we have seen, opposition to physicalism is often motivated by the conceivability of the pure physical truth obtaining in the absence of consciousness. Panqualityists add fundamental qualities into the mix to try to account for consciousness. But the problem is that, even after we have added fundamental qualities, the absence of consciousness is arguably still conceivable. It seems that we can conceive of a "panqualityist zombie world": a world that (i) is just like our world in its pure physical structures, and (ii) is composed of richly qualitied matter, but in which (iii) there is no subjective experience whatsoever (i.e., none of the qualities are *for* a subject). If such a world is conceivable, panqualityism shares the physicalist's inability to account for consciousness.[40]

For both of these reasons, panqualityism seems to me an unhappy halfway house between physicalism on the one hand and panpsychism/panprotopsychism on the other. I think the view deserves further consideration: if the previously discussed challenges could be responded to, then it offers an attractive theory of reality, avoiding some of the worries with panpsychism (the subject-summing problem) and panprotopsychism (the threat of noumenalism) that we will consider in the next chapter. However, the intuitions that lead one to reject physicalist accounts of qualitivity are unlikely to rest content with physicalist accounts of subjectivity:

> I am in blood stepped in so far that should I wade no more,
> Returning were as tedious as go o'er.[41]

---

[40] Chalmers (2015) makes this argument.
[41] *Macbeth*, Act III, Scene IV.

With some reservations, therefore, I will set aside panqualityism and focus only on panpsychism and panprotopsychism in what follows.

6.2.4 A Promising View

There are two big divisions among Russellian monists:

- Panpsychist forms versus panprotopsychist forms.
- Constitutive forms versus emergentist forms.

These divisions are orthogonal, leading to four forms of Russellian monism. By dividing emergentist forms into layered and fusionist varieties and adding panqualityism as a distinct form of constitutive Russellian monism, we end up with seven main forms of Russellian monism:

The seven forms of Russellian monism
- Constitutive panpsychism
- Layered emergentist panpsychism
- Fusionist panpsychism
- Constitutive panprotopsychism
- Layered emergentist panprotopsychism
- Fusionist panprotopsychism[42]
- Panqualityism

Physicalist forms of monism cannot account for consciousness. The hope is that Russellian monism may fare better in this regard. Moreover, Russellian monism provides a prima facie more unified and elegant picture of nature than other non-physicalist options:

- *Substance dualism*—Fundamental reality is divided into two very different kinds of thing: utterly non-mental matter on the one hand and utterly immaterial o-subjects on the other.
- *Brute emergentism*—O-consciousness arises from non-conscious matter in virtue of brute laws of nature.
- *Idealism*—Fundamental reality is exclusively composed of immaterial o-phenomenal subjects. Inanimate matter is grounded in facts

---

[42] As far as I know, this view has not thus far been defended by anyone.

involving the experiences and dispositions to have experiences of fundamental o-phenomenal subjects.[43]

Russellian monism provides a much more unified picture of reality than substance dualism. In contrast to brute emergentism, Russellian monism takes there to be intelligible connections from narrowly material facts to the o-phenomenal facts, thus giving us a more elegant picture of the world.

Idealism is at least as economical as Russellian monism. The problem with idealism is that it is hard to see how it can account for the structure of o-experience and the commonality of experience between different o-phenomenal minds. Why is it that you and I both experience a common world? Why is it that we both see a tree in the quad? The most straightforward explanation is that there is a tree in the quad, the existence of which is not dependent on o-phenomenal minds, and that that single tree causes both of our experiences; it is the common o-mind-independent world that explains the commonalities in experience between different o-minds. The Russellian monist, like the physicalist, accepts this straightforward explanation (for the panpsychist Russellian monist, the tree is dependent on certain fundamental narrowly material subjects, but it is not dependent on any o-subjects). The idealist in contrast seems to be left with a series of seemingly disconnected facts about what each individual subject is disposed to experience, with no explanation of how those facts "hang together."

Thus, once we have rejected physicalism, Russellian monism seems to be the most promising metaphysical theory, at least for those committed to respecting the Consciousness Constraint. Even its opponents have expressed admiration for its virtues; physicalist Alyssa Ney says of it: "This proposal strikes me, suspending disbelief about the ... theses that lead up to it, as at least as bold and exciting as Newton's proposed identification of terrestrial and cosmic reality."[44]

Constitutive Russellian monism is perhaps the ideal, given its capacity to reconcile the causal efficacy of human and animal feelings and emotions with micro-level causal closure. However, both emergentist and constitutive views provide us with an elegant and unified picture of the

---

[43] For a good recent defense of idealism, see Robinson (2016). See also Foster (1982).
[44] Ney 2015: 349.

world, in which all entities intelligibly arise in one way or another from the interactions of micro-level entities. Russellian monism is our best hope for finding a place in nature for consciousness.

In the next two chapters, we will explore some major challenges for the view.

7

Panpsychism versus Panprotopsychism and the Subject-Summing Problem

As we have discovered, Russellian monism is a very promising theory of fundamental reality and the place of consciousness within it. However, the view faces serious challenges, some of which we will explore in the next two chapters.

The most notorious problem facing Russellian monism is the *combination problem*, which is actually a family of problems. Each is a reflection of the following general concern. According to Russellian monism, o-subjects and o-consciousness—the kind of subjects and consciousness we pre-theoretically associate with humans and other animals—intelligibly arise from fundamental (proto)subjects and (proto)consciousness. On the most familiar versions, there are a huge number of micro-level (proto)subjects in your brain right now, each enjoying its own (proto) consciousness, which somehow come together to form, or to bring about, your mind and its consciousness.[1] The essence of the combination problem is simply this: how on earth is that possible? We feel we have some kind of grip on how bricks forms a house or parts of a car engine make up an engine, but we are at a loss trying to make sense of lots of "little" (proto)minds forming a "big" mind.[2]

We can divide the combination problem into two forms: bottom–up and top–down. Bottom–up versions of the combination problem focus

---

[1] I am not entirely happy with the word "proto-subject" as there is no sense in which a "proto-subject" is a kind of primitive subject. But it is useful to have a word for the bearers of protophenomenal properties, and so long as we remember that the word is just defined to mean *a bearer of protophenomenal properties* we shouldn't get into trouble. Perhaps the word "protophenomenal" itself is problematic for similar reasons, but it has a clear definition and so ought not to lead to confusion.

[2] The term "combination problem" is due to William Seager (1995), although the problem itself is usually traced back to a much discussed text by William James, which we will consider in what follows.

on the basic elements that (supposedly) enter into mental combination and raise doubts concerning their potential to intelligibly produce o-consciousness or o-subjects. The most powerful bottom–up combination problem, and the main focus of this chapter, is the *subject-summing problem*: the difficulty making sense of how "little" subjects could unify together to make a "big" subject.[3] The subject-summing problem is the paradigmatic form of the combination problem. Top–down versions of the combination problem, which we will discuss in the next chapter, focus instead on the putative results of mental combination (i.e., o-consciousness or o-subjects) and examine whether their nature is compatible with having been intelligibly produced from more basic elements of matter.

The subject-summing problem applies only to panpsychist forms of Russellian monism. Consequently, one might think that panprotopsychist forms are to be preferred. However, before getting to the combination problem, I want to discuss a quite separate difficulty for panprotopsychism: the worry that it threatens to resign us to *noumenalism*, the view that human beings, by their very nature, are unable to understand the deep nature of reality. Not only does panpsychism avoid this concern, but there is also, as we shall see, a powerful simplicity argument in favor of panpsychist interpretations of Russellian monism. All of this gives us strong motivation to try to find a solution to panpsychism's subject-summing problem.

7.1 The Threat of Noumenalism

An initial concern about panprotopsychism is that it seems to be an incomplete picture of the world. The essence of the view is that the deep nature of the physical consists of *protophenomenal properties*. But the definition of these properties is partly negative and partly indirect. Protophenomenal properties are those that are *not* phenomenal (the negative bit) but that somehow give rise to the phenomenal (the indirect bit). We are left wanting to know "Ok, but what are they? What are these consciousness-producing properties *in and of themselves?*"

---

[3] We will not be considering other bottom–up combination problems, but examples would be: worries about the potential for micro-experiential *properties* (as opposed to subjects) to combine, and the panqualityist's problem of how to make sense of unexperienced qualities combining to form a conscious subject.

It doesn't seem that we have any positive conception of a property that is not a feeling but that somehow entails the instantiation of feelings. To this extent, panprotopsychism gives us a rather unsatisfying account of fundamental reality and its relationship with consciousness. We ask the big question, "What is fundamental reality like, and how on earth does it give rise to consciousness?"; the panprotopsychist seems to answer, "I've no idea what fundamental reality is like, but, whatever it's like, it somehow gives rise to consciousness."

How permanent is this incompleteness? For some panprotopsychists, the positive nature of the protophenomenal is a detail to be filled in as the theory advances. Hence, while panpsychists, in characterizing fundamental stuff as consciousness-involving, have a head start characterizing the deep nature of matter, there is the hope that panprotopsychists will catch up as time advances. For other panprotopsychists, our failure to grasp the protophenomenal is a permanent feature of the human condition. Just as dogs aren't set up to understand mathematics, so human beings aren't set up to grasp protophenomenology. Colin McGinn is perhaps the best known of the second group of theorists, dubbed "mysterians" by Owen Flanagan, after the first Latino rock band to have a hit in the United States.[4]

McGinn does not describe his view as a form of Russellian monism, but it seems to have all the features of a protophenomenal version of Russellian monism: there is a deep nature of matter that does not itself involve forms of consciousness but that intelligibly produces consciousness. McGinn believes that there is a perfectly intelligible link from certain brain properties to the properties of consciousness but that we are constitutionally incapable of understanding that link. To put it in his jargon, we are "cognitively closed" to the brain properties that explain consciousness, a notion defined as follows:

A type of mind M is cognitively closed with respect to a property P (or a theory T), if and only if the concept-forming procedures at M's disposal cannot extend to a grasp of P (or an understanding of T). Conceiving minds come in different kinds, equipped with varying powers and limitations, biases and blindspots, so that properties (or theories) may be accessible to some minds but not to others.[5]

---

[4] McGinn 1989; Flanagan 1991.
[5] Pereboom 2011, 2015.

We can reasonably interpret McGinn as a panprotopsychist who holds that we are cognitively closed to protophenomenal properties. Panprotopsychism of this kind is a form of *noumenalism*, which we can now describe as the view that human beings are cognitively closed to the deep nature of fundamental reality.

For McGinn, the root of the difficulty is that we access consciousness on the one hand and matter on the other through two very different faculties: consciousness is accessed through introspection, matter through perception. Through introspection we find only consciousness; through perception we find only non-conscious properties that fail to entail consciousness. Through neither faculty can we discover properties of the brain that are not phenomenal but entail phenomenology. Human beings simply lack a faculty for accessing protophenomenal properties.

However, as has been pointed out by Derk Pereboom, there seems to be a gap in this argument.[6] Even if McGinn is right that we don't have any immediate awareness of, or acquaintance with, protophenomenal properties, it doesn't follow that we are unable to form a positive conception of them through our creative imagination. Perhaps future theorists might be able to construct possible candidates in imagination and maybe even formulate testable hypotheses involving such candidates. It seems that we do not *currently* have a positive conception of protophenomenal properties, but how can we draw limits on future conceptual innovation?

Perhaps there is no way of conclusively demonstrating that humans are cognitively closed to protophenomenal properties, but there may be reason to give some credence to the supposition that we are. It is plausible that a human who has not been acquainted with a token of phenomenal property type P is cognitively closed to phenomenal property type P; for example, a congenitally blind person is unable to form a positive idea of phenomenal color. It is not unreasonable to expect the same to be true of the protophenomenal properties that underlie phenomenal color; if we agree with McGinn that no human is acquainted with the protophenomenal property underlying phenomenal red, we can plausibly infer from this that no human is able to form a positive idea of that property.

Furthermore, reflect for a moment on what would be involving in positively conceiving of a protophenomenal property. A protophenomenal property is a third-person property, but it entails the instantiation of first-person properties. It seems that to conceive of it, or at least to

---

[6] McGinn 1989: 350.

conceive of it *qua* protophenomenal property, would involve first-person and third-person representational faculties employed in a unified conception of a single property. But our perceptual and introspective faculties don't seem capable of being integrated in this way. The more I reflect on what would be involved in conceiving of a protophenomenal property, the more I am struck by how awesome—in the British English sense of the word—it would be to behold such a property and the more I am inclined to think that beholding such beauty is beyond the reach of human minds, just as, say, visually imagining the infinite is beyond us.

Perhaps I have limited imagination regarding what it is possible for humans to imagine. Or perhaps a bit of surgery or drug-induced brain alteration could expand our powers of imagination. Unlike McGinn, I don't take what I have said to constitute a knock-down argument that humans will be forever incapable of grasping protophenomenal properties. It's just that, whereas Pereboom is cautiously optimistic, I am cautiously pessimistic. At the very least, the optimistic panprotopsychist relies on the hope of a monumental conceptual revolution to fill in the gaps in her theory of the world.[7]

7.2 The Simplicity Argument for Panpsychism

Of all metaphysical theories consistent with the reality of ordinary consciousness, panpsychist forms of Russellian monism are the most simple, elegant, and unified. As we discovered in the last chapter, although physics tells us much about the causal structure of matter, it leaves us completely in the dark about the categorical nature that underlies that causal structure. The only thing we know for certain about the deep nature of material entities is that at least some of them—for example, you and I—have a consciousness-involving nature.

We now have a theoretical choice. We can either suppose that the categorical nature of fundamental particles, such as electrons and quarks, is constituted of properties of the kind we are acquainted with, or we can suppose that they have some entirely unknown categorical nature. On the former supposition, the nature of macroscopic things is continuous

---

[7] As discussed in the last chapter, panqualityism solves this difficulty by offering a positive characterization of the deep nature of matter. However, as we have seen, this solution comes with some serious problems.

with the nature of microscopic things. The latter supposition leads us to complexity, discontinuity, and mystery. The theoretical imperative to form as simple and unified a view as is consistent with the data leads us quite straightforwardly in the direction of panpsychism.

The main objection one comes across to panpsychism is that it is "crazy" and "just obviously wrong." It is thought to be highly counterintuitive to suppose that there is something that it is like to be an electron, and this is taken to be a very strong reason to doubt the truth of panpsychism. But the view that time slows down at high speeds, that particles have determinate position only when measured, that the Earth goes round the sun, or that we have a common ancestor with apes were (indeed, still are) also highly counterintuitive, and to many "just obviously wrong." And yet the counter-commonsensicality of these views gives us little or no reason to think them false. It is hard to see why the fact that most Westerners living today happen to be pre-theoretically inclined to think panpsychism false constitutes a reason to think that it is false.

Probably the willingness of contemporary philosophers to accept special relativity, natural selection, and quantum mechanics, despite their strangeness from the point of view of pre-theoretical common sense, is a reflection of their respect for the scientific method. We are prepared to modify our view of the world if we take there to be good scientific reason to do so. But in the absence of hard experimental proof, philosophers are reluctant to attribute consciousness to electrons.

However, while there is perhaps no observational data that in itself support panpsychism, there is a hard datum that arguably counts in its favor: the existence of consciousness. The reality of consciousness is more evident to us than any empirical data. The existence of consciousness does not entail the truth of panpsychism, but if it turns out that panpsychism is the most unified picture of the world that is consistent both with the reality of consciousness and with our observational knowledge, then we have solid evidence in favor of the truth of panpsychism. Compare the datum that the speed of light is measured to be the same in all frames of reference. This datum does not entail the truth of special relativity, but it counts in its favor in the sense that special relativity is the most elegant picture of the world consistent with it. The evident reality of consciousness arguably supports the truth of panpsychism in much the same way that measurements of light support special relativity.

While in the mindset of thinking that physics is on its way to giving a complete picture of the fundamental nature of reality, panpsychism seems improbable as physics does not attribute experience to fundamental particles. But once we realize that physics leaves us completely in the dark about the deep nature of the entities it talks about, and indeed that the only thing we know for certain about the deep nature of the universe is that some of it is taken up with consciousness, things look very different. All we get from physics is this big black and white abstract structure, which we metaphysicians must somehow color in with concrete categorical nature. Assuming the falsity of substance dualism, we know how to color in one bit of it: the brains of organisms are colored in with consciousness. How to color in the rest? The most elegant, simple, sensible option is to color in the rest of the world with the same pen.[8]

7.3 The Subject-Summing Problem

At this stage, panpsychism has the advantage over panprotopsychism. Panpsychism provides unity where panprotopsychism introduces division. Panpsychism gives answers where panprotopsychism brings mystery. However, panpsychism faces a deep challenge that threatens to undermine its very coherence: the subject-summing problem. While all forms of Russellian monism face some form of the combination problem, the subject-summing problem is one of the most vicious, and it is faced only by panpsychists. If panpsychists are unable to mount a good defense against the subject-summing problem, the advantage may go back to panprotopsychism.

If the difficulty for the panprotopsychist is that she doesn't have enough to say about the fundamental constituents of reality, the difficulty for the panpsychist is she says too much. According to her theory of reality, the basic building blocks of reality are *subjects*.[9] And on a standard version of panpsychist Russellian monism these subjects combine to intelligibly produce o-subjects. We will explore in what follows a few ways of spelling out the subject-summing problem, but the starting point is just a deep intuition that *subjects aren't combinable*. The idea of lots of little conscious subjects coming together to form a big conscious subject

---

[8] This argument for panpsychism is taken from Goff (2016a). It is also made in Goff (2017a).

[9] I say "basic building blocks of reality," rather than "fundamental building blocks of reality," because for the emergentist Russellian monist o-subjects are fundamental too.

seems, at best, something we haven't yet been able to make sense of and, at worst, something of which sense cannot be made.

7.3.1 James's Anti-Subject-Summing Argument

The inspiration for the combination problem is the following much quoted passage from William James:

> Take a hundred of them [feelings], shuffle them and pack them as close together as you can (whatever that may mean); still each remains the same feeling it always was, shut in its own skin, windowless, ignorant of what the other feelings are and mean. There would be a hundred-and-first-feeling there, if, when a group or series of such feelings where set up, a consciousness *belonging to the group as such* should emerge. And this 101st feeling would be a totally new fact; the 100 feelings might, by a curious physical law, be a signal for its *creation*, when they came together; but they would have no substantial identity with it, nor it with them, and one could never deduce the one from the others, nor (in any intelligible sense) say that they *evolved* it.[10]

Many philosophers, under the influence of this passage, claim to find some special conceptual difficulty in the idea of mental entities combining. In fact, closer examination of the text surrounding this passage reveals that James' resistance to the summing of mental entities is grounded in a general resistance to the idea of *anything* combining:

> [N]o possible number of entities (call them as you like, whether forces, material particles, or mental elements) can sum *themselves* together. Each remains, in the sum, what it always was; and the sum itself exists only *for a bystander* who happens to overlook the units and to apprehend the sum as such; or else it exists in the shape of some other *effect* on an entity external to the sum itself. Let it not be objected that H_2 and O combine of themselves into "water," and thenceforward exhibit new properties. They do not. The "water" is just the old atoms in the new position, H-O-H; the "new properties" are just their combined

[10] James 1890/1981: 160.

effects, when in this position, upon external media, such as our sense-organs and the various reagents on which water may exert its properties and be known.[11]

Without much argument, James takes it to be evident that entities "combine" only in the sense that their acting in concert gives rise to some distinctive perception in observers. Combinations exist only in the eye of the beholder. The "combination problem" according to James goes as follows:

1. There are no combinations.
2. Therefore, there are no mental combinations.[12]

However, the more suggestive elements of the former paragraph have made more of an impression on contemporary philosophers than the argument of the latter paragraph. There does seem to be some deep difficulty making sense of distinct subjects of experience combining to intelligibly produce a greater subject, and in what follows I will explore two different ways of understanding this difficulty.

7.3.2 The Anti-Subject-Summing Conceivability Argument

7.3.2.1 The Argument

In the standard understanding of panpsychist Russellian monism, o-subjects are intelligibly produced by micro-level subjects, or "micro-subjects" as we might call them. Call this standard form of panpsychist Russellian monism "micropsychism."[13] The constitutive micropsychist holds that the intelligible production takes the form of constitutive grounding, while the emergentist micropsychist holds that the intelligible production is causal. But in both forms there is an a priori entailment from the micro-phenomenal truths—the consciousness-involving micro-level truths—to the o-phenomenal truths. And in both forms, the micro-phenomenal truths necessitate the o-phenomenal truths.

---

[11] James 1890/1981: 1. 158–9.

[12] Shani (2010) critiques James' argument on these grounds.

[13] This term comes from Galen Strawson 2006a. However, Strawson makes a distinction between "micropsychism" and "panpsychism" that I am not adopting here.

One way of reading the James passage sees it as speaking against the possibility of such intelligible production. For any group of subjects, it seems that we could conceive of just those subjects existing in the absence of some further subject. A panpsychist might suppose that my severe pain intelligibly arises from the slight pain of trillions of neurons. And yet, for any group of subjects feeling slight pain, it seems possible to conceive of just that number of slightly pained subjects existing in the absence of some further pained subject, whether slightly or severely pained.

Contrast with the case of a party. Once you've got people dancing and drinking and generally having a good time, you've got a party. It's impossible to conceive of people dancing and drinking and having fun without conceiving of a party; the two states of affairs cannot intelligibly be separated.[14] Similarly, it's impossible to conceive of a state of affairs in which bricks are arranged as they are in my house, but in which there is no building formed of those bricks. In contrast, whenever we conceive of two states of affairs involving distinct subjects, it seems that those two states of affairs can be intelligibly separated: either can be conceived of obtaining in the absence of the other.

We can put this in the form of a principle:

Conceivable Isolation of Subjects (CIS)—For any group of subjects, S_1, $S_2 \ldots S_n$, and any conscious states, E_1, $E_2 \ldots E_n$, the following scenario is conceivable: there are S_1, $S_2 \ldots S_n$ instantiating E_1, $E_2 \ldots E_n$, but it's not the case that there is a subject S^* such that S^* is not identical with any of S_1, $S_2 \ldots S_n$.

It might be objected that we only know CIS to obtain with respect to phenomenal qualities we are acquainted with and hence able to form phenomenal concepts of. Indeed, it is not clear that we can form phenomenal concepts of the phenomenal qualities instantiated by micro-subjects; and if we are unable to conceive of micro-subjects in terms of their determinate phenomenal nature, then we are unable to directly test whether

---

[14] Schaffer (forthcoming) holds that we require basic metaphysical principles to bridge the gap between micro-level entities and composite wholes. I know from conversation that he thinks the same about revelling and parties. However, in line with the grounding by analysis model, I am inclined to think that all it is for there to be a party is for there to be people revelling and that, consequently, we cannot conceive of there being people revelling without it being the case that there is a party.

CIS is true of actual micro-subjects, that is, whether or not actual micro-subjects, having the experience they actually have, can be conceived of in the absence of further subjects. Nonetheless, CIS seems true of any of the kinds of subject we can positively conceive of; varying the phenomenal character of the subjects we're conceiving of, in so far as we are able to do this, has no bearing on the conceivable isolation of the subjects being conceived of. Intuitively, CIS is a conceptual truth concerning the determinable property of *being a subject of experience* rather than any specific determinates of it.

I don't know how to demonstratively prove that there is not a possible set of subjects that constitute a counterexample to CIS, that is, a group of subjects of experience that cannot intelligibly be thought about in the absence of some further subject of experience. But reflection shows CIS to be true with regards to the many and varied kinds of consciousness we are able to conceive of and in a way that doesn't seem dependent on their specific phenomenal characters. I take it therefore that CIS is a principle we can reasonably take ourselves to know.

CIS constitutes a challenge for the micropsychist. If the micro-subjects in my brain, merely by existing with the conscious experiences they have, intelligibly produce the subject of my experience, then it is not conceivable that those micro-subjects exist (with the conscious experiences they have at a time when I am conscious) without the subject of my o-experience also existing. But it follows from CIS that it *is* conceivable that those micro-subjects exist (with the conscious experiences they have a time when I am conscious) without the subject of my experience also existing.

This line of reasoning assumes that the subject of my experience is not identical with one of the micro-subjects that intelligibly produce it. This is not true by definition as o-subjects are defined as the subjects of experience we pre-theoretically associate with macroscopic entities, such as people and animals. It is a conceptual possibility that the subject that common sense associates with me is identical with a single particle in my brain. Nonetheless, this is a conceptual possibility that it is reasonable to dismiss on empirical grounds and on grounds of general plausibility. There is no single micro-level entity in my brain that it is plausible to identify with my entire mind. And the thesis that my mind is identical with a single micro-level entity is tantamount to epiphenomenalism, as a single micro-level entity in the brain cannot on its own cause the behavior we pre-theoretically suppose is caused by my mind.

We could combine CIS with the Transparency Conceivability Principle to infer the corresponding modal principle:

Modal Isolation of Subjects (MIS)—For any group of subjects, S_1, S_2 ... S_n, and any conscious states, E_1, E_2 ... E_n, the following state of affairs is possible: there are S_1, S_2 ... S_n instantiating E_1, E_2 ... E_n, but it's not the case that there is a subject S^* such that S^* is not identical with any of S_1, S_2 ... S_n.

However, a move from conceivability to possibility is unnecessary given that Russellian monism has a claim about conceivability built into it. If the micro-level facts intelligibly produce the o-phenomenal facts, then the micro-level phenomenal facts cannot be conceived of in the absence of the o-phenomenal facts.

We should also note that this is just as much a problem for the layered emergentist Russellian (monist) panpsychist as it is for the constitutive Russellian (monist) panpsychist, as both take the connection between micro-level consciousness and o-consciousness to be intelligible.[15]

7.3.2.2 *Fusionism and the Anti-Subject-Summing Conceivability Argument*

Fusionist panpsychists agree with layered panpsychists that o-subjects are intelligibly produced by micro-subjects. However, the intelligible production is *diachronic* rather than synchronic. Compare: a causal structuralist holds that salt is essentially disposed to dissolve in water; the fact that salt has been placed in water at a given time intelligibly results in the salt dissolving *at a slightly later time*. Similarly, for the fusionist, o-subjects are formed by a process of diachronic intelligible production: the obtaining of certain facts concerning micro-subjects at a given time entails that there will be an o-subject at a slightly later time. Recall that for the fusionist the o-subject does not co-exist with the micro-subjects that produce it; the micro-subjects cease to exist at the moment the o-subject is formed.

While fusionist intelligible production is diachronic, it is natural to interpret CIS synchronically:

Synchronic interpretation of CIS—For any group of subjects, S_1, S_2 ... S_n, and any conscious states, E_1, E_2 ... E_n, the following scenario is

---

[15] I gave a version of the anti-subject-summing conceivability argument in Goff (2009).

conceivable: there are $S_1, S_2 \ldots S_n$ instantiating $E_1, E_2 \ldots E_n$ at time T, but it's not the case at T that there is a subject S^* such that S^* is not identical with any of $S_1, S_2 \ldots S_n$.

On this synchronic interpretation CIS is clearly no threat to fusionism, given that the fusionist does not think that the macro-level subject exists at the same time as the micro-subjects that formed it.

One could formulate a diachronic version of CIS:

Diachronic interpretation of CIS—For any group of subjects, $S_1, S_2 \ldots S_n$, and any conscious states, $E_1, E_2 \ldots E_n$, the following scenario is conceivable: there are $S_1, S_2 \ldots S_n$ instantiating $E_1, E_2 \ldots E_n$ at time T, but it's not the case at any time later than T that there is a subject S^* such that S^* is not identical with any of $S_1, S_2 \ldots S_n$.

However, it would not be unreasonable for the fusionist to build some ceteris paribus qualifiers into their claims of intelligible production. Their claim is likely to be that certain facts about micro-subjects at T1 intelligibly produce certain facts about a macro-subject at a slightly later time *so long as there are no intervening factors*. For example, if God decides to annihilate the universe a tiny fraction of a second after T1, then clearly there aren't going to be any o-subjects. Compare: even if salt is essentially such as to dissolve in water, if it's placed in water at T1, and God decides to destroy the world a moment later, that salt ain't going to dissolve.

Perhaps the problem can be posed in a slightly different way: for any micro-phenomenal state of affairs, it seems to be conceivable that it not give rise to the existence of an o-subject *even if nothing else gets in the way*. This may be just another instance of *the* Humean observation that, with respect to any causal connection, we seem to be able to conceive of the cause not giving rise to the effect. Still, the Russellian fusionist is supposed to be making sense of the *intelligible emergence* of o-subjects, and the presence of the Humean epistemic gap—even if it is present in all causal relations—seems to show that this can't be done. At the very least, this diachronic conceivability gap shows that the fusionist has work to do if she wants to show that o-subjects intelligibly result from the coming together of micro-level subjects.[16]

---

[16] Mørch (2014) defends a form of fusionism according to which the emergence of o-subjects from micro-subjects is *partially intelligible*.

Is there any way for the micropsychist, of either the emergentist or the constitutive variety, to respond to the subject-summing problem? Let us consider some options.

7.3.2.3 *The Ignorance Response*

It might perhaps be suggested that it is our ignorance of the nature of subjecthood—of what it is for something to be a subject—that explains our inability to grasp the combinability of subjects. The most straightforward version of this would be to adopt full-blown opacity concerning our concept of subjecthood, according to which we have no a priori grasp of what it is for something to be a subject. It could then be claimed that if we understood what it is for something to be a conscious subject, we would understand that subjects are the kind of things that combine to yield other subjects.

Imagine someone in the strange position of having opaque concepts of each of the pieces in a jigsaw puzzle of Ken Dodd, perhaps by having a list of numbers each of which refers to a piece of the puzzle. Not having a grasp of the shape and appearance of each of the pieces, such a person would be ignorant of how a certain fact involving the pieces a priori entails the complete image of a Ken. Similarly, for the proponent of the ignorance response, we have only opaque labels for subjecthood and hence fail to grasp all that is implied by the instantiation of that kind.

However, in chapter 5, I defended Direct Phenomenal Transparency, the thesis that direct phenomenal concepts reveal the essences of the states they denote. I take it that subjecthood is a determinable of which each conscious state is a determinate. For example, to be pained is to be a subject in some specific way; to have an experience of orange is to be a subject in some other way. I further take it that if one grasps the essence of a given determinate one thereby grasps the essence of the determinable of that determinate. For example, I couldn't understand what it is for something to be spherical without grasping what it is for something to be shaped, or what it is for something to be red without understanding what it is for something to be colored. It follows that, for any phenomenal property I conceive of under a direct phenomenal concept, in grasping the nature of that property I thereby grasp the nature of subjecthood. This is inconsistent with the ignorance response, at least in its most straightforward form. Moreover, if we have no a priori grasp of the nature of subjecthood, then we have no a priori grounds for denying that

that property is wholly physical, which would leave the panpsychist with no means of rejecting physicalism and would therefore undermine the crucial motivation for her view.

A panpsychist may try to claim that we are *partially ignorant* of the nature of subjecthood, perhaps by defending Direct Phenomenal Translucency: the thesis that direct phenomenal concepts reveal something significant but not everything about the nature of the states they denote.[17] In this way she will hope to walk a thin line: we have enough a priori insight into the nature of subjecthood to know that conscious subjects aren't physical, but not enough to grasp their combinability.

However, in chapter 5 I argued that a thesis of *Full*—rather than *Partial*—Revelation is required to properly account for our epistemic situation with respect to consciousness; and Full Revelation implies Phenomenal Transparency. At the very least, panpsychist proponents of Phenomenal Translucency owe us an account of it as detailed as the physicalist account offered by Robert Schroer. They need to tell us, for example, exactly which features of subjecthood are transparently revealed and which are hidden, and how this precise blend of transparency and opacity rules out physicalism while leaving mental combination a possibility. In my experience anti-physicalists in conversation often gesture at a commitment to Phenomenal Translucency, but I have never found in the literature a detailed non-physicalist account of it.

7.3.2.4 *The Consciousness+ Response*

One hypothesis easily confused with Phenomenal Translucency is the thesis that consciousness is an aspect of a greater property, of which we have only a partial understanding. Call this the "consciousness+ hypothesis." Crucially, the consciousness+ hypothesis is not the thesis that we are ignorant about any aspect of consciousness itself; rather, it is the thesis that we are partially ignorant about some property—call it "consciousness+"—of which consciousness is an aspect. Just as when thinking of proto-consciousness so when thinking about consciousness+, I am

---

[17] It is common to hear this kind of response from panpsychists in conversation. Galen Strawson (2006b) explicitly defends a form of partial ignorance about *consciousness*, in response to the form of the combination problem articulated in my 2006. This would seem to me to imply partial ignorance about subject-hood, given that specific conscious states just are specific ways of being a subject (as just discussed in the main text).

struck by how deeply beautiful such a property would be, enfolding experiential and non-experiential aspects into a single nature.

> But before I examine this matter with more care, and pass on to the consideration of other truths which may be derived from it, it seems to me right to pause for a while in order to contemplate ... to consider, and admire, and adore, the beauty of this light so resplendent, at least as far as the strength of my mind, which is in some measure dazzled by the sight, will allow me to do so.[18]

Back to the game. According to the response currently under consideration, the unknown part of consciousness+ is crucial to phenomenal combination, and our inability to make sense of phenomenal combination is the result of our ignorance of this aspect. The proponent of the consciousness+ hypothesis accepts CIS but denies the following principle:

> *Conceivable Isolation of Subjects+ (CIS+)*—For any group of subjects, S_1, $S_2 \ldots S_n$, and any conscious+ states, $E+_{1+1}$, $E+_2 \ldots E+_n$, the following scenario is conceivable: there are $S_1, S_2 \ldots S_n$ instantiating $E+_1, E+_2 \ldots$ $E+_n$, but it's not the case that there is a subject S^* such that S^* is not identical with any of $S_1, S_2 \ldots S_n$.

Given our lack of grasp of the + bit of consciousness+, we are not in a position to judge whether or not this principle is true.

A concern with the consciousness+ hypothesis is that it essentially reintroduces protophenomenal properties, which one might think removes the advantage panpsychism has over panprotopsychism. Why postulate protophenomenal and phenomenal properties at the micro-level, when we might as well just postulate protophenomenal properties? Of course, by definition, "consciousness+" properties are properties that involve micro-phenomenal properties. But if the choice is between postulating consciousness+ properties, involving phenomenal and protophenomenal elements, and only postulating protophenomenal properties, the latter would seem to be the simpler hypothesis.

While adopting the consciousness+ response does weaken the simplicity argument for panpsychism, I don't think it undermines it

---

[18] Descartes 1645/1996: 35–6.

entirely. The consciousness+ panpsychist has much less noumenalism in her world view than does the pure panprotopsychist: according to the former view, we have a partial understanding of the deep nature of every material property; according to the latter view, we have zero understanding of the deep nature of any (narrowly) material property. And the hypothesis (H1) that all material entities instantiate consciousness+ is simpler than the hypothesis (H2) that brains instantiate consciousness while things other than brains instantiate protophenomenal properties. Panpsychism assumes continuity while panprotopsychism assumes discontinuity.

If the panpsychist adopts the consciousness+ response, then we no longer have the simple contrast between panpsychism on the one hand—giving us (in principle) a completely transparent (i.e., non-noumenalist) picture of reality—and panprotopsychism on the other—giving us total noumenalism (at least about the deep nature of stuff outside of brains). Nonetheless, significant differences remain, and these differences favor panpsychism.

7.3.2.5 *The Spatial Relations Response*

CIS focuses on how subjects of experience are intrinsically and says nothing about how they are *related* to each other. The principle tells us that a plurality of subjects cannot, merely in virtue of how they are intrinsically, intelligibly produce another subject of experience. One might respond that this is not surprising, as combination as we know it always requires the things combining to be spatially related to each other in a certain way. At the very least things that are to combine generally need to be *near each other*: bricks could not form a house if they're scattered at different corners of the globe. And yet CIS does not even mention spatial proximity. The micropsychist may plausibly hold that to intelligibly produce an o-subject, micro-subjects must not only be a certain way intrinsically but must also be spatially related to each in a certain way. Given that CIS does not mention spatial relationships between subjects, its truth is no bar to mental combination so understood.

The initial difficulty with this response to CIS is that adding spatial relationships doesn't seem to close the gap. In so far as we can conceive of micro-subjects as occupying spatial relations and standing in certain spatial relationships with each other, doing so still seems to leave micro-subjects conceivably isolated from o-subjects.

We can make the point vividly by imagining *micro-experiential zombies*, defined as follows:

> *Micro-experiential zombies*—A micro-experiential zombie is (i) a duplicate of an actual human being in terms of its pure physical nature, (ii) such that each of its fundamental parts is a micro-subject, but also (iii) such that none of its macro-level parts is an o-subject.[19]

When we conceive of a regular zombie of, say, the great Liverpudlian comedian Ken Dodd, we conceive of something just like Ken but lacking any kind of consciousness. Take such a zombie and conceive of each of its micro-level parts instantiating, say, slight pain. It still seems conceivable that such a creature lacks the o-consciousness we pre-theoretically associate with Ken himself; indeed, it seems conceivable that it lacks o-consciousness of any form.

Perhaps it's not surprising that a multitude of instances of slight pain won't give rise to Ken's complex and sophisticated experience. But no matter what kind of consciousness we attribute to Ken's bits, the result still seems consistent with the absence of any macro-level consciousness. Suppose actual macro-subject Ken is currently staring at green grass, smelling its freshly cut odor, and listening to a lawn mower engine in the distance. We might imagine (obviously ludicrously oversimplifying to make the point vivid) that some of Ken's micro-subjects underlying relevant brain functioning have an experience as of staring at grass, some have an experience as of freshly cut grass smell, and some have an experience as of the sound of a distant lawnmower. Still, all of these micro-level goings on seem consistent with the absence of some subject having *a unified experience* as of seeing and smelling grass while hearing a distant lawnmower. No matter what weird and whacky conscious states we attribute to your micro-level bits, it seems conceivable that those micro-subjects exist in the absence of some further subject at the macro-level.

It might be pointed out that we cannot conceive of every form of consciousness, and probably we cannot conceive of the forms of consciousness instantiated by micro-level subjects. However, I suggested earlier that the fact that CIS holds for the many and varied forms

---

[19] I first discovered micro-experiential zombies in a 2005 expedition of a far corner of modal space, the findings of which were published in Goff (2009). They are defined slightly differently here.

of consciousness we are able to conceive of gives us good grounds for believing CIS. Similarly, I would suggest here that the fact that micro-experiential zombies remain conceivable whatever consciousness—from the many and varied forms we are able to conceive of—we imagine enjoyed by their micro-level parts, gives us good reason to think that all micro-experiential zombies are conceivable.

It follows that we have good reason to believe in a form of CIS that involves micro-subjects standing in pure physical relations:

Physicalized Conceivable Isolation of Subjects (P-CIS)—For any group of subjects, S_1, S_2 ... S_n, conscious states, E_1, E_2 ... E_n, and n-place pure physical relation P, the following scenario is conceivable: there are S_1, S_2 ... S_n, instantiating E_1, E_2 ... E_n, and standing in P, but it's not the case that there is a subject S^* such that S^* is not identical with any of S_1, S_2 ... S_n.

Assuming that spatial relations are a kind of pure physical relation, P-CIS implies a form of CIS that involves micro-subjects standing in spatial relations:

Spatialized Conceivable Isolation of Subjects (S-CIS)—For any group of subjects, S_1, S_2 ... S_n, conscious states, E_1, E_2 ... E_n, and n-place spatial relation R, the following scenario is conceivable: there are S_1, S_2 ... S_n instantiating E_1, E_2 ... E_n, and standing in R, but it's not the case that there is a subject S^* such that S^* is not identical with any of S_1, S_2 ... S_n.

This can be seen as a very depressing conclusion for the micropsychist. One is initially drawn to panpsychism on the grounds that the physical facts cannot account for consciousness: zombies are conceivable. And yet adding micro-subjects to the mix seems not to change anything: zombies are still conceivable. We seem to have got nowhere.

Despite all this, I think the spatial relations response is defensible. What must be appreciated is that we have good reason to think that we lack a transparent understanding of spatial relationships. We discussed at length in the last chapter the distinction between the causal structural characterization of matter we get from physics and the deep nature of matter that underlies that structure. But space and spatial relations are just as much a part of concrete reality as matter. Indeed, in general relativity, space impacts and is impacted on by the material entities that occupy it. Our scientific understanding of spatial relations is mediated by mathematical models. But for spatial relations to be part of concrete reality, they must have a more than mathematical categorical nature.[20]

If micro-subjects do combine, the ways in which they are spatially related will surely be relevant. But spatial relations will be relevant in virtue of their full nature, not merely the mathematical structures they realize. In the light of this, we can appreciate that our conception of a micro-experiential zombie is most likely non-transparent: our conception of the intrinsic nature of its micro-subjects is potentially transparent (or at least we have a transparent grip on their determinable nature), but our conception of the ways in which micro-subjects are spatially related may be opaque or translucent. It is perhaps not so surprising that this partially opaque conception fails to reveal the intelligible connection between the micro-phenomenal facts and o-phenomenal facts, if indeed there is one.

We can see, then, that there is an ambiguity in S-CIS. It might be a claim about what is conceivable when spatial relations are conceived of in terms of their pure physical nature:

*Physicalistically Spatialized Conceivable Isolation of Subjects (PS-CIS)—*For any group of subjects, $S_1, S_2 \ldots S_n$, conscious states, $E_1, E_2 \ldots E_n$, and n-place spatial relations R_p—where R_p is conceived of under pure a pure physical concept—the following scenario is conceivable: there are $S_1, S_2 \ldots S_n$ instantiating $E_1, E_2 \ldots E_n$, standing in R_p, but it's not the case that there is a subject S^* such that S^* is not identical with any of $S_1, S_2 \ldots S_n$.

Alternatively, it might be a claim about what is conceivable when spatial relations are conceived of under transparent concepts:

*Transparently Spatialized Conceivable Isolation of Subjects (TS-CIS)—*For any group of subjects, $S_1, S_2 \ldots S_n$, total conscious states, $E_1, E_2 \ldots E_n$, and n-place spatial relation R_T—where R_T is conceived of under a transparent concept—the following scenario is conceivable: there are $S_1, S_2 \ldots S_n$, instantiating $E_1, E_2 \ldots E_n$, standing in R_T, but it's not the

---

[20] If spatial relations are not fundamental, as is the case in the priority monist views we will discuss in chapter 9, there is perhaps less pressure to think that they must have a deep nature of their own.

case that there is a subject S* such that S* is not identical with any of $S_1, S_2 \ldots S_n$.

We have good reason to think that PS-CIS is true, but we have no good reason to think TS-CIS is true. Lacking a transparent conception of spatial relationships, we have no grounds for denying that micro-subjects, spatially related, intelligibly produce o-subjects.

The micropsychist can reasonably argue, therefore, that the subject-summing problem results from our lack of understanding of the deep nature of the spatial relation. If we transparently understood the nature of spatial relationships, then it would be clear to us how micro-subjects bond to make o-subjects. The gap between the micro-phenomenal and the o-phenomenal plausibly results from the gap in our understanding of space.

Thus, as with the consciousness+ response, the spatial relations response threatens to introduce an element of noumenalism into panpsychism. The deep nature of spatial relations shows up neither in perception nor in introspection, which makes me cautiously pessimistic about the prospects of our ever reaching positive grasp of it, just as I am cautiously pessimistic about the prospects of our grasping the nature of protophenomenal properties (if there are such things). I think, however, that the spatial relations response is to be preferred over the consciousness+ response. The consciousness+ hypothesis adds mystery merely for the sake of explaining mental combination, whereas there are good reasons independent of mental combination to adopt noumenalism about spatial relations. And by confining noumenalism to relations, this approach allows that we have complete understanding of the deep nature of intrinsic properties. The simplicity argument favors consciousness+ panpsychism over panprotopsychism, but it favors panpsychism in conjunction with the spatial relations response over consciousness+ panpsychism.[21]

---

[21] In chapter 9 I will give reasons independent of mental combination to adopt the consciousness+ hypothesis, pertaining to the need to account for the causal efficacy of consciousness. Accepting these reasons removes the advantage of the spatial relations response over the consciousness+ response. However, I am keen to distinguish independent dialectical considerations. Humean panpsychists and those committed to Armstrong-Dretske-Tooley strong laws (Armstrong 1978, 1983; Dretske 1977; Tooley 1977) will not accept these reasons (outlined in chapter 9) to adopt the consciousness+ hypothesis, and so may accept the reasons outlined in this chapter for favoring the spatial relations response.

I don't want to completely rule out the possibility of human beings one day coming to understand the real nature of spatial relations, or indeed the full nature of consciousness+, and, on the basis of this, securing a more satisfying account of the summing of subjects.[22] Perhaps it simply requires some great conceptual innovation or a bit of neural rewiring. However, I am inclined to be cautiously pessimistic in this regard for the same reason I was cautiously pessimistic about the panprotopsychist's hopes for discovering a positive conception of protophenomenality (as discussed in section 7.2). It's hard to see how we could somehow guess at the deep nature of a feature of reality we are not acquainted with, just as it's hard to see how a congenitally blind woman could somehow guess at the phenomenal nature of red.

Whether or not my pessimism is justified, there is still plenty of hope for theoretical progress. Empirical investigation may be able to reveal what kind of spatial relationships result in combination and the production of an o-subject. Even if we are unable to fully grasp an intelligible connection between the micro-level phenomenal facts and the macro-level phenomenal facts, theoretical success with a micropsychist model may deepen our conviction that there is such an intelligible connection.

In conclusion, the subject-summing problem does not give us reason to doubt panpsychism. It merely draws our attention to an epistemic gap that we would expect to be there anyway given our ignorance concerning the deep nature of spatial relations.

7.3.2.6 *The Gap Is Here to Stay*

It should now be clear that in my view any solution to the combination problem will involve an element of noumenalism and hence a gap in our picture of reality. Some panpsychists, most notably Galen Strawson,[23] defend panpsychism in terms of its capacity to render the existence of human and animal consciousness intelligible. However, the postulation of micro-level consciousness cannot do this on its own, and hence the

---

[22] In this next chapter I will argue, for quite distinct reasons flowing from the subject irreducibility problem, that constitutive subject-summing is impossible. However, this will not rule out the possibility of emergentist subject-summing.

[23] Strawson (2006a: 73) is not optimistic that human beings will one day themselves possess a transparent understanding of macro-level consciousness in terms of micro-level consciousness; nonetheless, he thinks that the panpsychist, but not the panprotopsychist, can avoid being committed to intelligibility gaps in nature.

panpsychist must add further elements to her conception of fundamental reality in order to account for o-consciousness; and those further elements are unlikely to be ones that humans have a positive conception of.[24] Panpsychism is, I have argued, to be preferred over panprotopsychism, but this is because the former is simpler and involves less of a commitment to noumenalism. Neither panpsychism nor panprotopsychism is able to provide us with a completely transparent account of the existence of o-consciousness, at least not yet.[25]

Isn't a gap in a theory a sign of giving up, of "nay-saying" to use Churchland's expression (from section 1.1.2)? Gaps are indeed a downside of a theory, to be minimized if at all possible. Panpsychism fares better than panprotopsychism in this regard. However, the presence of gaps does not necessarily imply that the theory in question is on the wrong tracks, as there is no good reason to presume that human beings are equipped with the faculties necessary to uncover the complete nature of fundamental reality. Churchland's argument is grounded in a narrative concerning the success of physical science. However, while the success of physical science gives us reason to think that human beings are good at mapping the world's causal structure, it gives us no reason to think we will be especially good at discovering its deep nature.

7.3.3 Coleman's Anti-Subject-Summing Argument

Thus far we have been considering the conceivability argument against intelligible subject-summing. There are other arguments that attempt to show more directly that the notion of a conscious whole formed from conscious parts is implausible or incoherent. In an early paper of mine— before my conversion to panpsychism—I argued that even if we can make sense of subject-summing, the experience of each micro-subject must feature in the experience of the macro-subject, and that appreciating this casts doubt on the coherence of micropsychism:

> For the experiential being of some little experiencing thing "LITTLE" to be part of the experiential being some big

---

[24] This is related to the arguments I made in Goff (2006, 2009).

[25] Doesn't this admission put physicalism and Russellian monism on an equal footing, given that both involve a gap? The difference is that the Russellian monist gap is an *epistemic gap*, due to our ignorance of certain features of reality, while the physicalist gap (as demonstrated by the arguments of the first half of this book) is *metaphysical*.

experiencing thing "BIG" is for what it is like to be LITTLE to be a part of what it is like to be BIG. But if follows from this that BIG feels how LITTLE does (even if it also feels other things). Correspondingly, for the experiential being of some BIG to be wholly constituted by the experiential being of LITTLE 1, LITTLE 2, LITTLE 3 ... (again assuming this makes any sense at all) can be nothing other than for BIG to feel how it feels to be all those LITTLES and to feel nothing else. Even if it is intelligible how experiential states can *sum* together, it is contradictory to suppose that they could sum together to form some novel conscious state.

If my experiential being were constituted by the experiential being of billions of experience-involving ultimates ["ultimate" is Galen Strawson's term for a fundamental material entity],[26] then what it is like to be each of those ultimates would be part of what it is like to be me. I would literally feel how each of those ultimates feels, somehow all at the same time. Assuming that my experiential being is *wholly* constituted by the experiential being of a billion experience-involving ultimates, then what it is like to be me can be nothing other than what it is like to be each of those billion ultimates (somehow experienced all at the same time).

But this surely cannot be right. My experience is of a three dimensional world of people, cars, buildings, etc. The phenomenal character of my experience is surely very different from the phenomenal character of something that feels as a billion ultimates feel.[27]

Even if this argument were successful in demonstrating that the experience of each micro-subject is present in the experience of the o-subject they form, perhaps we should see the argument as presenting a challenge to the micropsychist to accommodate this fact into her view rather than being a decisive argument that micropsychism is incoherent.

However, more recently Sam Coleman has formulated an ingenious argument to the conclusion that, whatever the nature of the consciousness allegedly instantiated at the micro and macro level, subject-summing

---

[26] Strawson 2006a.
[27] Goff 2006: 58–9; emphasis in the original.

is incoherent.[28] His argument relies on the idea that the essence of a subject's point of view is given not just by the fact that the subject has certain conscious states, but by the fact that it has certain conscious states *and not any others*. Like the holy sacrament of marriage, subjectivity demands exclusivity. Coleman considers for illustration the putative possibility of combining a micro-subject instantiating only phenomenal red—which he calls "Red"—and a micro-subject instantiating only phenomenal blue—which he calls "Blue"—into an "uber-subject":

> Consider the original duo's point of view. One—*Blue's*—is pervaded by a unitary blueness, the other—*Red's*—by redness, and that is all they experience respectively. To say these points of view were present as components in the experiential perspective of the uber-subject ("Ub") would therefore be to say that *Ub* experienced a unitary phenomenal blueness and a unitary phenomenal redness, i.e. had synchronous experiences as of each of these qualities alone, *to the exclusion of all others*. For it is these qualities each *on their own* that characterise, respectively, the perspectives of the original duo. Experience excludes, as well as includes. Yet nowhere does *Ub* have any such experiences: he precisely *combines* his predecessors' qualitative experiential contents. *Ub* doesn't experience red-to-the-exclusion-of-(blue-and)-all-else, nor blue-to-the-exclusion-of-(red-and)-all-else, let alone—impossibly—both *together*. Thus, the original points of view are not ingredients in *Ub's* subjectivity.[29]

Both of these arguments rely on equating the following two things:

- Phenomenal quality/point of view X is *partially constituted* by—that is, partly grounded in—phenomenal quality/point of view Y.
- Phenomenal quality/point of view X is *partially characterized* by phenomenal quality/point of view Y—that is, Y is phenomenal present—or "shows up" in X's experience.

In my argument I was assuming that if my experience is partially constituted by, say, a slight pain, then that slight pain must characterize my

---

[28] Coleman (2014).
[29] Coleman 2014: 33; emphasis in the original.

experience: it must be a feature of what it's like to be me. In Coleman's argument, he assumes that if a lesser point of view partially constitutes a greater point of view, then the lesser point of view must be phenomenally present in the greater point of view (which he tries to show is incoherent). In both cases, the equation of partial constitution with partial characterization is crucial. However, this equation can be coherently denied.

To try to make sense of this, consider a standard form of panprotopsychism. On this view, a given o-experiential state is constituted of certain protophenomenal properties, but those protophenomenal properties don't themselves characterize the resulting o-experience. Protophenomenal properties, not being phenomenal, are not the kind of properties that can characterize experiences. One might dispute the truth of this kind of view, but we can't reject it simply because of its implication that the qualities that constitute experience don't also characterize experience. Nor for that matter could we rule out the truth of physicalism on these grounds. It seems coherent, therefore, to hold that a property can play a role in constituting a given experience without playing a role in characterizing that experience.

One might object that it's one thing to hold that a *non-experiential* micro-level property can partially constitute an o-experience without partially characterizing that experience, and quite another to hold that an *experiential* micro-level property can partly constitute without partially characterizing an o-experience. However, once we have allowed that partial characterizing and partially constituting can come apart, it seems that we can coherently suppose that they can come apart in the case of the relationship between the micro-level phenomenal and the o-phenomenal. At the very least we are owed an argument as to why this couldn't be the case.

We might see the arguments against subject-summing currently under consideration as relying on an ambiguity in the phrase "being part of what it's like to be subject." A given micro-experience can be "part of what it's like to be me" in the sense that it constitutes my experience or can be "part of what it's like to be me" in the sense that it characterizes my experience. Distinguishing these two meanings disarms the arguments. Regarding my 2006 argument, one could hold that the experience of each of a huge number of micro-subjects constitutes without characterizing my experience, and thereby avoid the counterintuitive conclusion that "what it is like to be me can be nothing other than what it is like to be each of those billion ultimates (somehow experienced all at the same time)." Regarding Coleman's argument, one could hold that *Blue* and *Red* constitute (i.e., partially ground) the *Ub*'s point of view but without being phenomenally present in that viewpoint (i.e., without "showing up" in *Ub*'s experience), and hence avoid the incoherent scenario of *Ub* experiencing both red-to-the-exclusion-of-(blue-and)-all-else and blue-to-the-exclusion-of-(red-and)-all-else.

I think there's a more general moral to be drawn here. I would be cautious about any argument against subject-summing that implicitly relies on a sense that we have a transparent understanding of the part–whole relation. We feel intuitively we have a grip on what it is for one thing to be part of another thing, just as we feel we have a grip on what it is for things to be spatially related, or for things to be solid. Certainly in the case of solidity, our everyday sense of what it is for matter to be solid has been decisively refuted by modern science, given that "solid" matter is mostly empty space. But more generally, as Russellian monists, we accept that our grip on the world beyond our own consciousness is mediated by abstract mathematical models. When concerned with the more than mathematical nature of fundamental reality, the default position should be an assumption of ignorance.

Russellian monists have thus far not appreciated that this general assumption of ignorance ought to hold in consideration of mereological relations. Appreciating this opens up possibilities. Just as has proved to be the case with respect to solidity, the part–whole relation might turn out to be radically different from our pre-theoretical conception of it. Suppose layered emergentist panpsychism is true, such that a given o-subject BIG is intelligibly caused by a number of micro-subject SMALLS. We might naturally be inclined to think:

> Given that the SMALLS *cause* BIG, they cannot also be *part* of BIG. For a whole is nothing over and above its parts, while an effect is ontologically additional to its cause.

Once made explicit, it is clear that this argument relies on an assumption that we have a significant grip on the nature of the part–whole relation, the very assumption I am suggesting a Russellian monist ought not to make. It is rather like arguing, "Given that the table is solid, it cannot be mostly empty space." Like solidity, mereological relations are out there in the world; they are not created in the image of what we have in our minds. We identify a part–whole relation by pointing: "*Those things* (we point at some small things) are parts of *that thing* (we point at a large thing filling roughly the same region of space as the little things)." It could turn out that the little things we call "parts of Bill's brain" intelligibly cause the big thing we call "Bill's brain." In this case it would turn out, not that that the little things we call "parts" are not really parts at all, but rather that—at least in this case—the relationship between parts and whole is causal rather than constitutive. The whole is something over and above its parts.

It is even clearer that Coleman's anti-subject summing argument fails if the relationship between micro-subjects and o-subjects is causal rather than constitutive. The fact that a given micro-phenomenal quality is partially causally responsible for my experience does not tempt us into thinking that that micro-phenomenal quality must partially characterize my experience. To be clear, I'm not suggesting that Coleman intended his argument to refute emergentist panpsychism; he was simply trying to refute the thesis that human subjects are composed of micro-subjects. But my point is that it might turn out that *composition*—in its deep nature—is a form of emergence, and this would undermine Coleman's attempted refutation of subject-to-subject composition.[30]

Thus, in formulating this solution to Coleman's anti-subject-summing argument, I do not take myself merely to be rescuing constitutive micropsychism from his argument, but also articulating a form of emergentist micropsychism. This point is important, as while I ultimately think that constitutive micropsychism is unworkable (for reasons distinct from the subject-summing problem, which we will get to in the next chapter), emergentist micropsychism seems to me perfectly coherent.

---

[30] Just to be clear: I also think the argument fails against constitutive panpsychism, for the reasons I have already given.

8

Top–Down Combination Problems

Russellian monists postulate narrowly material subjects or proto-subjects, of which we are not familiar, to explain ordinary experience, of which we are familiar. In the last chapter we focused on what the micropsychist takes to be the basic elements of mental combination—micro-subjects—and considered doubts about their potential to combine. In this chapter we focus on the putative results of (proto)mental combination: our own minds. Is it possible that my mind and the conscious experience I am enjoying right now is grounded in, or intelligibly emerges from, more fundamental elements? Or do I have conclusive grounds for thinking that my conscious mind is fundamental or irreducible? Reflection on ordinary consciousness—o-consciousness as I have been calling it throughout the book—poses considerable challenges to the Russellian monist; I call these challenges "top–down combination problems." We will examine three:

- The palette problem
- The structural mismatch problem
- The subject irreducibility problem

8.1 The Palette Problem

The first difficulty we shall consider begins from the observation that o-experience is extraordinarily rich and diverse. Even within a single sense modality, such as vision, there are a vast range of kinds of experiences. More strikingly, the experiences of different sense modalities seem of wildly different kinds, with no commonality between them; there seems, for example, to be an unbridgeable gulf between an experience of taste and an experience of color.

This richness and variety is a problem for the Russellian monist because she is committed to o-experience arising from a relatively small number of properties. Recall that according to Russellian monism the explanatorily basic properties of the universe are material properties: the properties picked out by fundamental physics, such as mass, spin, and charge. There is more to the nature of these fundamental properties than is revealed by physics: they are the deep nature of matter. Nonetheless, they are the properties *named* by fundamental physics, and those properties are relatively few in number. Hence, if Russellian monism is true, the vast range of kinds of consciousness—from colors, to tastes, to the experience of echo-location—must emerge from, as it were, a tiny palette of qualities. This seems prima facie an implausible, perhaps even impossible, supposition. I will follow Chalmers in calling this "the palette problem."[1]

We may take the palette problem in one of two ways. On a stronger understanding, the palette problem takes the form of an argument to the conclusion that Russellian monism is impossible, as the variety of o-experience could not possibly result from a relatively small number of properties. The milder understanding of the palette problem takes the form of a challenge to the Russellian monist, a demand to explain how o-consciousness in all its variety could come from half a dozen or so properties. Let us take each of these in turn.

8.1.1 The Strong Palette Problem

There are certainly similarities between different experiences within a sense modality: the experience of red is similar to the experience of orange, to return to an example we explored in chapter 5. And there is some prima facie plausibility to the idea that these similarities result from *common phenomenal elements*: intuitively, phenomenal orange is what you get when you mix phenomenal red with phenomenal yellow. Noting such similarities and commonalities may give the constitutive Russellian monist hope for the prospects of a kind of "mental chemistry," a science of how more complex phenomenal qualities result from combinations of more simple kinds.[2]

---

[1] Chalmers 2016. Barry Dainton (2011a: 246) calls the palette problem "the derivation problem."
[2] Cf. Coleman 2012.

Unfortunately, such hope is cruelly disappointed when we compare and contrast phenomenal qualities from distinct sense modalities. There may perhaps be structural or representational commonality between distinct senses: I can represent the shape of a ball with vision and with touch. But the media in which these representations are formed seem entirely unlike. On the face of it, the taste of mint on the one hand and the experience of red on the other have nothing whatsoever in common. How then could they be built up from the same elements?

We could press the strong palette problem against the constitutive Russellian monist with the following argument:

The palette argument

1. If constitutive Russellian monism is true, then for any two o-conscious experiences X and Y, X and Y have common constituents (assuming the basic properties of matter, mass, spin, charge, etc. are present in all macro-level properties of matter).
2. Minty phenomenology and red phenomenology have nothing in common.
3. Therefore, constitutive Russellian monism is false.

The emergentist Russellian monist thinks that o-experience is intelligibly caused by, rather than built up from, micro-(proto)experiential elements. One might find baffling the idea that qualities as diverse and dissimilar as those we find in o-experience intelligibly arise from a small number of properties. However, although it is prima facie difficult to see how this could be so, it's also difficult to see how one could demonstrate that it could not be so. Thus, the emergentist Russellian monist is subject only to the mild form of the palette, which will give her an advantage over the constitutive Russellian monist unless the latter has an effective response to the argument just outlined.

Luke Roelofs has argued that there may be elements of our experience that we are in a sense unaware of due to what he calls "confusion," a notion he draws from Spinoza and Leibniz:

> The perceptions of our senses even when they are clear must necessarily contain certain confused elements . . . [for] while our senses respond to everything, our soul cannot pay attention to every particular . . . It is almost like the confused murmuring

which is heard by those who approach the shore of a sea. It comes from the continual beatings of innumerable waves.[3]

The human body, being limited, is only capable of distinctly forming a certain number of images within itself at the same time; if this number be exceeded, the images will begin to be confused; if this number . . . be largely exceeded, all will become entirely confused one with another. . . . When the images become quite confused in the body, the mind also imagines all bodies confusedly without any distinction, and will comprehend them, as it were, under one attribute.[4]

As Roelofs understands the notion of confusion, a subject is confused with respect to two mental elements when she is able to attend to or think about those two elements together, but unable to attend to or think about them individually.[5]

Let us illustrate the notion of confusion with respect to an imagined alien race, the Kenzars. When a Kenzar smells a rose, she has an experience qualitatively just like the experience a human being has when she smells a rose: call that experience the "R-experience." But she also has—when smelling a rose—an experience qualitatively just like the experience a human being has when she hears middle C: call that the "C-experience." Suppose that, as a matter of contingent fact, a Kenzar never has an R-experience without also having a C-experience. Suppose further that Kenzar's brains are wired such that, although they are able to attend to and think about both the R-experience and the C-experience together, for example, when they smell a rose, they are unable to think about or attend to R-experiences without also thinking about/attending to C-experiences. In Roelofs' terms, the Kenzars are *confused* with respect to R-experiences and C-experiences.[6]

It might be natural to infer from this that the Kenzars would take the experience they have when they smell a rose to be a primitive, irreducible

---

[3] Leibniz 1686/2012: 96.

[4] Spinoza 1677/1994: 140.

[5] Roelofs 2014/2015: ch. 5. Roelofs does not claim that this notion of confusion captures exactly what either Leibniz or Spinoza understand by the term in the quotations.

[6] Roelofs distinguishes between a number of different kinds of confusion, and his central notion of *radical confusion* is not quite the one I am employing here. My notion is asymmetric as the Kenzars can think about C-experiences without thinking about R-experiences, for example, when they think about S-experiences. I do this so that I can discuss the possibility of being ignorant of a common element of experiences; I don't think this affects the argument.

experience—call it an "RC-experience"—and would be unaware that it is composed of two distinct elements: R-experiences and C-experiences. To develop the example, we can imagine that when Kenzars taste sugar they have an experience qualitatively just like the experience a human being has when she tastes sugar—call it the "S-experience"—but they also have a C-experience. As in the case of smelling roses, although they can attend to and think about S-experiences and C-experiences together, they are unable to attend to/think about S-experiences without also attending to/thinking about C-experiences. It might be natural to infer that the Kenzars take the experience they have when they taste sugar— SC experience—and the experience they have when they smell a rose— RC experience—to both be primitive, irreducible experiences with no elements in common. Contrary to this supposition, these experiences are composite and have a common element: C-experience.

If all this makes sense, we might suppose that something similar is true of human beings. Perhaps whenever we see red we actually have two experiences—an X experience and a Y experience—but are confusedly unable to think about or attend to X and Y individually. Similarly, whenever we taste mint we have two experiences—an X experience and a Z experience—but are confusedly unable think about or attend to X and Y individually. We are thus unable to discern the common element—X-experience—in red experiences and minty experiences.

There is a worry that this ingenious solution to the strong palette problem is inconsistent with Phenomenal Transparency. I am able to attend to and form direct phenomenal concepts of both minty experiences and red experiences. Given Phenomenal Transparency, these concepts reveal the complete essences of those experiences. If there is an essential element in common between these experiences, then that common element ought to be a priori accessible to someone who has both concepts. This common element may be difficult to discern, but it is inconsistent with Phenomenal Transparency to suppose it utterly inaccessible to reason.

However, what is being assumed in this worry is that the constituents of a given experience are *essential* to that experience, and we need not take this to be so. Compare: *being a heart* is a functional property that is grounded in certain specific biological properties in human beings. But the biological nature of a human heart is not essential to the general property of *being a heart*. The hearts of other organisms have a different biological nature, and indeed we can suppose that in the future some humans may have wholly prosthetic hearts. I can completely understand the essence of the property of being a heart, by understanding the functional role required for there to be a heart, without understanding anything of the biological goings-on that ground that property in human beings.

Now red experiences are not functional properties, but it may be that like red experiences they are *multiply realizable*: in humans they are grounded in experiences X and Y, while in other creatures they may be grounded in certain other experiences or proto-experiences. In this case, I can completely understand the essence of red experience—what it is for something to have a red experience—while knowing nothing about the phenomenal or protophenomenal properties that ground that property in human beings. In general, grasping the essence of a property does not entail grasping the essence of the properties that ground it.[7]

One might object that if X-phenomenology partly constitutes red phenomenology, then X-phenomenology is part of what it's like to have red phenomenology, and thus ought to be in principle introspectively discernible to someone having a red experience. However, this plays on an ambiguity already discussed in our consideration of Coleman's anti-subject-summing argument in the last chapter. To say that X-phenomenology is "part of" red-phenomenology might mean that X-phenomenology partly *characterizes* red-phenomenology—that X-phenomenology is phenomenally present in red-phenomenology—but it might merely mean that X-phenomenology party *constitutes* minty-phenomenology, and the latter does not obviously imply the former.

Once we appreciate this, we can see that a commitment to confusion is not required in order to make sense of our ignorance concerning the constituents of our experiences, for the constituents of my experiences may not be experienced by me at all. Roelofs' view seems to be that:

1. Each o-experiential property is *identical* with the property of having a large number of specific micro-experiential properties (perhaps standing in certain relations to one another). In our imaginary example, for a Kenzar to have an RC experience just is for her to have an R-experience at the same time as a C-experience. In the case of actual human beings, Roelofs' view seems to be that to have a red experience just is to instantiate a huge number of specific micro-experiential properties

---

[7] Chalmers (2016) makes this point in response to the revelation argument. We will return to the revelation argument in the next chapter.

at the same time (and perhaps for the micro-experiential property instances to stand in certain relations to one another).

2. Confusion renders me unable to think individually about any of the micro-experiential properties that constitute my o-phenomenology.

This view is indeed inconsistent with Phenomenal Transparency: we have direct phenomenal concepts of many o-experiences, and hence if they were identical with complex micro-experiential states, our direct phenomenal concepts of those states would reveal this to us (assuming Phenomenal Transparency). Of course we might reject the argument I have given in support of Phenomenal Transparency, but if direct phenomenal concepts do not reveal the natures of o-conscious states, then we have no a priori grounds for denying that those states have entirely physical natures, and hence we lose our motivation for adopting panpsychism (I will not repeat here the arguments I gave in chapter 5 against the halfway house of Phenomenal Translucency.)

However, if we suppose that o-phenomenal states are grounded in, rather than identical with, certain micro-experiential states, then we need not suppose that those micro-experiential states are experiences of any human being, and so we need not suppose that they are experiences any human being is aware of. We can reject premise 2 of the palette argument. Although we entirely grasp the nature of red phenomenology and minty phenomenology, we may be entirely ignorant of the nature of their experiential or proto-experiential components. Hence, we have no introspective grounds for supposing that minty phenomenology and red phenomenology states are not constructed from common experiential or proto-experiential elements.

8.1.2 The Mild Palette Problem

Even if it fails to present a knock-down argument against Russellian monism, the palette problem clearly poses a serious challenge for a Russellian monist, of either constitutive or emergentist stripe, wanting to fill in the details of her view. How might it be that such diversity results from a small number of properties? The ideal Russellian monist theory would postulate a specific explanatorily basic phenomenal or protophenomenal property for each of the properties of fundamental physics; it would then provide, for each of the qualities we encounter in our experience, an explanation as to how that quality arises from those basic phenomenal/protophenomenal properties. A less ambitious way of responding to the palette problem would be to give a broad-brush-strokes account of how such seemingly radically diverse qualities might result from a small number of elements.

Work has already begun to address the challenge of the palette problem. Sam Coleman, drawing on the work of Charles Hartshorne, argues that the gap between sensory modalities might not be as unbridgeable as we imagine.[8] Perhaps we think there is an unbridge-able gap between colors and tastes simply because we lack the experiences that would bridge that gap. Perhaps there is a certain range of possible experiences (not had by humans) that lie in between auditory experiences and colors experiences, such that if we instantiated those "in between" experiences we would be able move in imagination from colors to sounds as seamlessly as we move between shades of blue. And maybe future brain science will find a way of inducing in us these "in between" experiences.

There may also be more commonality than strikes us at first glance between the experiences we already have. Coleman suggests the following subtle commonalities between experiences of distinct sensory modalities:

> Sometimes, especially when falling asleep, I am uncertain whether I *heard* or *felt* something thud somewhere (it doesn't seem to be *both*): auditory/tactile overlap thus seems quite feasible. Again, one thinks of the experience of deep bass drumming. This suggests the possibility that tactile sensations are (qualitatively speaking) just "strong," more "impactful," forms of auditory qualia. Additionally, one might take seriously empirical data indicating that what we commonly think of as the "flavour" of things is really a composite of smell and taste qualia (from receptors in the nose and tongue respectively). It's very easy to separate out the taste element, just hold your nose while eating. Is our failure to notice this fusion experientially because these two species of qualia overlap qualitatively?[9]

[8] Coleman 2015; Hartshorne 1934.

[9] This is an extract from an early draft of Coleman (2015; emphasis in the original), which was later removed.

Coleman, following Hartshorne, speculates that, contrary to initial appearances, all experiential qualities may lie on a single continuum. If future research could identify such a continuum and the location of our experiences within it, then we could perhaps come to understand how a relatively small number of properties could "hone in on" a certain point on that spectrum, and thereby explain the nature of resultant o-experiences.

An alternative approach to the palette problem is to try to reconceive the relationship between micro-experiences and o-experiences. Perhaps the emergence of o-experiences from micro-experiences is not so much a process of composition but of distillation. Keith Turausky speculates that the qualitative nature of each and every possible o-experience may be in some sense already present in the experience of each and every particle, in something like the way that all the colors of the spectrum are present in white light:

> [I]nstead of postulating that phenomenology "fades out" as one moves down the scale of complexity, we might consider that the simplest, most fundamental phenomenology is a sort of "white out." In other words, perhaps experientiality in its most basic form is modally, intentionally, and informationally *undifferentiated*: not watered-down at all, but rather a super-saturated ... experientiality. Consider what it would be like to experience *everything at once*: hot and cold, rising and falling, quiet and loud, light and dark, wet and dry, happy and sad, etc. *ad infinitum*. Not, again, that we wish to claim the humble electron actually feels any of *those* specific things; the point, rather is to get a sense for "experiencing everything at once" actually implies: an utter *undifferentiation* that is, in a certain sense, the antithesis of consciousness as we know it. To experience experiential state *E* with every experiential state *not-E* would be to have *no useful content* concerning either oneself or one's environment. It would be a senseless seething stasis of phenomenology—but phenomenology it would be![10]

Admittedly these are all extremely speculative stabs in the dark. But this is early days in a wholly new research program. Neuroscience has come

---

[10] Turausky (n.d.; emphasis is original).

a long way in the last 80 years, but we have also wasted a lot of time on consciousness-denying neuro-fundamentalist approaches to dealing with phenomenology, and precious little time has been devoted to working in a framework that takes both matter and mind seriously. Darwin's theory of natural selection was a very general biological hypothesis; filling in the details has taken a long time, and we've still got a long way to go. Russellian monism is an extremely elegant unification of mind and matter, but it is also a very general hypothesis, and it will take time to fill in the details.

The Russellian approach has enjoyed a small revival within contemporary analytic philosophy of mind. But it is still not a well-known view, and it is almost completely unknown in other relevant disciplines. Decades of serious work within a Darwinian framework led to the development of genetics. It will presumably take at least several decades of serious interdisciplinary effort within a Russellian framework before we have any kind of real understanding as to how everyday conscious experience emerges from the fundamental components of matter. We are a long way from even beginning to do what is required. It is ironic that the very people who accuse anti-physicalists of being "naysayers" are the quickest to claim they know a priori that a panpsychist or panprotopsychist research program will never bear fruit.[11]

Having said that, it is quite possible that the details will forever elude us. The success of the physical sciences has given us great confidence about our powers to uncover the essential nature of space, time, and matter. However, as we have discovered in chapters 1 and 6, this is false confidence: the success of the physical sciences is precisely due to the fact that since the scientific revolution they have *not* been in the business of finding out the essential nature of space, time, and matter. From Galileo onward, physicists have ignored the concrete categorical nature of matter and just focused on mapping its causal structure. We human beings have no idea how much potential we have for finding out the deep nature of the world we live in. Assuming our faculties evolved for survival in a state of nature rather than for uncovering the essential nature of matter, it is perhaps more likely than not that we won't get very far.

---

[11] For more about "naysaying," see my discussion of Churchland in section 1.1.2. I am, in part, basing my comments here on lively (but friendly!) discussions with Daniel Dennett, Patricia and Paul Churchland, and other neuro-fundamentalists.

It's well worth trying to develop a better understanding of why we have the kind of consciousness we do, and we may yet surprise ourselves. If theorizing within the Russellian framework produces detailed panpsychist/panprotopsychist theories that accurately predict the nature of a given subject's o-conscious on the basis of more fundamental material goings-on, then this would provide powerful evidence for these theories. However, it may be that we end up having to accept some degree of noumenalism about the deep nature of matter; I argued in the last chapter that this is likely with respect to the deep nature of spatial relations. At the very least, the business of investigating the deep nature of matter is likely to involve a great deal more speculation and educated guessing than we are used to in the physical sciences.

Even if this proves to be the case, I would argue that the elegant way in which Russellian monism brings together in a unified theory both what we know about reality introspectively and what we know about reality empirically, gives us strong reason to believe it to be true. Even if humans prove to be incapable of filling in the details, Russellian monism in its general form remains our best guess as to the nature of reality.

8.2 The Structural Mismatch Problem

Like physicalists, most constitutive Russellian monists believe that o-experience results from micro-level goings-on in the brain. Indeed, assuming that the macro-level brain is intelligibly produced by such micro-level goings-on, it is natural for the constitutive Russellian monist to identify the human brain and (certain of) its macro-level states with the o-conscious subject and its o-conscious states. Of course, the mind and the brain seem like very different things, but the Russellian monist puts this down to the fact that from the outside we only get at the causal structure of the brain, while the mind is identical with the deep material entity underlying that structure.

A problem remains, however, as while the physical sciences don't reveal the concrete categorical nature of the brain, they do reveal its structure. And on the face of it, the structure of the brain seems radically unlike the structure of the o-conscious mind as revealed through introspection. But if the mind and brain are identical, or at least grounded in the same micro-level base, one might expect them to have the same structure.

David Chalmers puts the intuitive sense that mind and brain have different structures as follows:

> Our phenomenology has a rich and specific structure: it is unified, bounded, differentiated into many different aspects, but with an underlying homogeneity to many of the aspects, and appears to have a single subject of experience. It is not easy to see how a distribution of a large number of individual microphysical systems, each with their own protophenomenal properties, could somehow add up to this rich and specific structure. Should one not expect something more like a disunified, jagged collection of phenomenal spikes?[12]

As with the palette problem, the structural mismatch problem can be taken in either a stronger or a milder form.[13] In its milder form, it is a challenge to the Russellian monist to explain how something with the structure of the o-conscious mind could possibly arise from something with the structure of the micro-level brain. This is not an argument against Russellian monism but a target for future research. In its stronger form, the structural mismatch problem takes the form of a deductively valid argument to the conclusion that Russellian monism is false. Chalmers expresses the stronger form as follows:

The structural mismatch argument

1. If constitutive Russellian monism is true, micro-level (proto)phenomenal structure is isomorphic to micro-level pure physical structure.
2. If constitutive Russellian monism is true, micro-level (proto)phenomenal (and micro-level pure physical) structure constitutes o-phenomenal structure.
3. Micro-level pure physical structure constitutes only macro-level pure physical structure.
4. If micro-level (proto)phenomenal structure is isomorphic to micro-level pure physical structure, then any structure constituted by micro-level (proto)phenomenal structure (and micro-level material structure) is isomorphic to a structure constituted by micro-level pure physical structure.

---

[12] Chalmers 2002: 266.
[13] This term is from Stoljar (2001; cf. Lockwood, 1993; Foster 1991: 119–30).

5. O-phenomenal structure is not isomorphic to macro-level pure physical structure.

6. Constitutive Russellian monism is false.[14]

This argument is aimed at constitutive Russellian monism in particular. According to emergentist Russellian monism, o-experience is causally brought about by micro-(proto)experience, and there is no reason to think that an effect need be structurally isomorphic with its cause. Compare: I was causally brought into being by my parents, but my shape and size are quite different to that of my parents. Having said that, standardly emergentist Russellian monists take o-conscious states to be the deep nature of macro-level brain states. In this way, they can avoid the worry that macro-level brain states causally exclude o-conscious states, even if they can't so easily avoid the worry that micro-level brain states causally exclude o-conscious state. But if o-conscious states are the deep nature of brain states, it seems to follow that there must be brain states structurally isomorphic with o-conscious states. And so the emergentist is likely to face essentially the same challenge as the constitutivist: brain states don't seem to have the same structure as o-conscious states.

Premise 1 of Chalmers' argument may be questioned. Physics captures the causal structure of micro-(proto)phenomenal properties, but the categorical nature of these properties may involve structure that goes beyond their causal structure. More importantly, we have good reason to think that premise 5 is false. This is because we have good reason, as Chalmers is well aware, to think that the structure of o-consciousness is captured in information states realized by the brain. Indeed, in the article and then the book on which he made his name,[15] Chalmers defended what he called the "Principle of Structural Coherence" as a constraint on an adequate theory of consciousness:

Whenever there is conscious experience, there is some corresponding information in the cognitive system that is available in the control of behaviour, and available for verbal report.... [T]he geometrical structure of the visual field [for example] is directly reflected in a structure that can be recovered from visual

---

[14] Chalmers (2016: 7.8). I have framed the argument using my terminology.
[15] Chalmers 1995, 1996.

processing. Every geometrical relation corresponds to something that can be reported and is therefore cognitively represented. If we were given only the story about information-processing in an agent's visual and cognitive system, we couldn't *directly* observe that agent's visual experiences, but we could nevertheless infer those experiences' structural properties.[16]

The basic point is that a person is able to report on the structure of their conscious experience, which seems to imply that that structure is represented in the information structures of that person's brain.

Appreciating this, we can see that the "structural mismatch" problem is, at best, misnamed. There is no structural mismatch, as the relevant structures are there in the brain. Indeed, Chalmers goes on to acknowledge that the Russellian monist may exploit this fact in responding to his argument:

> Perhaps the best way to respond to the argument is to say that it equivocates on "macro[pure]physical structure." We might say that *narrowly macro[pure]physical structure* is macrophysical structure characterized in terms of physics: for example, in terms of space, time, mass, charge, and so on. *Broadly macro[pure]physical* structure is any structure constituted by microphysics: for example, chemical, biological, and computational structure .... The structure of consciousness is not isomorphic to the spatiotemporal and other narrowly macrophysical structures of the brain, but it may well be isomorphic to other sorts of macrophysical structures there .... Most obviously, one can suggest macrophenomenal structure is isomorphic to certain *information stuctures* in the brain .... I think something like this has to be the best option for the pan[proto]psychist: It seems clear that the structure of the visual field corresponds to information structure in the brain and not to spatial or qualitative structure.[17]

Adopting this strategy leaves the Russellian monist with a challenge, and that is to explain why phenomenology corresponds to abstract and

---

[16] Chalmers 1995, 212–13; emphasis in original.

[17] Chalmers 2016: 208–9. From earlier to later drafts, the writing of this section of the book and of the corresponding section of Chalmers' paper have to a certain extent evolved through mutual interaction.

highly specific information states that don't seem notable from the perspective of physics. We can make the point clearer with an analogy. Consider the property of being a table-shaped material object, which I suggested in chapter 2 might be analyzed in terms of a certain (difficult to articulate) pattern of penetration resistance among spatial regions. That is a real material property, which objects out there in the mind-independent world really have. But it is a quite abstract, rarefied kind of property. It would be weird if some fundamental or significant truth about the universe depended on the distribution of *table-shaped-objecthood*, for example, if that property featured in fundamental physical laws. Similarly, although there are information states corresponding to the structure of o-consciousness, those information states seem, at least from the third-person perspective, to be highly abstract and rarefied. It seems odd that an important property such as o-consciousness should correlate with states of this kind.

How should we respond to this difficulty? Luke Roelofs argues for the coherence of the following line: o-experience really does have the incredibly complex structure we might expect it to have given its grounding in the micro-level structure of the brain, but confusion (in the technical sense explicated in the previous discussion of the palette problem) renders us unaware of much of that structure. We are unable to think about the components of our experiences in isolation, and thus we are blinded to their complexity.[18] But this approach is inconsistent with Phenomenal Transparency. In so far as I can form direct phenomenal concepts of my o-conscious states, those concepts accurately represent the essential nature and thereby the structure of those states.

What are we to make then of the fact that our o-conscious states share the structure of highly rarefied information states rather than the structure of more natural and fundamental macro-level brain states? I think the moral to be drawn is that o-phenomenology is not the unique or privileged kind of property we ordinarily take it to be; it is only one of many forms of consciousness in the macro-level brain. If we suppose that there is a vast multiplicity of kinds of consciousness corresponding to a vast multiplicity of structures in the brain, the mystery as to why there is a form of consciousness mirroring a seemingly quite arbitrary brain-structure disappears; many macro-level brain structures correspond to phenomenology, and the information states corresponding to

---

[18] Roelofs 2015: 182–97.

o-consciousness are just one among this many. If we suppose that there is one, or few, kinds of consciousness at the macro-level of the brain, it is extremely odd that there should be consciousness corresponding to high-level information states. This gives us strong reason to suppose that there are, in fact, many forms of consciousness instantiated in the macro-level brain.

One might object that surely our conscious experience *is* special and privileged. Certainly o-consciousness is special *for us*. My o-consciousness is the form of consciousness that corresponds to the information states that govern the overall behavior of my body. It is not surprising that this is the kind of consciousness that gets to call itself "my consciousness" and that other people think of as such. O-consciousness is special from the perspective of those interested in human society. But from the God's eye point of view, it may be a highly arbitrary and uninteresting slice from a world teeming with phenomenology. We have become used to the Copernican idea that we are not at the center of the universe but simply one planet among many. Perhaps it's time for a Copernican revolution about our own consciousness.

Of course, there is always the response: "But it's really weird to think that there is so much consciousness." A similar "it's just too weird" response could be given to the theories of Darwin, Einstein, or Heisenberg. The rational metaphysician values theoretical virtue over common sense, and the previous considerations demonstrate that the supposition that there is only one mind in the macro-level brain, although it's what we ordinarily think, is too improbable to be taken seriously.[19]

A question remains, which is how a Russellian monist should think about the relationship between o-conscious states—which we have discovered correspond to highly rarefied information states of the brain—and the conscious states that correspond to more basic material states of the brain. As Chalmers puts it:

.... it remains unclear [on the panpsychist option outlined in the last quotation I gave from Chalmers] just why phenomenal microquiddities ["quiddities" is the term Chalmers uses for the concrete categorical properties that realize pure physical structures] should give rise to broad phenomenal macroquiddities. It

---

[19] The problem of the many (Unger 1980) also provides us with a reason to think that there are many conscious subjects involved in the brain.

also remains unclear how these broad phenomenal macroquiddities relate to narrow phenomenal macroquiddities. In particular how can these two sorts of macroquiddity stand in the constitutive relation that is plausibly required to avoid causal exclusion worries?[20]

The version of Russellian monism I ultimately want to defend has answers to these questions. But for that we will have to wait until the next chapter—specifically, section 9.3.2—after I have outlined my preferred view in some detail.

8.3 The Subject Irreducibility Problem

In the last chapter we considered the subject-summing problem as a bottom–up problem: from what we know about the nature of micro-subjects, is there any reason to think that they cannot sum to form a composite subject? When considered in this way, I don't think we find any conclusive arguments against the possibility of subject-summing. However, we will now consider the possibility of mental (or proto-mental) composition starting with the allegedly composite subject itself, that is, with the human conscious mind. Our question is: Is there anything we know about the human conscious mind that rules out its reality being constitutively grounded in micro-level facts? When the issue is posed in this way, I believe we do meet insuperable challenges. The problem is that we have very good reason to think that subjects are irreducible. (N.B. In contrast to the discussion of the subject-summing problem in the last chapter, I am here focusing exclusively on mental composition as *constitution*. Nothing I say in this section rules out emergentist views of mental composition.)

I will use the term "Subject Irreducibility" to denote the following thesis: *What it is for there to be a conscious subject S cannot be analyzed into facts not involving S.* It is the thesis that *there are no deflationary analyses of subjecthood*, that is, no true analyses of the following form:

General Form of a Deflationary Analysis of Subjecthood—For it to be the case that there is a conscious subject X is for it to be the

---

[20] Chalmers 2016: 210.

case that there are Ys that are F, where X need not be one of the Ys (or for it to be the case that there is a Y that is F, where X need not be identical with Y).

To make this clearer, contrast with the case of parties, which do admit of deflationary analysis:

> *Deflationary Analysis of Partyhood*—For it to be the case that there is a party is for it to be the case that there are people revelling.

A person is not a party; hence, in this analysis we define what it is for a given party to exist in terms of things that are not that party. Subject Irreducibility tells us that the same cannot be done with subjects: we cannot analyze what it is for a given subject to exist in terms of things that are not that subject.

Physicalists have ways of avoiding Subject Irreducibility. Analytic functionalists would offer the following a priori analysis:

> *Analytic Functionalist Deflationary Analysis*—For it to be the case that there is a conscious subject X is for it to be the case that there are Ys that perform such and such a functional role.

The conscious subject itself will not be among the Ys; they will ultimately be certain particles in the body and brain of the conscious subject acting in concert. Thus, what it is for the conscious subject to exist is analyzed in terms of things that are not that subject. Type-B physicalists are likely to hold that there is a deflationary analysis of subjecthood, in either physical or functional terms, but that it is only available a posteriori.

Of course, these possibilities have been ruled out by premises already defended in the first half of the book. The epistemic gap—defended in chapter 3—rules out analytic functionalism, and Direct Phenomenal Transparency—defended in chapter 5—rules out a posteriori physicalism. Furthermore, as I explained in section 7.3.2.3, Direct Phenomenal Transparency entails that the analysis of subjecthood is a priori accessible. This is because the property of being a conscious subject is a determinable of which any conscious state is a determinate; feeling pain, for example, is a specific way of being a conscious subject. And if one grasps the essence of a given determinate, one thereby grasps the essence of the determinable of that determinate. For example, I couldn't understand what it is for something to be spherical without grasping what it is for something to be shaped, or what it is for something to be red without thereby understanding what it is for something to be colored. According to Direct Phenomenal Transparency, I am able to grasp the essence of any phenomenal property I conceive of under a direct phenomenal concept; in grasping the nature of that property I thereby grasp the nature of subjecthood.

So much for physicalist proposals for deflationary accounts of subjecthood. Can Russellian monists fare any better? It is important to bear in mind that we are not looking merely for a *reductive analysis* of subjecthood, which could be of the following form:

> *General Form of a Non-Deflationary but Reductive Analysis of Subjecthood*—For it to be the case that there is a conscious subject *x* is for it to be the case that *x* is F, where "F" expresses a property non-identical with the property of being a conscious subject.

If we were merely looking for a reductive analysis of subjecthood, the proposal (considered in the discussion of panqualityism in section 6.3.2) that consciousness can be analyzed into *subjectivity* and *qualitivity* would suffice:

> *Sample Reductive Analysis of Subjecthood*—For it to be the case that there is a conscious subject *x* is for it to be the case that there are certain qualitative contents that are subjectively presented to *x*.

This analysis is not deflationary, as the bearer of consciousness has not been analyzed away. Recall that we are looking for is an analysis of the following form:

> *General Form of a Deflationary Analysis of Subjecthood*—For it to be the case that there is a conscious subject X is for it to be the case that there are Ys that are F, where X need not be one of the Ys (or for it to be the case that there is a Y that is F, where X need not be identical with Y).

What kind of analysis could the constitutive Russellian monist offer? It would natural for the micropsychist to offer something like the following:

> *Micropsychist Analysis*—For it to be the case that there is a conscious subject X is for it to be the case that there are microsubjects $S_1, S_2 \ldots S_n$, none of which is identical with X, standing in n-place relation R.

The first problem with such an analysis is that it's hard to see how we might complete the proposal by saying what relation R is. In the last chapter we speculated that there might be some unknown relation—the deep nature of the spatial relation—that somehow bonds subjects together such that they produce a further subject. However, in this context (assuming Phenomenal Transparency), we are looking for a relationship that is *available* a priori. Armchair reflection on the nature of subjecthood does not seem to reveal such a relation.

More generally, if the analysis of subjecthood is a priori, then it must be in some implicit sense what we *mean* when we judge that there is a conscious subject. What is it for me to judge that there is a conscious subject—call it "Jane"? It is simply not plausible that my judgment that there is a conscious subject Jane consists in the judgment that there are a large number of micro-subjects, none of which is identical with Jane, standing in some relation.

Finally, given that this is a general analysis of what it is for there to be a conscious subject, it ought to apply also to the micro-subjects themselves, such that the existence of each micro-subject consists in the fact that there are further micro-subjects standing in R; and the existence of each of those further micro-subjects must consist in the fact that there are further micro-subjects standing in R, and so on ad infinitum. Something seems to have gone wrong.

The panpsychist might try to avoid these concerns by giving an analysis not in terms of micro-subjects themselves but in terms of the *experiences* of micro-subjects. What relation between experiences ties them together into a subject? Barry Dainton has proposed the *co-consciousness* relation: the relation two experiences bear to each other when they are *experienced together*.[21] Following this line of thought, we might be led to the following analysis:

> *Co-Consciousness Analysis (1st formulation)*—For it to be the case that there is conscious subject X is for it to be the case that there are certain experiences that are co-conscious with each other.[22]

[21] Dainton 2011a.

[22] I am grateful to Umrao Sethi for prompting me explore this kind of view by raising an objection pertaining to the bundle theory of the self.

The panpsychist could then hold that (i) a large number of the experiences had by the micro-subjects making up my brain bear the co-consciousness relationship to each other, and that (ii) it is in virtue of this that my conscious mind exists.

This proposal analyzes subjects into experiences. But what is an experience? Following Martina Nida-Rümelin, I am inclined to think that phenomenological reflection reveals an experience to be nothing other than an event of a certain subject bearing certain experiential properties.[23] Consider for example my experience of pain. All it is for that experience of pain to exist is for it to be the case that I feel pain of a certain kind at a certain time. If this is correct, then experiences are analyzed in terms of subjects, which rules out an analysis of subjects into experiences.

Perhaps the proponent of the co-consciousness analysis could try the following:

> *Co-Consciousness Analysis (2nd formulation)*—For it to be the case that there is conscious subject X is for it to be the case that there are certain experiential properties that are co-conscious with each other.

But what is it for certain experiential properties to be "co-conscious"? It is surely nothing other than for those properties to be experienced by a single subject. For the experiential property of pain and the experiential property of anxiety to be "co-conscious" is for there to be a single subject that both feels pain and feels anxiety. This turns our analysis into the following:

> *Co-Consciousness Analysis (3rd formulation)*—For it to be the case that there is conscious subject X is for it to be the case that there are certain experiential properties that are had by a single subject.

The problem of course is that the "single subject" can be nothing other than X itself. We have failed to analyze away the bearer of subjecthood and hence failed to give a deflationary analysis of subjecthood.[24] These

---

[23] Nida-Rümelin 2016.

[24] This argument is influenced by criticisms of co-consciousness solutions to the combination problem in Coleman (2016).

panpsychist options seem prima facie plausible but on deeper reflection turn out to be either incoherent or not really deflationary.

The problem for the Russellian monism is that no other options seem available. Once we have set aside functionalist analyses, there seems to be no other candidates for being an *a priori accessible deflationary analysis of subjecthood*. What is it for Jane to exist as a conscious individual? An initial answer: it is for Jane to exist and to have experience, for there to be something that it's like to be Jane. Can we analyze this without quantifying over Jane? A functionalist could say that all that is essentially required for Jane to exist as a conscious individual is for certain entities (non-identical with Jane) to be acting in concert to play such and such a functional role. But once we reject functionalism, there just doesn't seem to be any way of a priori analyzing what it is for there to be conscious Jane without quantifying over Jane.

Maybe we just haven't thought of the correct deflationary analysis yet? Even if one has a transparent concept of a property, certain implications of its nature can be difficult to derive. It is pertinent at this point to consider Arnauld's famous objection to Descartes:

> Suppose someone knows for certain that the angle in a semi-circle is a right angle, and hence that the triangle formed by this angle and the diameter of the circle is right-angled. In spite of this, he may doubt, or not yet have grasped for certain, that the square on the hypotenuse is equal to the squares on the other two sides; indeed he may even deny this if he is misled by some fallacy.[25]

Perhaps the deflationary analysis of subjecthood is subtle and difficult to discern, just as Pythagoras' theorem is a not easily discernible implication of the essence of triangularity. Perhaps Russellian monists can look forward to the day when the "Pythagoras of consciousness" works it out.

However, what is being demanded here is not some subtle implication of the essence of subjecthood but simply what is essentially required for there to be a conscious subject (for there to be an x such that x is a conscious subject). A more appropriate analogy would be to suggest that someone could have a transparent concept of a triangle without knowing that for there to be triangle is for there to be an object with three sides.

[25] Descartes 1645/1996: 109.

Of course, there are many cases in which we have an implicit grasp of what is required for property P to be instantiated, and yet find it very difficult to fully articulate that requirement as necessary and sufficient conditions for there to be a token of P. Consider, for example, the ongoing travails of philosophers trying to give a precise definition of the everyday concept of knowledge. If several decades of our greatest conceptual analysts beavering away cannot give us necessary and sufficient conditions for the instantiation of knowledge, something of which we plausibly have a transparent concept, then maybe it's not so implausible to think that Phenomenal Transparency is consistent with our failure to fully articulate the essence of subjecthood in such a way as to reveal its deflationary essence.

However, while it may be unreasonable to demand of the constitutive Russellian monist precise necessary and sufficient conditions for the instantiation of subjecthood, it is not unreasonable to demand some kind a gesture toward what is required. When it comes to those properties of which we have a transparent concept, although we generally find it hard to express what is required for there to be a token of the property as precise necessary and sufficient conditions, we can always formulate some rough and ready approximation of what is required. For there to be knowledge is roughly for there to be true and justified belief. For there to be a party is roughly for there to be people gathered together having a good time. There are, of course, counterexamples to these rough definitions, but they serve to communicate the idea, and, in doing so, they give us a sense of how the entity might be constitutively grounded in more fundamental features of reality. On the basis of such examples, Theodore Sider argues that a reductionist is obliged to offer a "toy" reductive analysis, to give credence to her belief that a fully spelled out reductive analysis is available to God if not to us.[26]

However, in the case of subjecthood, we're not able even to gesture at its supposed deflationary analysis. Perhaps this is not a knock-down argument for Subject Irreducibility, but the fact that sustained and careful consideration yields no sign of a non-functionalist a priori accessible deflationary analysis of subjecthood makes the thesis that there is one seem like an unsupported and implausible leap of faith.

---

[26] Sider 2012: 117–18. Sider puts the point in terms of the notion of "metaphysical truth conditions," which is central to his framework, but the substance is the same. I show in Goff (2015a) and Goff (2016b) how the argument of this section can be put in terms of Sider's framework.

Thus, I think the following is a powerful argument for Subject Irreducibility:

The argument for Subject Irreducibility

Premise 1—If the analysis of subjecthood is a priori, then it is deflationary only if analytic functionalism is true.

Premise 2—Analytic functionalism is false.

Premise 3—The analysis of subjecthood is a priori (implied by Phenomenal Transparency).

Conclusion—The analysis of subjecthood is not deflationary (i.e., Subject Irreducibility).

Why does it matter that subjects are irreducible? In section 6.3.1 we defined constitutive Russellian monism in terms of constitutive grounding, and in section 2.2.2 we decided that—unless and until we could find some other way of satisfying the Free Lunch Constraint (discussed in section 2.2.1)—we would be understanding constitutive grounding in terms of grounding by analysis. The details of grounding by analysis haven't been important until now, so let us remind ourselves of them:

Fact X is grounded by analysis in fact Y iff:

- X is grounded in Y, and
- Y logically entails what is essentially required for the entities contained in X (including property and kind instances) to be part of reality.

To take a concrete example, the fact (F1) that there is a party is grounded by analysis in the fact (F2) that Rod, Jane, and Freddy are revelling because:

- F1 is grounded in F2, and
- The fact that Rod, Jenny, and Freddy are revelling logically entails what is essentially required for a party to exist, that is, that there are people revelling.

Now if we cannot analyze what it is for Jane to exist as a conscious subject without quantifying over Jane, then the micro-level facts could logically entail *what is essentially required* for the reality of conscious

Jane—for the reality of that specific instance of subjecthood—only if they logically entail the existence of Jane. In other words, the reality of conscious Jane is grounded by analysis in the micro-level facts only if the non-existence of Jane is logically inconsistent with the obtaining of the micro-level facts.

The trouble is that compositional nihilism—the view that there are no objects with proper parts—is logically coherent.[27] There is no contradiction in the assertion that there are particles arranged table-wise, planet-wise, and so on, but there are no tables, planets, and so on. And thus, assuming that o-subjects are macro-level entities, we can pose the following argument against constitutive Russellian monism:

The subject irreducibility argument against constitutive Russellian monism

Premise 1—The fact that Jane exists as a conscious subject is grounded by analysis in the micro-level facts only if the micro-level facts logically entail what is essentially required for Jane to exist as a conscious subject. (This premise follows from the definition of grounding by analysis.)

Premise 2 (Subject Irreducibility)—What is essentially required for there to be an x such that x is a conscious individual cannot be analyzed into facts not involving x.

Conclusion 1—The fact that Jane exists as a conscious subject can be grounded by analysis in the micro-level facts only if the micro-level facts logically entail the existence of Jane.

Premise 3—Jane is a macro-level entity, and hence her non-existence is logically consistent with the complete micro-level facts.

Conclusion 2—The fact that Jane exists is not grounded by analysis in the micro-level facts.

Why doesn't this form of argument apply quite generally to rule out the grounding of any macro-level entities? Or to put it another way, why does it not follow from the logical coherence of compositional nihilism that facts about micro-level entities *never* ground the existence of macro-level

---

[27] I would distinguish *logical coherence*, the absence of contradiction that can be demonstrated in a formal system, from the more general notion of *a priori coherence*.

entities? Because, in general, the essences of macro-level entities are rich enough to account for their grounding in the micro-level facts. As we discussed in section 2.2.2, it is plausible that all that is required for there to be a table (or at least a table-shaped material object) is for there to be a certain (difficult to precisely specify) pattern of penetration resistance among regions of space, such that the micro-level facts logically entail the reality of that pattern. Thus, even though the micro-level facts in and of themselves do not logically entail the existence of tables, the micro-level facts logically entail a certain condition C, and tablehood is such that C is what is essentially required for there are tables. Once we "unpack" the nature of the grounded entities, we secure the logical entailment. The problem in the case of conscious subjects is that, if Subject Irreducibility is true, the nature of subjecthood is not rich enough to "reach out" to the micro-level facts in this way.

I am thus inclined to think that mental combination—when understood as a form of constitution—is indeed impossible, but that the impossibility is apparent only when we approach the combination problem top–down rather than bottom–up. When the focus is on the work that stuff at the bottom has to do, the noumenalist panprotopsychist may declare: "We have no idea what the nature of micro-level protophenomenal properties are. Hence, how on earth could we rule out that they have some weird and wonderful nature that somehow produces consciousness?" Likewise, Russellian panpsychists might announce: "We have no clue as to the deep nature of spatial relations, so how could we possibly know that their nature is not sufficient to bind micro-subject into o-subjects?" Fair enough, as far as it goes. But attention to the details of grounding by analysis reminds us that the constituents of the *grounded fact* must also play their part in cases of constitutive grounding; it takes both sides of the grounding relation to produce an ontological free lunch (at least as regards cases of grounding by analysis). And given Phenomenal Transparency, it is not an option to be a noumenalist about the grounded reality of subjecthood; we cannot get rid of the problem by saying "We have no clue as to the nature of subjecthood, and hence no way of ruling out that it admits of deflationary analysis."[28]

---

[28] Consciousness may be an aspect of a more expansive property, a view we will discuss at length in the next chapter. But this does not remove the need to account for (i) the grounding of the experiential aspect of that more expansive property, and (ii) the bearer of that experiential aspect (qua bearer of experience). The non-deflationary of subjecthood renders it impossible to do this via grounding by analysis.

None of this threatens emergentist forms of Russellian monism, as the emergentist takes conscious subjects to be fundamental and unanalyzable entities that causally arise from the narrowly material. However, this is an extremely powerful challenge to constitutive Russellian monism, and I can't see how the forms we have so far considered can survive it. We need a metaphysical picture that can accept that conscious subjects are *irreducible*, while at the same time make sense of their being *non-fundamental*, that is to say, grounded in more fundamental features of reality. Fortunately, I think there is metaphysical view that is able to square this circle. This will be the subject of the next chapter.

9

A Conscious Universe

We ended the last chapter with the subject irreducibility problem, which arises from the plausibility of the thesis that we can't analyze what it is for there to be a conscious subject in more fundamental terms. Once we accept Phenomenal Transparency and anti-functionalism—the core premises in the anti-physicalist argument of the first half of this book—I think we have very good grounds for accepting the irreducibility of subjects. And once we accept the irreducibility of subjects, we cannot make sense of the grounding by analysis of o-subjects in micro-level facts.

One might be tempted at this point to give up on constitutive Russellian monism. If subjects are irreducible, then it's hard to see how they could be grounded in more fundamental facts. Emergentism seems to be the only option. Perhaps this is where we will end up. But in this chapter I want to explore the potential of an alternative form of constitutive grounding, which I will call "grounding by subsumption." The hope is that if we understand constitutive grounding in terms of grounding by subsumption rather than grounding by analysis, we might (i) find a coherent way to make sense of the grounding of conscious subjects, and (ii) thereby render coherent some form of constitutive Russellian monism.

9.1 Grounding by Subsumption

Grounding by subsumption is in the first instance a relation between *entities* (N.B. I am using "entity" in a broad sense to mean any kind of worldly thing: individuals, properties, events, states of affairs, and so on). We can define it as follows:

Entity X grounds by subsumption entity Y iff (i) X grounds Y, and (ii) X is a unity of which Y is an aspect.[1]

I take *unity* and *aspect* to be primitives not admitting of more fundamental analysis. As with the other primitive employed throughout this book—consciousness, grounding, metaphysical analysis—the best way to get a grip on the notion is through examples. Here are four:

9.1.1 Grounding by Subsumption of Experiences

In some sense an experience has "parts"; my current experience, for example, involves visual experience of colors, auditory experiences of sounds, and emotional experiences of joy. One view is that one's total experience is a composite event of having many partial experiences, or perhaps of having many partial experiences related in a certain way. An alternative to this "bottom–up" analysis of total experience, to my mind more plausible, is the view that what is more fundamental is the total experience: the total experience is a unity of which the experiential parts are aspects. If you can even make sense of the latter view, then you can make sense of the thesis that partial experiences are grounded by subsumption in total experiences.[2]

9.1.2 Grounding by Subsumption of Hue, Saturation, and Lightness in Color

A specific shade of orange—call it "orange 7"—involves red hue and yellow hue as well as a certain degree of saturation and a certain degree of lightness. One might suppose that orange 7 is a composite property made up of red hue, yellow hue, such and such a degree of saturation, and such and such a degree of lightness. Alternately, one might take orange 7 to be a unified property of which those constituents are aspects. If you can make sense of the latter view, you can make sense of the thesis that instances of hue, saturation, and lightness are grounded by subsumption in instances of color.[3]

---

[1] I am grateful to Greg Miller for making me see the importance of explicitly specifying in the definition that there is a grounding relationship.

[2] Brentano (1874/1973) and Bayne and Chalmers (2003) defend views in this ballpark.

[3] I am grateful to Angela Mendelovici for offering me this example of grounding by subsumption. We could also consider these options with respect to the experiential qualities involved in color experiences, which arguably involve experiential equivalents of hue, saturation, and lightness.

9.1.3 Grounding by Subsumption of Properties in States of Affairs

It is an old philosophical conundrum what to say about the relationship between an object and its properties, for example, between a given electron E and negative charge. A natural first move is to postulate the relation of instantiation to "glue" E and negative charge together. But the mere postulation of the instantiation relation is not sufficient to ground the fact that E is negatively charged; E, negative charge, and the electron could all exist without it being the case that E is negatively charged, for example, if the instantiation relation related negative charge to some other entity.[4] Perhaps then we need to postulate a third relation, instantiation*, to relate E, negative charge, and instantiation. But, of course, just as the mere postulation of instantiation does not guarantee that it relates E and negative charge, so the mere postulation of instantiation* does not guarantee that it relates E, negative charge, and instantiation. No matter how many relations we postulate, they will never add up to the *unity of the fact that E is negatively charged*. This notorious difficulty has become known in recent times as "Bradley's regress."[5]

A plausible solution to this problem, defended in slightly different ways by C. B. Martin, E. J. Lowe and D. M. Armstrong, is to start with the unity of the fact.[6] What is fundamental is not objects and properties, somehow glued together, but *objects-having-properties* (you have to say it really quickly!). To express the view with a theological metaphor, when God created the fact that E has negative charge, She didn't create E, then create negative charge, and then stick them together; rather she created *e-having-negative-charge*. The state of affairs of *E-having-negative-charge* is a fundamental unity, of which negative charge, and the substratum that bears negative charge (what Armstrong calls "the thin particular") are aspects.[7] If you can even make sense of this view, you can make sense

---

[4] One might object that negative charge is an essential property of E and hence E could not exist without it. To avoid this worry, we could focus on an example involving an object and one of its contingent properties.

[5] The worry is rooted in Bradley's famous regress argument against the possibility of external relations (Bradley 1935: 643; van Inwagen 1993: 35–6).

[6] Martin 1980; Lowe 2000; Armstrong 1997.

[7] The term "aspect" is not always explicit in the way Martin, Armstrong, and Lowe describe these views. Martin talks about the properties and the substratum being "about" the object, which seems to be what I am getting at with the word "aspect." All three characterize properties as what we are aware of when we "partially consider," adopting Locke's terminology. But partial consideration is an epistemological notion; the reality that we are aware of when we partially consider is an aspect.

of properties and substrata being grounded by subsumption in states of affairs.[8]

9.1.4 Grounding by Subsumption of Regions of Space in the Whole of Space

The central debate in philosophy of space is that between *substantivalists* and *relationists*. Substantivalists believe that, at the fundamental level, space (or spacetime, or regions of space/spacetime) exists as an entity(s) in its own right. Again, a theological metaphor can help make things clear. According to standard substantivalism, prominently defended by Isaac Newton, when God created the world She first created space—the Great Container, as it were—and then created the things *in* space, such as stars and planets.[9] For the relationalism in contrast, God's only task was to create the stars, planets, and so on, and ensure that they bear certain spatiotemporal relationships to each other. Facts about space are grounded in facts about concrete entities and the relationships between them. Leibniz famously challenged Newton not only on the matter of which of them first came up with calculus, but also by defending relationalism (although in a non-materialist form).

Substantivalists face the following question: Are facts about larger regions of space grounded in facts about smaller regions, or vice versa? The substantivalist could hold that (i) certain very small regions of space are the fundamental building blocks of reality, and that (ii) space as a whole is built up from such "spatial atoms." Alternatively, she might (i) take the whole of space to be a fundamental unity, and (ii) take specific regions of space to be *aspects of* this fundamental unity. In so far as you can make sense of the latter view—call it "holistic substantivalism"—you

---

[8] Martin does not talk about states of affairs; however, he describes the object as *property-bearer-properties-borne*, which sounds to me more like a state of affairs than an object. Lowe modifies Martin's view by identifying—rightly in my view—the property bearer with the object. But he nonetheless seems to hold that the properties are aspects of the object. I find this view hard to make sense of for two reasons. First, if the properties are aspects of but do not exhaust the being of the object, then there must be some other aspect to the being of the object. But it's hard to see what that could be if not a substratum. Second, it seems wrong to say that the properties are aspects of the property bearer. For these reasons, I prefer Armstrong's version of the view (although I also find problems with it, which I hope to deal with in future work). In any case, any of these views will do for the purpose of illustrating a case of grounding by subsumption.

[9] Schaffer (2009b) casts doubt on the conventional wisdom that Newton was a substantivalist.

can make sense of regions of space being grounded by subsumption in the whole of space.

Super-substantivalism is the view that (i) space (or spacetime, or regions of space/spacetime) is an entity in its own right, and that (ii) material objects are identical to regions of space/spacetime.[10] Regions of space we think of as "filled" may be very different from regions we think of as "empty," which is presumably because they have quite different properties. But in both cases the bearer of the properties is the region of space itself, not some distinct object contained within the region. As Jonathan Schaffer puts it, properties are "pinned" directly to space itself.[11] We could perhaps identify material objects with mass-instantiating regions of space.[12]

Consider the combination of holistic substantivalism and super-substantivalism. Such a view would be a form of what Jonathan Schaffer calls "priority monism," the view that there is only one fundamental individual. For the holistic supersubstantivalist, material objects are identical with regions of space, and regions of space are aspects of space as a whole. Thus, all being is ultimately derived from the fundamental unity that is space considered as a whole.

What are the properties of this one fundamental object? One plausible proposal is *distributional properties* of the kind we discussed in characterizing fusionism in section 6.3.1 (holistic super-substantivalism could be thought of as fusionism blown up to the level of the whole universe).[13] To remind ourselves: distributional properties are properties that concern how an object is spatially filled in, e.g., *being polka-dotted, being striped*. We naturally think of distributional properties of an object as non-fundamental, grounded in the properties of its proper parts; for example, we tend to think that the carpet is *red polka-dotted* because certain little round bits of it are colored red while surrounding areas have a different color. Conceivably though, the ontological priority could go the other way around. It could be that the carpet has the primitive property

[10] We might also construe super-substantivalism as the view that facts about material objects are *grounded in* facts about space or spacetime.

[11] Schaffer 2009b.

[12] The term "super-substantivalism" comes from Sklar (1974). See Skow (2005) and Schaffer (2009b) for extended discussion and defense of super-substantivalism.

[13] Parsons 2004. Schaffer favors the view that the properties of the one fundamental object are distributional properties, although he also offers two alternatives (Schaffer 2010c: 59–60).

of *being red polka-dotted*, and in virtue of this the smaller parts of the carpet are colored as they are.[14]

Now imagine a universe with a nice tidy polka-dotted distribution of mass throughout space. As with the carpet example, we might naturally assume that a universe with a polka-dotted distribution of mass has that distribution in virtue of having mass-instantiated regions arranged in a neat polka-dotted pattern. But it is coherent to suppose that the onto-logical priority goes the other way: space is a fundamental unity with a fundamental distributional property of *having a polka-dotted distribution of mass*, and the mass-instantiating regions, together with their mass, are aspects of this fundamental unity. If you can make sense of this view, then you can make sense of regions of space and their properties being grounded by subsumption in the whole of space and its distributional properties.

9.1.5 What Is an Aspect?

What unifies all four cases? We reach the core of the notion of an aspect when we allow for the possibility that fundamental entities can be *structured* rather than homogeneous blobs, and we reflect on what is required for that to be the case. So long as a fundamental entity is structured, it will involve various constituents that can be considered in isolation from the whole, but which are (at least contingently) dependent for their exis-tence on the whole of which they are constituents. This is precisely what I mean by my talk of "aspects."[15]

In some cases, aspects are *incomplete beings*—"*unsaturated*" to use Frege's term—such that we cannot capture the essence of the aspect without reference to the whole of which it is an aspect.[16] This is plausi-bly the case with respect to the view that properties and substrata are aspects of states of affairs, and the view that hues are aspects of colors. We need not suppose, however, that all aspects are unsaturated beings. Suppose that my current experience of red is an aspect of my whole con-scious experience. It is nonetheless possible that that very red experience might have exhausted my entire experience, and in that counterfactual

---

[14] Parsons (2004) thinks of extended objects distributional properties as lacking parts, but I find it hard to make sense of the idea of a structured object that lacks constituents of any kind.

[15] I do not mean to say that non-fundamental entities cannot have aspects, just that the core of the notion is most clear when we reflect on the case of structured fundamental entities.

[16] Frege 1951.

scenario it would (or at least might) not have been an aspect of anything else. (Conversely, my whole current actual experience might have been subsumed in a more expansive experience.) To take another example, the thesis that our space—call it "S"—is fundamental is compatible with there being a possible world in which S is subsumed in a more expansive space with a greater number of dimensions. The fact that an entity is, or could be, subsumed in a more expansive entity is compatible with its being a complete unity in its own right.[17]

9.1.6 Free Lunch without Analysis

We can draw two morals from this discussion of grounding by subsumption. Firstly, cases of grounding by subsumption involve an ontological free lunch; it is in the nature of an aspect that it is nothing over and above the unity of which it is an aspect. If my experience of red is an aspect of my total visual experience, then my experience of red is nothing over and above my total visual experience. If property instances are aspects of states of affairs, then property instances are nothing over and above states of affairs. If region R is an aspect of the whole of space S, then R is nothing over and above S. Grounding by subsumption clearly satisfies the Free Lunch Constraint outlined in section 2.2.1: the requirement that sense be made of the ontological free lunch without appeal to identity.

Secondly, and crucial for our purposes, securing this ontological free lunch does not require *analysis* of grounded entities in more fundamental terms. It is only because we can analyze *what is essentially required* for there to be a party in terms of facts about revellers that facts about parties are nothing over and above facts about specific revellers. It is only because we can analyze *what is essentially required* for there to be a table in terms of facts about patterns of penetration resistance among regions of space that facts about tables are nothing over and above the facts of fundamental physics.[18] However, in the cases we have been considering of

---

[17] This point becomes important when we get to the grounding by subsumption of conscious subjects. Brian Cutter (2016) has (pre-emptively!) criticized my view on the grounds that Revelation entails that we would know if conscious states were metaphysically derivative. Indeed, I have myself previously argued against constitutive Russellian monism along these lines (Goff 2010a). If we can make sense of certain entities being aspects *contingently*, then this worry goes away, as an entity's status as aspect or non-aspect might not be part of its nature. I address another aspect of Cutter's worry about my view in section 9.3.2.

[18] To be more precise, facts about table-shaped objects (see section 2.2.2).

grounding by subsumption, the ontological free lunch would be secured even if the less fundamental entities are irreducible. Suppose what it is for something to experience red cannot be analyzed in more fundamental terms. It could nonetheless be that my experience of red is an aspect of my total visual experience, and hence my experience of red is nothing over and above my total visual experience. Suppose what it is for there to be an R-shaped region of space cannot be analyzed in more fundamental terms. It could nonetheless be that a given R-shaped region R is an aspect of space as a whole S; if so, R is nothing over and above S. In such cases the aspect is *irreducibly subsumed* in a more expansive whole.

Perhaps some aspects do admit of analysis, but this is not required to secure an ontological free lunch. It is the notion of an *aspect* that secures the free lunch, leaving analysis without any work to do.

We turn now to the question of whether this form of grounding can help us make sense of the grounding of conscious subjects.

9.2 Subject-Subsumption and the Decombination Problem

Grounding by analysis requires that less fundamental entities admit of analysis. This method of securing the ontological free lunch ran into trouble when it came to the grounding of subjects, given Subject Irreducibility (the thesis that the existence of a given subject S cannot be analyzed into facts not involving the existence of S). As we have just observed, grounding by subsumption does not require that less fundamental entities admit of analysis. The hope, as the reader might by now have anticipated, is that grounding by subsumption offers a way of grounding conscious subjects that is compatible with their irreducibility.

What I would like to examine, then, is whether we can make sense of following:

> *Subject-Subsumption*—Each state of affairs of a particular o-conscious subject bearing certain experiential properties is grounded by subsumption in some more expansive unity.

It is natural to ask what the nature of the more expansive entity could be. Could it perhaps be another experience? Can we make sense of the idea of one experiencing subject being an aspect of another? We could imagine the following toy example (in which states of affairs are referred to by sentences in curly brackets):

Subject-Subsumption Scenario—{subject BIG feeling pain, anxiety, and experiencing red} grounds by subsumption {subject $LITTLE_1$ feeling pain}, {$LITTLE_2$ feeling anxious}, and {subject $LITTLE_3$ experiencing red}.

In the Subject-Subsumption Scenario, the state of affairs of BIG having such and such experience is a fundamental unity of which the LITTLE subjects and their experiential properties are aspects. Each subject exists and has the experience it has in virtue of the fact that BIG exists having the experience it has. In the first instance, I will assume that BIG is a "pure" subject, that is, a Cartesian mind whose nature is exhausted by consciousness.

Analogs of the subject-summing problems we considered in chapter 7 reoccur in this context, except that we are now trying to ground parts in wholes rather than wholes in parts. Instead of a "combination problem," we have a "decombination problem."[19] Itay Shani has suggested that an analog of Coleman's anti-subject-summing argument is at the heart of the decombination problem.[20] As I said in section 7.3.3, I believe the problem with Coleman's argument is that he assumes without warrant that the fact that subject X *constitutively grounds* subject Y entails that X is *phenomenally present* (i.e., "shows up") in the experience of subject Y. In the context of Subject-Subsumption, it is particularly clear that this inference cannot be drawn: $LITTLE_1$ is grounded in BIG in virtue of being an aspect of BIG; it does not follow that BIG is phenomenally present within $LITTLE_1$.

It is more likely that what Shani has in mind is not that BIG should be phenomenally present in $LITTLE_1$, but that $LITTLE_1$ should be phenomenally present in BIG. One might pose the following Coleman-esque argument against the coherence of the Subject-Subsumption Scenario:

$LITTLE_1$'s point of view is a matter of its having *pain-to-the-exclusion-of-all-else*; this point of view is not an aspect of BIG's point of view, as the latter experiences pain co-consciously with anxiety and redness.

---

[19] Miri Albahari (forthcoming) uses this term. Chalmers (2015) calls it the "decomposition problem," and Nagasawa and Wager (2016) call it the "derivation problem."

[20] Shani 2015.

I am not persuaded that this argument has force. Consider the following parody against the possibility that an object X that has 4 grams of mass could have a part Y that has 2 grams of mass:

Y has *2 grams of mass and no more*; hence, Y cannot be a constituent of X, as X has more than 2 grams of mass.

Clearly, this is not a good argument. Why is it any different in the case of the Subject-Summing Scenario? What it's like to be $LITTLE_1$ is given by the fact that it has pain and no other conscious states. Why can't that point of view—limited in itself—be an aspect of a more expansive point of view? The idea of one conscious mind being an aspect of another conscious mind is something we find difficult to get our heads around (so to speak). But is there an argument that it is incoherent?

I think a more worrying threat to the coherence of the Subject-Subsumption Scenario comes from a conceivability argument analogous to the anti-subjects-summing conceivability argument also considered in chapter 7:

The anti-subject-subsumption conceivability argument

Premise 1—"{BIG feeling pain, anxiety, and experiencing red} obtains in the absence of {$LITTLE_1$ feeling pain}" is conceivably true. (We can infer this from the CIS principle introduced in section 7.3.2.1.)

Premise 2—If BIG and X are conceived of as pure subjects, "{BIG feeling pain, anxiety, and experiencing red} obtains in the absence of {$LITTLE_1$ feeling pain}" is a transparent sentence.

Premise 3—*Transparency Conceivability Principle (TCP)*—If a transparent sentence is conceivably true, then it's possibly true.

Conclusion 1—Therefore, "{BIG feeling pain, anxiety, and experiencing red} obtains in the absence of {$LITTLE_1$ feeling pain}" is possibly true.

Premise 4—*Necessitation*: If fact/entity X grounds Y, then necessarily if X exists/obtains, then Y exists/obtains.

Conclusion 2—Therefore, it's not the case that {BIG feeling pain, anxiety and experiencing red} grounds {$LITTLE_1$ feeling pain}.[21]

---

[21] A similar conceivability argument is given in Chalmers (2015). I am grateful to David Pitt and David Chalmers for persuading me of the soundness of this kind of argument. Having said that, it's

Just as in the case of conceivability combination problem, to avoid the conceivability decombination problem, I think we need to admit some nature beyond consciousness into the grounding base. In the case of the combination problem, I suggested adding spatial relations with a noumenal deep nature. But with respect to the decombination problem our fundamental fact involves just a single entity, and hence adding more nature to the fundamental fact will involve adding some intrinsic nature to the fundamental entity over and above its consciousness; it will require, in other words, that the fundamental entity is an *impure subject*.

Return again to the hypothesis (considered in section 7.3.2.4) that consciousness is one aspect of a more expansive property, a property we called "consciousness+"; consciousness+ enfolds experiential and non-experiential aspects in a single unified property. If the subject BIG being conceived of in the Subject-Grounding-Scenario is taken to be an impure subject, instantiating consciousness+ rather than consciousness, then we are not conceiving of it in terms of its complete nature when we conceive of it merely as a bearer of consciousness. In this case, the sentence "{BIG feeling pain, anxiety, and experiencing red} obtains in the absence of {LITTLE$_1$ feeling pain}" is not a transparent sentence, and hence the move from conceivability to possibility is blocked.

We are thus led to consider the following possibility:

Consciousness+ Subject-Subsumption—{subject X bearing such and such consciousness+ properties} grounds by subsumption {Subject Y bearing such and such experiential properties}.[22]

This proposal entails a significant degree of noumenalism about fundamental reality. The attraction of a pure form of panpsychism, according to which the only intrinsic properties are forms of consciousness, is that the general form of fundamental reality is transparently known to us (at least in its non-relational nature). But in so far as we lack a positive conception of the non-experiential aspects of consciousness+, we lack a general understanding of the deep nature of matter. The spatial relations

kind of annoying, as I had initially hoped (a hope expressed in Goff 2017b) that cosmopsychism avoided altogether this kind of concern.

[22] Of course, we might also suppose that the less fundamental subjects are bearers of consciousness+, and I am inclined to think this for reasons pertaining to mental causation, which I will discuss in what follows. But this is not required to block the Anti-Subject-Subsumption Conceivability Argument.

response to the subject-summing problem adopted in chapter 7 already involved us in a certain degree of noumenalism, but only concerning relational properties.

Would it be an option to adopt a panprotopsychist, rather than a panpsychist, conception of subject-subsumption?

Panprotopsychist Subject-Subsumption—{subject X bearing such and such protophenomenal properties} grounds by subsumption {subject Y bearing such and such experiential properties}.

Panprotopsychist subject-subsumption doesn't seem to me to be coherent, at least once we accept that conscious subjects are irreducible. It seems self-evident that if there is an entity X that has an experiencing mind as an irreducible aspect of its nature, then X must itself be an experiencing mind. I am not here committing the fallacy of composition: clearly something can have a *part* that is conscious without itself being conscious; for example, a wall made up of living human beings has conscious parts but might not itself be conscious. But for an entity E to have a unified nature of which one aspect is a consciously experiencing mind M is for E's unified nature to incorporate M within itself. And surely E cannot incorporate a conscious mind within its nature without itself being conscious.

I think therefore we are left with consciousness+ subject-subsumption as the only coherent way of making sense of the grounding by subsumption of conscious subjects. The element of noumenalism is, of course, not epistemically ideal; it would be nice to have a picture of the world with all gaps filled in. But, to return to a much repeated theme of this book, we must remind ourselves that, as naturally evolved creatures, there is no reason to expect that all of nature's secrets will be laid bare to us. The collective forgetting that physical science records only causal structure has made us overly optimistic about what we are capable of.

Moreover, we perhaps have good reason, independent of the need to make sense of the grounding of conscious subjects, to suppose that conscious subjects are not pure. I will argue in section 9.4 for Power Realism: the thesis that laws of nature are grounded in the causal powers of objects. And yet the categorical nature of a conscious state does not seem to essentially involve causal power, as evidenced by the fact that epiphenomenalism is coherent. If (i) direct phenomenal concepts reveal the essence of our conscious states, and yet (ii) direct phenomenal concepts do not reveal our conscious states to essentially involve causal power, how can we avoid the conclusion that our conscious states are epiphenomenal?[23]

This is a very deep problem, but the consciousness+ hypothesis can perhaps help us with it. For the believer in consciousness+ can hold that although in and of itself consciousness does not ground causal power, it is an aspect of a property—consciousness+—that does ground causal power. For example, my pain might be an aspect of pain+, such that if one had a transparent conception of pain+, it would be apparent that it grounds certain causal powers. (Doesn't this mean that it is *pain+* that does the causal work, dragging pain along as an epiphenomenal dead weight? I feel this worry, but the hope is that *as an aspect of pain+* pain makes an essential causal contribution, but that this contribution can be discerned only when pain+ as a whole is transparently conceived of.)[24]

Even if all this works out, one might wonder what the advantage is of grounding subjects by subsumption, if we end up knee-deep in noumenalism just as we were in earlier chapters. In what sense has turning to grounding by subsumption allowed us to make progress? The point is that our other strategy for grounding subjects—grounding by analysis—is *simply not an option*, given the irreducibility of subjects. Because grounding by subsumption does not require non-fundamental entities to admit of analysis, it offers us a way of accounting for the grounding of subjects consistent with their irreducibility. Put simply: we have good reason to rule out the possibility that subjects are grounded by analysis, but we have no good reason to rule out the possibility that subjects are grounded by subsumption. We can't entirely make sense to ourselves of the thesis that subjects are grounded by subsumption, but we have no reason to think it's impossible.

But do we need to think that subjects are grounded at all? Why not adopt the emergentist view that the irreducibility of subjects seems to point us toward? In section 9.4 I will try to answer this question. But

---

[23] Pereboom (2011, 2015) raises a related worry about whether micro-phenomenal properties are able to ground pure physical dispositions.

[24] The problem would also be solved, without a commitment to consciousness+, if we adopted the Armstrong–Dretske–Tooley commitment to strong laws (Armstrong 1978, 1983; Dretske 1977; Tooley 1977). For we could then say that the causal powers of conscious states flow not from their essential nature alone but from their essential nature in conjunction with the contingent strong laws. I am persuaded by the arguments in Strawson (1987) that individuals that lack an essentially powerful nature are as incoherent as individuals exhausted by powers, but I don't have space to discuss these arguments here.

for the moment let us explore what view results if we do suppose that human and animal subjects are grounded by subsumption.

9.3 Constitutive Cosmopsychism

Most of the discussion of this book has been framed against a background assumption of *smallism*: the view that the fundamental building blocks of reality exist at the micro-level and hence that all facts are grounded in micro-level facts.[25] To return to our theological metaphor, according to smallism, God created the world by creating certain micro-level components and relating them in certain ways. Everything that is—tables, people, planets, and stars—exists and is the way it is because its micro-level parts exist and are the way they are.

Smallism fits naturally with a grounding by analysis conception of constitutive grounding. On such a view, the micro-level facts logically entail what is essentially required for the reality of macro-level entities. We have seen that this conception of grounding runs into trouble when it comes to the grounding of conscious subjects.

There has recently been a revival of enthusiasm for *priority monism*, the view (discussed in section 9.1.4) according to which the one and only fundamental entity is *the cosmos*. This revival is largely due to a wide-ranging exploration and defense carried out by Jonathan Schaffer in a number of articles.[26] For the priority monist, God created the world by creating the cosmos and giving it certain properties. Everything within the universe—particles, people, rocks, planets—exists and is the way it is because the universe exists and is the way it is.[27] The holistic super-substantivalism previously discussed, according to which the universe is identical with the whole of space, is one form of priority monism.

Is priority monism consistent with materialism? Strictly speaking, it is not consistent with the definition from chapter 2: there we characterized materialism as the thesis that all facts are grounded in facts concerning

---

[25] This terms is from Coleman 2006.

[26] Schaffer 2007, 2009b, 2010a, 2010b, 2010c, 2012, 2013. Horgan and Potrč (2008, 2012) defend *existence monism*, the more radical view that the cosmos is the only thing that exists. There is a dialogue between Schaffer and Horgan and Potrč in Goff (2012b).

[27] Schaffer sets up the debate between monists and *pluralists*, rather than between monists and smallists—pluralism being the view that there is more than one fundamental individual. It suits my purposes to set things up the way I do, as the empirical argument I develop in the following

entities at low levels of complexity, while according to priority monism everything is grounded in facts about the most complex entity. However, the aim of this definition was to characterize materialism as an anti-emergentist thesis, and there is a clear sense in which priority monism is also an anti-emergentist thesis: all fundamental entities reside at a single level of reality. For the priority monist, fundamental reality is flat rather than layered; it's just that that flat reality is at the top rather than the bottom. It seems to me appropriate, therefore, to make room for priority monism in the definition of materialism, which we can do by extending our definition of narrowly material/physical facts to include cosmic-level as well as micro-level facts. In this extended definition, priority monism is a form of materialism, and forms of priority monism that deny the fundamental reality of (proto)mentality and value-laden causation are forms of physicalism.

Priority monism fits naturally with a grounding by subsumption conception of constitutive grounding. On such a view, the universe is a fundamental unified whole, and all other material entities are aspects of that whole. The adoption of some form of priority monism seems to be the most simple and elegant way of accommodating the thesis that o-subjects are grounded by subsumption.[28] We can suppose that the universe is a fundamental unified subject, a bearer of consciousness+, and that states of affairs involving o-subjects having such and such states of consciousness+ are aspects of states of affairs of the universe having such and such states of consciousness+. The result is a form of the view that has become known as "cosmopsychism."[29]

discussion has the conclusion that either priority monism is true or smallism is true (or a hybrid of the two). Emergentist dualism is a kind of pluralism that is ruled out by this argument.

[28] Priority monism is not the only view that can account for the grounding by subsumption of o-subjects. We could imagine the following kind of view: (i) the Milky Way is a fundamental conscious subject, of which my conscious mind is an aspect, and (ii) the universe is an aggregate of galaxy-size subjects. However, in the absence of some empirical reason for thinking that there are fundamental unities above the biological level but below the cosmic level, a priority monist form of cosmopsychism is to be preferred on grounds of theoretical virtue. Furthermore, the empirical support for the disjunction of smallism and priority monism (or a hybrid thereof) given in the following discussion provides further reason to doubt the kind of view just outlined.

[29] I define "cosmopsychism" as the view that the universe is conscious. Forms of cosmopsychism are proposed by Jaskolla and Buck (2012), Mathews (2011), Itay Shani (2015), Nagasawa and Wager (2016), and Albahari (forthcoming). There is historical precedent for the view in Green (1888), Bradley (1897), Royce (1901), and Sprigge (1983, 2006). There are chapters on Green and Royce in Sprigge 2006.

Some might be tempted to describe cosmopsychism as "idealism." But if we can conceive of it as a form of constitutive Russellian monism, then we can equally describe it as a form of materialism. Let us call this view 'constitutive cosmopsychism.' For the constitutive cosmopsychist, the cosmos is a material entity, as are the o-subjects it subsumes. While physical science describes the causal structure of the cosmos, its deep nature is constituted of consciousness+. Neuroscience describes the causal structure of the brain, but in its deep nature it is a bearer of consciousness+, and that bearer of consciousness+ is an irreducible aspect of the consciousness+-bearing universe. We might further spell out the view in terms of the holistic super-substantivalism previously outlined (although I have reservations, discussed in the next chapter, about the four-dimensionalist view of time super-substantivalism pushes us toward).[30]

9.3.1 Does Cosmopsychism Require Brute Laws?

Adam Pautz has recently argued that constitutive cosmopsychism, and indeed any form of priority monism, suffers from the theoretical vice of being a viciously *complex* theory of the world. This complexity, according to Pautz, results in the fact that the cosmopsychist is obliged to postulate a huge number of *"big-to-small grounding laws."* Consider the relationship between the determinate state of consciousness+ instantiated by the universe right now—call it "consciousness+$_{BIG1}$"—and the determinate state of consciousness+ instantiated by my brain right now—call it "consciousness+$_{LITTLE1}$." Pautz suggests that the constitutive cosmopsychist is forced to explain the grounding relationship between these two properties in terms of the brute big-to-small grounding law that if there is something that instantiates consciousness+$_{BIG1}$, then it grounds the existence of something instantiating consciousness+$_{LITTLE1}$.

Taking this route leads us into trouble, as a huge number of such laws are going to be required. For at the next moment the universe will be in

---

[30] Why not three-dimensionalist super-substantivalism? The worry is that it's hard to see how such a view could account for the movement of objects, as regions of space don't move. One could ground by analysis certain facts about moving objects in facts about non-moving regions of space. But I would like to also make sense of the thesis that irreducible aspects of fundamental reality— such as my conscious mind—can move, and this seems inconsistent with those irreducible aspects being identical with regions of space. I am instead attracted to the view that material objects are identical with aspects of the cosmos and space is an abstraction from the extension of the cosmos, the latter being a bit like lines of latitude and longitude around the Earth.

another determinate state of consciousness—call it consciousness+$_{BIG2}$—
and I will be in another determinate states of consciousness—call it
consciousness+$_{LITTLE2}$—and so we must account for this grounding relationship in terms of the big-to-small grounding law that if something has
consciousness+$_{BIG2}$, then it grounds the existence of something having
consciousness+$_{LITTLE2}$, and so on. For every possible determinate state of
the cosmos X and every corresponding determinate state of me Y, it must
be a basic law that if something has X, then it grounds the existence of
something having Y. And, of course, we need to explain not only possible
states of me but also possible states of any subject and indeed possible
states of any material entity. The resulting huge number of grounding
laws, Pautz argues, constitute an extreme theoretical vice.[31]

I deny that such grounding laws are required in a cosmopsychist world.
I suspect that Pautz feels that they are needed because he is thinking of
the fundamental properties of the universe as *blobby*, that is, lacking in
any kind of structure. But on the form of constitutive cosmopsychism
that I take seriously, the fundamental properties of the universe have *rich
structure*; although each property is fundamentally unified, that unity
subsumes many aspects. And the cosmos itself, although a fundamental
unity, subsumes a huge number of dependent parts as aspects. The state
of affairs of the universe instantiating consciousness+$_{BIG1}$ is a unity of
which the state of affairs of me instantiating consciousness+$_{LITTLE1}$ is an
aspect. There is therefore no need to add brute grounding laws to get
from the former state of affairs to the latter; the latter state of affairs is
already contained within the former as an aspect.[32]

Compare with the previously discussed view that properties are
grounded by subsumption in states of affairs, according to which, say,
negative charge is an aspect of the state of affairs of {electron-e-having-
negative-charge}. There is no need to add the brute grounding law that if
{electron-e-having-negative-charge} exists, then it grounds an instance
of negative charge; an instance of negative charge is already contained
within {electron-e-having-negative-charge} as an aspect. Or compare to
the view that my current experience of red is an aspect of my overall
conscious experience E. There is no need to add the grounding law that

---

[31] Pautz 2015: footnote 47. Pautz accepts that these laws could be grounded in the essences
of the properties in question, along the lines of the grounding via essence model considered in
chapter 2, but argues plausibly that this would not remove the vicious complexity.

[32] In this respect, my understanding of monism differs from that of Schaffer, who does postulate
grounding laws to get from facts about the cosmos to facts about its parts (see Schaffer forthcoming).

experiences of such and such a type ground red experiences; the red experience is already contained within the overall experience as an aspect.

However, I would make the following concession to Pautz (and this may be a useful clarification): constitutive cosmopsychism as I envisage it is no more parsimonious than emergentism. The relationship between constitutive cosmopsychism and panpsychist emergentism is a bit like the relationship between Armstrong's view of states of affairs and a view according to which substrata and properties are fundamental. On Armstrong's view, properties and substrata are not fundamental; states of affairs are fundamental. But states of affairs involve properties and substrata as irreducible constituents, and, because of this, the thesis that fundamentally there are substrata-having-properties is no more parsimonious than the thesis that fundamentally there are substrata and properties.[33] Committing to entities that contain properties and substrata as irreducible aspects is as ontologically costly as the combined price of a commitment to properties and a commitment to substrata.

By analogy, compare constitutive cosmopsychism and emergentism. For the constitutive cosmopsychist, o-subjects are not fundamental; the cosmos alone is fundamental. But the cosmos involves o-subjects as irreducible constituents. And committing to an entity that contains o-subjects as irreducible aspects is just as expensive as committing to fundamental o-subjects. Hence, constitutive cosmopsychism is much more expensive than a view according to which o-subjects can be analyzed away (just as Armstrong's view is much more costly than any view according to which properties can be analyzed away). Unfortunately, o-subjects cannot be analyzed away; we're stuck with them.

Aren't I going back on my previous claim (section 9.1.6) that grounding by subsumption satisfies the Free Lunch Constraint? No: grounding by subsumption gets us an ontological free lunch, but this is only because we have incorporated lunch into breakfast. My aim is to solve the causal exclusion problem not to save ontological dollars. If subjects are irreducible, which I think they are, then they must be paid for handsomely.

However, I think Pautz's worry is not really about parsimony but about *elegance*. If the fundamental properties of the universe are blobby, then any law connecting such a blobby property to some complex facts

---

[33] Perhaps the Armstrong view removes the need for an instantiation relation, but the opposing view may also dispense with this need by taking it to be a fundamental fact that certain substrata instantiate certain properties.

concerning a huge number of entities with such and such properties is going to seem arbitrary and unsatisfying, not a good place to stop a theory. In fact, constitutive cosmopsychism has reality bottoming out in a single unified state of affairs with rich structure. Moreover, despite being equally matched with respect to parsimony, constitutive cosmopsychism has an important advantage over emergentism (which we will return to): it is better equipped to deal with the causal exclusion problem.

9.3.2 The Revelation Argument

While I definitely want to deny that o-subjects are grounded by analysis, it could be that other features of reality are. Consider the case of micro-level particles. The cosmopsychist need not take such things to be conscious subjects. If they are conscious subjects, then they are grounded by subsumption in facts about the cosmos. But if they are not, then we perhaps have the option of taking them to be grounded by analysis in facts about the cosmos. Electrons are characterized in physics by their nomic role. Perhaps that nomic role corresponds not to a fundamental entity but to a pattern in the distributional properties of the universe, such that all it is for electrons to exist is for that pattern to be instantiated.[34]

Whether we can give such analyses of all entities other than the cosmos and o-subjects probably depends on whether we have grounds for thinking that any entities other than o-subjects and the cosmos are conscious. Parsimony and common sense urge us not to attribute consciousness to inanimate entities (including the cosmos ideally, but on the view under consideration that commitment is obligatory). But there may be reasons of elegance pushing in the other direction. I have already raised, in the discussion of the structural mismatch problem in chapter 8, reasons to think that there is more consciousness in the brain than we ordinarily think. Furthermore, assuming it is not a vague matter whether or not something is conscious, the thesis that (apart from the cosmos) only organic entities are conscious will inevitably lead to there being implausibly precise cut-off points between the conditions that are and are not sufficient for the existence of a non-cosmic subject. We would have to suppose, for example, that some utterly precise change—involving some

---

[34] Although the nomic role we use to pick out electrons is expressed by the terms of physics, the fact (if it is one) that it corresponds to a pattern in the distributional properties of the universe—and hence the analysis of what it is for there to be an electron—presumably isn't.

tiny micro-level alteration[35]—ensures the transition from non-conscious to conscious fetus, and it is going to seem implausibly arbitrary that that utterly precise change was what made the difference.[36]

For these reasons, it seems to me likely that working out the details of the cosmopsychist model will involve a commitment to there being conscious subjects in addition to the cosmos and o-subjects. Suppose we end up thinking that the micro-level essentially involves consciousness. Doesn't this lead to problems given our commitment to Phenomenal Transparency? For if my pain is c-fiber firing, and c-fiber firing essentially involves a huge number of micro-level conscious properties, and I have a complete grasp of the nature of my pain, shouldn't it be apparent to me that my pain essentially involves a huge number of micro-level properties? This is the so-called revelation argument against panpsychism, which I have previously leveled against Galen Strawson's smallist panpsychism, and which Brian Cutter has recently raised against my form of constitutive cosmopsychism.[37]

To respond to this concern, we need to distinguish between different kinds of aspect. In the cosmopsychist universe as I envisage it, for any object o with irreducible entities as proper parts $x_1, x_2 \ldots x_n$, $x_1, x_2 \ldots x_n$ are aspects of o. Let us call such aspects—proper parts that are aspects of the whole of which they are proper parts—"vertical aspects." But at any mereological level, a given vertical aspect may itself have aspects that, as it were, abstract away from some of its richness; we can call these "horizontal aspects." Let us take a concrete example to illustrate. A brain is a vertical aspect of the cosmos: it is an extremely complex and richly structured vertical aspect of the cosmos; if you abstract away from some of that richness and conceive of the brain in terms of certain of its computational properties, you are thereby conceiving of a horizontal aspect of the vertical aspect that is the brain. The cosmos and its parts are particulars, but we can suppose that there is an analogous distinction between aspects

[35] Of course, assuming constitutive cosmopsychism, the more fundamental story will be in terms of some utterly precise change in the distributional properties of the universe.

[36] I give this argument in much more detail in Goff 2013. It is influenced by the Lewis-Sider vagueness argument for compositional universalism (Lewis 1986: 212–13; Sider 2001: chapter 4, section 9).

[37] Goff 2006, Cutter 2016. Actually Cutter runs the revelation argument in a slightly different way, which I address in footnote 17. See also Chalmers 2016. Strawson tends to set things up as though he were a smallist panpsychism, but in fact I know from conversation with him that he is agnostic between smallism and priority monism. The disagreement between us is that I believe that there is strong reason to think that smallism is false.

that are properties. The utterly determinate material nature of the brain is a vertical aspect of the utterly determinate material state of the universe; the computational properties of the brain are a horizontal aspect of the vertical aspect that is the utterly determinate physical nature of the brain.

In the cases of Subject-Subsumption previously considered, we imagined subjects/experiences as vertical aspects of other subjects/experiences. But we might equally suppose that some subjects/experiences are horizontal aspects of other subjects/experiences, where the latter experiences are comparatively rich and the former experiences abstract away from some of that richness.[38] We cannot imagine two subjects/experiences standing in such a relationship, but there doesn't seem to be any contradiction or incoherence in the idea. Compare: we cannot imagine a four-dimensional object, but such a thing is nonetheless coherent.

If this all makes sense, then the constitutive cosmopsychist should identify o-subjects not with brains but with horizontal aspects of brains. O-conscious states are not brain states—at least not if brain states are the utterly determinate properties of the vertical aspect of the cosmos that is the brain; o-conscious states are horizontal aspects of brain states.[39]

This supposition solves two problems at once:

- *The structural mismatch problem*—In our discussion of the structural mismatch problem, we found reason to think that o-conscious states are the deep nature of highly rarefied properties of the brain, corresponding to certain information states. We ended that discussion with a question: what is the nature of the constitutive relationship between o-conscious states and the (proto)consciousness of more basic states of the brain, and how does the nature of that relationship allow us to avoid causal exclusion worries? We now have an answer: basic conscious states in the brain are vertical aspects of the cosmos;

---

[38] Talk of "abstractions" suggests entities that are not fully real, but I don't mean the word to have this implication. For Armstrong, properties are horizontal aspects of states of affairs (one attends to properties when one "partially considers" a given state of affairs) but they are nonetheless irreducible entities in their own right. Similarly, on my view, some subjects are horizontal aspects of other subjects: from the God's eye perspective one could perceive subjects that are horizontal aspects by partially considering subjects that are vertical aspects of the cosmos. Nonetheless, subjects that are horizontal aspects are irreducible beings in their own right.

[39] Do horizontal aspects of brain states do any causal work? I can see no reason to deny this. The causal exclusion problem is motivated by the threat of over-determination, but there is no problematic over-determination given that my conscious states are nothing over and above my brain states, and (assuming cosmopsychism) my brain states are nothing over and above the states of the universe that do the fundamental causal work.

o-conscious states are horizontal aspects of those vertical aspects. As aspects of the basic conscious states of the brain, my o-conscious states are nothing over and above those more basic conscious states, and hence causal exclusion concerns are avoided.

- *The revelation argument*—We now have an explanation of why my experiential states do not present themselves as involving a huge number of micro-experiential properties. Basic conscious states of my brain do essentially involve experiential states involving a huge number of micro-experiential properties, but my o-conscious states are horizontal aspects of those more basic conscious states, and as such they abstract away from much of the richness of the more basic conscious states of the brain. Thus, the relationship between my consciousness and my brain's consciousness is analogous to the relationship between software and hardware. Just as you can know the computational properties of a system without knowing its determinate physical properties—as computational properties abstract away from some of the specificity of determinate physical properties—so I can have revelatory access to the nature of my consciousness without thereby having revelatory access to the nature of my brain's consciousness.[40]

9.3.3 Sharing Thoughts with the Cosmos

If my pain is an (horizontal) aspect of an (vertical) aspect of the cosmos, it would seem to follow that my pain is an aspect of the cosmos, which seems, in turn, to imply that the universe feels my pain.[41] And, of course, if that's right, the same will be true of every other conscious state felt by me or anyone else; the universe at each moment instantiates the consciousness had by each and every person at that moment. Miri Albahari has argued that this implication of constitutive cosmopsychism is incoherent. She gives the following example in support of this:

> Consider Fiona's intense and pervasive fear that she will be annihilated upon death, a fear whose first-personal character

---

[40] My notion of a horizontal aspect is somewhat similar to Pereboom's notion of a compositional property (Pereboom 2011: ch. 8). I am extremely grateful to Hedda Hassel Mørch for helping me develop these ideas (I think she came up with the "horizontal" and "vertical" terminology in discussion).

[41] See my reasons for rejecting panprotopsychist subject-subsumption in 9.2 for why I accept that this is indeed an implication of constitutive cosmopsychism.

is partly owed to its mind-dominating nature. Goff's cosmic subject must directly experience not only Fiona's intense fear of dying but also Fred's overwhelming excitement at his impending reincarnation. Yet qualifying just a fraction of the cosmic mind, it's hard to envisage how each emotion could, from the personal cosmic perspective, retain their defining first-personal characters *as* intense and dominating, and hence as those particular emotions. It is also difficult to conceive of how the cosmic subject could first-personally harbour what would, to its singular conscious perspective, be the mass of everyone's contradicting beliefs and identities, e.g. "there is only one life," "there is more than one life," "I am Fiona," "I am Fred." These epistemic considerations make Goff's subject-grounding scenario not only unimaginable, but I suggest, incoherent.[42]

The first thing to note about Albahari's objection is that it assumes a strong commitment to phenomenal intentionality: the view that intentionality is grounded in consciousness.[43] Indeed, it assumes a fairly strong variety, according to which thoughts are grounded in consciousness. An easy way for the cosmopsychist to avoid this objection is just to deny this assumption. However, I am myself inclined to endorse this strong form of phenomenal intentionality and hence am not inclined to avoid Albahari's objection in this way.

One way of reading this worry is as a version of the Shani/Coleman interpretation of the decombination problem discussed in section 9.2 (indeed, Albahari takes herself to be building on these arguments by Shani and Coleman). When we talk about the "mind-dominating nature" of Fiona's fear, we may be referring to something irreducibly phenomenological, with its own distinct character. Or we may be referring to the fact that Fiona has fear and nothing much other than fear in her conscious mind. On the latter understanding the "mind-dominating nature" is not itself a conscious state, which the cosmos must share. Rather the "mind-dominating nature" of the fear is cashed out in terms of the absence of any other forceful phenomenology in Fiona's mind. And the fact that Fiona has "fear and no other forceful experience" does not bar her from

---

[42] Albahari forthcoming.

[43] Kriegel (2013) is a good collection of essays on phenomenal intentionality.

being subsumed in a more expansive conscious mind (which may include other forceful experiences) any more than the fact that my little finger is "ten grams and no more" is a bar to its being a part of a body with a much greater mass.

What about the point that the cosmos will involves states of conscious cognition with profoundly contradictory content? My reply to that would be: so what? Cosmopsychism does not entail pantheism. We need not think of the universe as a supremely intelligent rational agent. Intelligence and agency are characteristics of highly evolved conscious creatures, which the universe is not. It is more plausible that the consciousness of the universe is simply a mess. It may be hard for us to *imagine* a single mental state involving such wildly conflicting contents, but I see no reason to think that such a thing is impossible.

9.4 Emergence or Constitution?

If these speculations are coherent, which I freely admit they may not be on closer examination, then we have reached a coherent way of making sense of the non-fundamentality of o-subjects. If we have empirical grounds for thinking that o-subjects are indeed non-fundamental, then we will have some support for the picture of the world developed in the previous sections of this chapter. In this section we will examine whether such empirical grounds exist.

As discussed in section 6.3.2, many arguments for physicalism begin with an assertion of the causal closure of the micro-physical: the thesis that every caused event has a sufficient micro-physical cause.[44] I now want to examine in more detail (i) the evidence philosophers have put forth in favor of this thesis, and (ii) precisely what picture of the world they lead us to. Although causal closure is often appealed to, actual arguments for it are rare. It is fairly common to hear philosophers claim that causal closure of the physical is implied by the principle of the conservation of energy. Here is Paul Churchland arguing against non-epiphenomenalist dualism from the conversation of energy (and seeming

---

[44] To repeat the qualification made in footnote 31 of chapter 6: if physical causation is non-deterministic, we can construe micro-level causal closure as the thesis that the chances of material happenings are fully determined by prior micro-level events (see appendix of Papineau 2002).

to equate conservation of energy/momentum with causal closure of the physical):

> [A]s has been known for more than fifty years ... [non-epiphenomenalist] forms of Dualism ... fly in the face of basic Physics itself ... since any position that includes non-physical elements in the causal dynamics of the brain must violate both the law that energy is neither created nor destroyed, and the law that the total momentum in any closed system is always conserved. In short, you simply can't get a change in any aspect of the physical brain (for that would causally require both energy changes and momentum changes) save by a compensatory change in some other *physical* aspect of the brain, which will thereby lay claim to being the cause at issue. There is simply no room in a physical system for ghosts of any kind to intervene in some fashion to change its dynamical behavior. Any physical system is "dynamically closed" under the laws of Physics. (Indeed, it was this very difficulty, over a century ago, that initially motivated the desperate invention of Epiphenomenalism in the first place.)[45]

This argument is far too hasty. As David Papineau has pointed out, emergent forces, such as fundamental biological or mental forces, need not constitute a counterexample to conservation principles, so long as those forces *act conservatively*; so long as they "operate in such a way as to 'pay back' all the energy they 'borrow' and vice-versa":[46]

> [T]he conservation of energy in itself does not tell which basic forces operate in the physical universe. Are gravity and impact the only basic forces? What about electro-magnetism? Nuclear forces? And so on. Clearly the conservation of energy as such leaves it open exactly which basic forces exist. It requires only that, whatever they are, they operate deterministically and conservatively.[47]

Despite their consistency with conservation of energy, Papineau offers a more careful argument against emergent forces. He claims that the fact

---

[45] Churchland 2013. A similar argument is given in Dennett (1991), although I managed to persuade him (while on a sailing boat in the Arctic as he carved a stick on deck) that the argument doesn't work, for the reasons I give here.

[46] Papineau 2002: 252.

[47] Papineau 2002: 259.

that cellular biology and neurophysiology have never revealed any sign of emergent forces gives us a strong inductive case to think that there are no such forces. His argument is worth quoting at length:

> During the first half of the century the catalytic role and pro-
> tein constitution of enzymes were recognised, basic biochemi-
> cal cycles were identified, and the structure of proteins analysed,
> culminating in the discovery of DNA. In the same period, neu-
> rophysiological research mapped the body's neuronal activity,
> and analysed the electrical mechanisms responsible for neuronal
> activity. Together, these developments made it difficult to go on
> maintaining that special forces operate inside living bodies. If
> there were such forces, they could be expected to display some
> manifestation of their presence. But detailed physiological inves-
> tigation failed to uncover evidence of anything except familiar
> physical forces.[48]

Elsewhere in the same book Papineau explicitly defines the word "physical" in "physical forces" to mean "identifiable non-mentally-*and*-non-
biologically, or 'inanimate' for short."[49] Hence the claim is that we have
good inductive grounds for thinking that everything that happens, if it
can be causally explained at all, can be explained in terms of laws that
govern both animate and inanimate entities. There is nothing that happens in cells or bodies or brains that could not, in principle, be causally
explained in terms of the laws that apply to particles and rock and planets.

We could put this as the following principle:

> *Nomic Generality*—There is a set of laws that govern both animate
> and inanimate entities—call these the "the general laws"—such
> that every event that has a causal explanation can be causally
> explained in terms of those laws.[50]

Nomic Generality does not imply that there are no laws that apply only to
a subset of physical systems, such as biological or mental systems. There

---

[48] Papineau 2002: 253–4.

[49] Papineau 2002: 41.

[50] To pre-empt a couple of fiddly objections: (i) we can take it that each of these laws governs the
behavior of both animate and inanimate entities, and (ii) a law can govern the behaviour of an entity
without directly applying to that entity, for example, by governing the behavior of its parts.

may very well be law-like generalizations that hold in the biological, mental, or sociological realm that fail to hold in the inanimate realm. Nomic Generality entails, however, that any token event that can be explained in terms of special science laws could also, in principle, be explained in terms of laws that also apply in the inanimate realm. It is no doubt easier to explain sociological events (e.g., why the British Labour Party won a landslide victory in 1997) in terms of what voters at the time believed and desired in conjunction with the "psychological law" that people tend to do what they want in light of what they believe. But Nomic Generality implies that the physical events involved in this happening (e.g., each person's walking to the polling booth and ticking the relevant box) could, in principle, be explained in terms of laws that also apply to inanimate entities.

Suppose we do have good evidence for the truth of Nomic Generality: what can we infer from it about the fundamental causal workings of the universe? Does Nomic Generality give us reason to believe that the fundamental causal workings of the universe reside at the micro-level, which would give us reason to doubt priority monism? Actually, I think Nomic Generality supports *anti-emergentism*, where emergentism is understood as the view that fundamental properties emerge at specific levels of complexity between the micro and the cosmic levels, such as the chemical or the biological. Clearly, on this definition of "emergentism," priority monism is just as much an anti-emergentist view as smallism: for the smallist, fundamental properties reside only at the micro-level; for the priority monist, fundamental properties reside only at the cosmic-level.

Indeed, I will argue not only that Nomic Generality gives us no reason to doubt priority monism, but that it leads to us a powerful argument to the conclusion that *either* smallism is true *or* priority monism is true (or a hybrid of the two according to which both the cosmos and certain micro-level entities are fundamental). If, as I have argued, o-conscious facts cannot possibly be grounded in micro-level facts, then we reach an argument, partly a priori and partly empirical, for the thesis that our conscious states are grounded in facts about the cosmos. I will spend the rest of this section outlining this argument.

The argument depends on a robust realism about causal powers:

Power Realism—For any law L that governs the universe, the fact that L governs the universe is ultimately grounded in the causal powers of some fundamental entity or entities.

While a Humean takes fundamental laws to record brute patterns or regularities that obtain among concrete entities, the Power Realist insists that such patterns must be *explained*, and does so in terms of the causal powers of certain fundamental entities. Which entities are plausible candidates for being the fundamental entities whose causal powers ground the general laws (i.e., the laws that, according to Nomic Generality, govern both animate and inanimate entities and can explain every event that has a causal explanation)?

Such entities must be capable of determining the behavior of all entities, both animate and inanimate.[51] One plausible candidate is micro-level entities. One could plausibly suppose that there are a relatively small number of fundamental micro-level entities that are present in each and every material entity—both animate and inanimate—and that those fundamental micro-level entities ground the behavior and causal structure of each and every material entity, making each material entity such as to behave in accordance with the general laws. Assuming the coherence of priority monism, another plausible candidate is the cosmos. It could be that the causal powers of the universe determine that the universe evolves in accordance with the general laws.[52]

There don't seem to be any other plausible candidates, at least not if we are restricting ourselves to something non-supernatural. Certainly nothing that exists only in the animate realm (e.g., human beings) could plausibly be thought to ground the general laws that govern inanimate entities in far-off galaxies. And, in the inanimate realm, there don't seem to be any entities that (i) stand out in such a way as to be plausibly fundamental, and (ii) are widely distributed enough to ground laws in terms of which every token event can be causally explained. Therefore, I take the following to be a plausible premise:

Plausible Candidates—Assuming materialism, the only plausible candidates for fundamental entities the causal powers of which ground the general laws are (i) widely distributed micro-level entities, and (ii) the cosmos.

---

[51] Note that I am using "animate" to refer to something living; if there are conscious particles, they are not "animate" as I am using the term.

[52] As Jonathan Schaffer pointed out to me, it could also be that the cosmos and the micro-level divide up the laws between them.

We are now in a position to argue in the following way:

Argument for the disjunction of smallism and priority monism (or a hybrid of the two)

Premise 1: Nomic Generality—There is a set of laws that govern both animate and inanimate entities—the general laws—such that every event that has a causal explanation can be causally explained in terms of those laws.

Premise 2: Power Realism—For any law L that governs the universe, the fact that L governs the universe is ultimately grounded in the causal powers of some fundamental entity or entities.

Premise 3: Plausible Candidates—Assuming materialism, the only plausible candidates for fundamental entities the causal powers of which ground the general laws are (i) widely distributed micro-level entities, and (ii) the cosmos.

Conclusion 1 (1st formulation): Therefore, each general law is grounded either in the causal powers of the fundamental cosmos, or in the causal powers of certain widely distributed fundamental micro-level entities.

This does not quite get us to the disjunction of smallism and priority monism (and a hybrid of the two), as Conclusion 1 is consistent with there also being fundamental entities at levels between micro and cosmic levels, for example, fundamental biological and mental entities.

However, we can bring in familiar causal exclusion considerations (discussed in section 6.3.2) to complete the argument as follows:

Conclusion 1 (2nd formulation): Each general law is grounded either in the causal powers of the fundamental cosmos or in the causal powers of certain widely distributed fundamental micro-level entities. And therefore everything that happens can be causally explained either in terms of the causal powers of certain micro-level entities or in terms of the causal powers of the cosmos. It follows that any property that is not either a micro-level property or a cosmic-level property is either (i) epiphenomenal, (ii) non-fundamental, or (iii) has its effects problematically over-determined either by the causal powers of certain micro-level entities or by the cosmos.

[*Problematic over-determination*: Property p has its effects problematically over-determined iff (i) p is fundamental and (ii) for any event e that can be causally explained in terms of instances of p, e can also be causally explained in terms of instances of some wholly distinct fundamental property]

Premise 4: There are no epiphenomenal properties.

Premise 5: There are no properties that have their effects problematically over-determined.

Conclusion 2: Therefore, for any fundamental property p, p exists at either the micro-level or the cosmic-level.

Premise 6: All fundamental individuals instantiate at least some fundamental properties.

Conclusion 3—Therefore, for any fundamental individual i, i is either a micro-level entity or the cosmos.[53]

According to the cosmopsychist view outlined in this chapter, states of affairs involving o-conscious minds are aspects of—and hence nothing over above—states of affairs involving the universe. Consequently, the actions of o-subjects are aspects of—and hence are nothing over and above—the "actions" of the universe. The causal exclusion problem is avoided.

How can the universe do anything if there is nothing outside of it for it to act on? The idea is that the causal powers of the universe result in its changing itself from moment to moment. For the cosmopsychist, this is the fundamental causal story of reality, in which all other causal stories are grounded.

How can we just justify the commitment to Power Realism that is appealed to in the argument just outlined? The alternative is Humeanism,

---

[53] We could run the argument with premise 2 expressing a commitment to the Armstrong–Dretske–Tooley view (Armstrong 1978, 1983; Dretske 1977; Tooley 1977) that there are strong laws that ground all weak laws (weak laws being law-like regularities in the universe that are not strong laws). Premise 3 would then state that the strong laws that ground the general laws plausibly concern either micro-level entities or the cosmos. In footnote 24, I expressed reservations about the Armstrong–Dretske–Tooley view.

which I take to be the view that fundamental reality does not involve causal powers or natural necessity.[54] For the power realist, the fundamental regularities that obtain in the world are to be explained in terms of the causal powers of objects. But for the Humean, fundamental regularities are brute and unexplained. Galen Strawson has argued that this implication of Humeanism is deeply implausible:

> According to [Humeanism] . . . the regularity of the world's behaviour is, in a clear sense, a complete and continuous fluke. . . . the theory is utterly implausible in asserting categorically that there is no reason in the nature of things for the regularity of the world. . . . [I]t is absurd to say—to insist—that there is definitely no reason in the nature of things why regularity rather than chaos . . . occurs from moment to moment. Such a view is typical dogmatically anti-realist overshoot: a strict empiricist epistemological claim about what we can observe flowers into a vast and spectacular metaphysical claim about the nature of things.[55]

Explanation has to end somewhere. But the Humean seems to stop with something that cries out for explanation. Why on earth does the universe continue from moment to moment to respect Schrodinger's equation? If there is nothing in the nature of things to ensure that it does so, then isn't it an implausible fluke that, out of all the possible ways the universe might evolve in the next moment, it continues—in that moment, and the next and the next . . . —to behave in such a way as to respect a quite specific set of rules?

I am sympathetic to this argument, but it is arguably rooted in a dynamic conception of time, according to which new states of affairs are continuously coming into being (for the cosmopsychist dynamist, these would be new states of affairs involving the three-dimensional cosmos). Assuming this kind of view, we require an explanation as to why the states of affairs that keep coming into existence always do so

[54] The Armstrong–Dretske–Tooley commitment to strong laws (Armstrong 1978, 1983; Dretske 1977; Tooley 1977) is also an alternative to Power Realism. I express reservations about this view in footnote 24, but in any case the argument could be set up in terms of this view, as I explain in the last footnote.

[55] Strawson 1987: 21–22. Cf. Chalmers 2012: 336–40. Strawson dislikes the word "Humeanism," as he believes it to be based on a misinterpretation of Hume. I take no stand on this issue but continue to use the word in what has become its standard sense.

in a way that respects a quite specific set of laws. But if we adopt the four-dimensionalist view that fundamental reality is a four-dimensional "block" of spacetime, such that the entire 4D block is (in an intuitive sense) "all there" from the God's eye point of view, then there seems no reason why there should not be certain patterns across that block. If we suppose that simpler and more elegant states of affairs are more probable, then we might even suppose that it is more likely that the block universe will be regular rather than chaotic.

Whether or not Humeanism is a plausible option may then depend, among other considerations, on whether we adopt a dynamic or a static view of time. In the next chapter I offer some support for a dynamic, presentist view of time. But in any case, causal exclusion concerns have little force for the Humean. For the Humean, causation is simply a matter of certain regularities obtaining or certain counterfactuals being true. It is perfectly consistent to hold that the relevant regularities/counterfactually defined relationships required for causation hold between (i) some micro-level event and my avoidance behavior, and that they also hold between (ii) my pain and my avoidance behavior; in this case, the two causal stories can co-exist in harmony. There is no need to suppose that the two stories need to compete to be the *real* causal story. It is only if we take causation to be an irreducible relation of one event bringing another into existence that systematic over-determination becomes improbable. It is a strange coincidence if all of the events my conscious mind brings into existence are also brought into existence by distinct entities at some other level of reality.[56]

Thus, for the Humean, the truth of Nomic Generality would give us little or no reason to deny emergentism. Considerations of economy may count against it, but these consideration fall away once we give up the possibility of analyzing away o-subjects. It is only when combined with Power Realism that Nomic Generality gives strong support to the disjunction of smallism and priority monism, and hence rules out emergentism.

Turning finally to Nomic Generality itself, I am somewhat agnostic as to whether or not we currently have a strong inductive case for accepting it. Andrew Melnyk has argued in some detail that there is a strong inductive case that what goes on at the chemical and biological level can be explained in terms of laws that hold quite generally. However, he

---

[56] Loewer (2001) and O'Conner and Churchill (2010) have previously argued that the causal exclusion argument has no force against the Humean.

reluctantly concedes that our sciences of the mind are not yet advanced to the extent that we can have confidence that the same is true of the mental level:

> It would be really impressive if we could take a relatively spe-
> cific and detailed fact about the (human) mind, such as that most
> people are much better at figuring out what follows from prem-
> ises of the form "All Fs are Gs, and all Gs are Hs" than they are at
> figuring out what follows from premises of the form "All Fs and
> Gs, and no Hs are Fs," and then show that exactly this pattern
> of response to presented premise pairs was to be *expected*, given
> our knowledge of neuronal behaviour, and of the human brain's
> neuronal composition and arrangement. If we could achieve this
> feat, and others like it, we would be in a position, with regard to
> the mind, analogous to the position that, as we saw earlier, we
> are actually in with regard to the heart: with the brain demon-
> strably capable (solely in virtue of its cellular constitution) of
> doing mind-like things, we could then argue that construing the
> mind as *more* than physical or physically realised was a hypoth-
> esis of which we have no need. Alas, we are not yet able—as far
> as I am aware—to achieve such feats as this.[57]

Of course, I don't agree with Melnyk's view as to what we could conclude if we were able to give these kind of neurophysiological explanations. Perhaps we would then have evidence that the mind is nothing over and above the material, but this is perfectly consistent with Russellian monism. What I think these neurophysiological successes would give us reason to believe is the following disjunction: either (i) the causal pow-ers of the mind are nothing over and above causal powers instantiated at the micro-level, or (ii) the causal powers of the mind are nothing over and above causal powers instantiated at the cosmic-level. Given that we have strong a priori reason to think that o-subjects are something over and above anything going on at the micro-level, we would be forced to the second disjunct.

I am not sure whether Melnyk is right that we don't yet have suffi-cient grounds for holding that Nomic Generality applies even to the

---

[57] Melnyk 2003: 282.

mind or Papineau is right that we do currently have such evidence. My claim is rather about what would follow if there were evidence for Nomic Generality, either now or at some future time. Specifically my claim is the following:

> Conscious subjects are irreducible, and hence o-conscious facts are not grounded in micro-level facts. As a result, if Power Realism is true, then evidence for Nomic Generality is evidence that o-phenomenal facts are grounded in facts about the cosmos.[58]

9.5 The Incredulous Stare

Panpsychism is becoming more acceptable in the analytic philosophy community, but one still finds oneself receiving the odd incredulous stare (or worse!). No doubt it will be even harder to persuade analytic philosophers to take seriously the thesis that the universe has experience.

It is important to divide such resistance into two categories:

- The view that it is incoherent to attribute experience to basic particles/the universe.
- The view that it is deeply counter-intuitive to attribute experience to basic particles/the universe.

With regards to the first kind of resistance, the onus is on resisters to make a case that the determinable of consciousness has essential features that could not possibly be instantiated by basic particles/the universe. For example, it could be argued that (i) consciousness necessarily involves intentionality, and that (ii) intentionality necessarily involves certain forms of behavior not exhibited by basic particles/the universe. But on the face of it, experience seems to be an extremely flexible determinable that could exist in very basic forms, perhaps more basic than we are able to imagine. The adoption of panpsychism involves a "Copernican revolution" with respect to consciousness, after which we conceive of o-consciousness as an extremely rare, highly evolved form of experience, with little in common with the consciousness filling most of the universe.

---

[58] I am implicitly assuming here that o-phenomenal properties are neither epiphenomenal nor micro-level properties.

What of the second kind of resistance? It is important to bear in mind that the intuitive resistance to panpsychism reflects, at least in part, its cultural connotations. It has a "new age" feel, and no doubt in popular culture it has been defended for less than rigorous reasons. But it should go without saying that just because a view has been defended with bad arguments, it does not follow that there is not also a very good argument for that same position. And when matters are looked at plainly, panpsychism, even in its cosmopsychist form, is no more profligate or problematic than many other views analytic metaphysicians are happy to take seriously. If we are serious about having our best guess at what reality is like, we should be careful not to be affected by such cultural associations, which are surely not relevant to serious metaphysics. We should not get lost in flights of fancy, but we should approach the arguments without prejudice.

Indeed, once we have set aside the cultural associations of cosmopsychism, the motivations can be seen to be continuous with those that have in recent times drawn philosophers to physicalism. In 1959 the physicalist pioneer J. J. C. Smart made the following bold declaration:

> [S]cience is increasingly giving us a viewpoint whereby organisms are able to be seen as physico-chemical mechanisms. . . . There does seem to be, so far as science is concerned, nothing in the world but increasingly complex arrangements of physical constituents. All except for one place; in consciousness. . . . That everything should be explicable in terms of the laws of physics . . . except the occurrence of sensations seems to me to be frankly unbelievable.[59]

In fact, the physical sciences tell us nothing about the concrete categorical nature of the material world, and hence nothing that rules out the ubiquity of consciousness. But the physical sciences do have authority concerning the *causal structure* of fundamental reality. If the behavior of organisms turns out to be entirely explicable in terms of general laws, we must infer that human and animals minds are not, at a fundamental level, involved in shaping the causal evolution of the material universe. Rather the fundamental motor of reality is located at either the micro or the cosmic level.

[59] Smart 1959: 142.

It may well be that science is telling us that human subjects are not fundamental. But we know from philosophy that conscious subjects are irreducible. The only theory that can account for both of these data is one according to which o-subjects are grounded by subsumption. And the most promising form of such a view is constitutive cosmopsychism.

10

Analytic Phenomenology

A Metaphysical Manifesto

10.1 The State of Contemporary Metaphysics

There is a concern that metaphysics hasn't got anywhere. We've been doing it for thousands of years and still don't seem to have reached conclusive answers on any of the big questions. For many, the track record of metaphysics is especially troubling in relation to that of the physical sciences, which are able to boast a history of continual progress and a substantial body of broadly agreed information to teach to their undergraduates. Perhaps because of such comparisons the public no longer takes metaphysics seriously; most don't even know what it is.

We have seen throughout the book (particularly chapters 1 and 6) that this comparison to the physical sciences is misguided. Physics has been so successful precisely because, from Galileo onward, it stopped trying to tell us what matter *is* and just focused on telling us what it *does*. Detailed information about the causal structure of the natural world has produced extraordinary technology. But physics has revealed to us nothing about the concrete categorical nature of the stuff that has that causal structure.

Even dropping allegedly unfavorable comparisons to physics, the lack of progress in metaphysics can still seem worrying. How can those with faith in metaphysics explain this? One thing to appreciate is that even though the physical sciences are not the same thing as metaphysics, they arguably provide a crucial source of data for metaphysics. We saw in the last chapter that whether or not emergentism is an option is a largely empirical question. And many believe that special relativity casts doubt on dynamical conceptions of time, to take another example. If metaphysical knowledge is dependent on knowledge in the physical sciences, it could be argued that progress in metaphysics was impossible until the physical sciences had reached a fairly developed state. This could explain the lack of progress from the pre-Socratics to the eighteenth century.

We can also note that in the eighteenth century there emerged an extremely influential line of thought through Hume and Kant according to which metaphysics as we traditionally understand it is impossible. In the final paragraph of the *Enquiry Concerning Human Understanding*, Hume urges us to "commit to the flames" all attempts to settle matters of fact a priori.[1] Picking up the baton from Hume, Kant encouraged philosophers to give up on attempts to uncover the world as it is in and of itself, and to confine their focus to the necessary structure of experience. And, of course, when we reach the twentieth century, we reach a high point of antipathy toward metaphysics in philosophy, with Wittgenstein and the logical positivists in their different ways dismissing metaphysical questions as not only impossible to answer but also meaningless. Taking all this into account, it becomes far from clear that metaphysics has been given enough of a go.

Recent history has been interesting. From the mid-1970s, we start to see, cautious at first, the return of attempts in analytic philosophy to do something like traditional metaphysics. And, in the twenty-first century, we find our most respected metaphysicians rediscovering traditional metaphysical notions of *essence, fundamentality*, the distinction between those concepts that do and those concepts that don't *carve nature at the joints*, and even the *Principle of Sufficient Reason*.[2] In this increasingly traditional framework, extremely intelligent women and men have put their minds to serious, sustained, scientifically informed, rigorous attempts to evaluate the relative worth of various metaphysical hypotheses.

How is the inquiry conducted? Perhaps the biggest influence on the practice of contemporary analytic metaphysics is David Lewis. Lewis holds that metaphysics must begin with *common sense*. Descartes tried to ground all metaphysics in that which cannot be doubted. It is universally

---

[1] Hume 1748/2000.

[2] This rediscovery of traditional metaphysical notions arguably begins with Lewis's 1982 defense of the idea that a certain subset of properties—the "natural" or "sparse" properties—are metaphysically privileged. Sider extends the basic Lewisian idea of metaphysical privilege from properties to other metaphysical categories, most notably existence: for Sider a subset of entities "exist" in a metaphysically privileged sense. Two other important milestones are Fine's 1994 arguments for a non-modal notion of *essence*, and his 2001 defense of the notion of *grounding* and of a metaphysically privileged notion of "*Reality*." Dasgupta (2016) explores a version of the Principle of Sufficient Reason built on the notion of grounding.

acknowledged that his project, for all its virtues, did not succeed. Perhaps one day philosophers will conclusively prove the existence of the external world or the reality of other minds, and thus provide us with firm foundations for metaphysics. But until that happens I am in sympathy with Lewis's view that we must help ourselves to certain commonsense assumptions simply because we have no other choice:

> [I]t is pointless to build a theory, however nicely systematised, that it would be unreasonable to believe. And a theory cannot earn credence just by its unity and economy. What credence it cannot earn, it must inherit. It is far beyond our power to weave a brand new fabric of adequate theory *ex nihilo*, so we must perforce conserve the one we've got [by which Lewis means the theory that is implicit in common sense].[3]

If this seems indulgent or unwarranted, we can note that natural science seems to be in the same boat. Neither metaphysics, nor science, nor daily living can get off the ground without making a whole host of commitments that are extremely difficult to justify, either empirically or by a priori argument:

- All things being equal, theories with greater simplicity are more likely to be true.
- Systematic regularities that have obtained in the past will continue to obtain in the future.
- There are no contradictory states of affairs.
- Solipsism is false.
- Other people have minds.

As John Locke put it:

> He that in the ordinary affairs of life, would admit of nothing but direct plain demonstration, would be sure of nothing in this world but of perishing quickly.[4]

---

[3] Lewis 1986: 134.
[4] Locke 1689/2008, book IV, chapter X1, section 10.

The need to begin where we are, epistemically speaking, is made vivid with an analogy due to Otto Neurath, in which knowledge is compared to a boat that must be repaired at sea.[5] We can improve the ship we have, attending to rotting planks one by one, but we cannot—as Descartes desired—dive off and try to build a new ship from scratch. We would drown before we had time to nail two planks together.

Crucially, starting with common sense doesn't meaning ending with common sense. Lewis thinks that if upon reflection the theory implicit in common sense can be *improved upon*, in terms of the theoretical virtues we appeal to in natural science—elegance, parsimony, and simplicity— then we are entitled to revise our pre-theoretical view of reality. But we have to *start* from common sense, if only we don't have anything better:

> It's not that the folk know in their blood what the highfalutin' philosophers may forget. And it's not that common sense speaks with the voice of some infallible faculty of "intuition". It's just that theoretical conservatism is the only sensible policy of theo- rists of limited powers, who are duly modest about what they could accomplish after a fresh start.[6]

The Lewisian method, then, can be summed up with the following imperative:

> *The Lewisian Method*—Start with the theory implicit in common sense, and move beyond it by appeal to theoretical virtues.

A few decades of hard work with this method, or slight variations on it, has not led to consensus among the practitioners of metaphysics, and the public outside of academia is still almost completely unaware that any of it's going on. Perhaps because of this there has also been in the last decade a growing interest in philosophical reflection on the foun- dations of metaphysics, in "metametaphysics" as it has become known, and once again the suspicion that metaphysics is a confused activity has resurfaced.[7] Despite the universal rejection of positivism, there has been

---

[5] Neurath 1932/1983: 92.

[6] Lewis 1986: 134.

[7] See Chalmers, Manley, and Wasserman (2009) for a number of essays that articulate and explore this suspicion.

renewed defense of the claim that metaphysical discussions are in some sense defective, and of the Carnapian position that central debates in contemporary metaphysics concerning the nature of material objects are merely verbal.[8] Eli Hirsch is one of the leading proponents of this "neo-Carnapian" movement:

> I know someone, whom I'll call A, who claimed that a standard drinking glass is a cup. "Just as a cat is a kind of animal," she said, "a glass is a kind of cup." Everyone else whom I've asked about this agrees with me that a glass is not a cup. Clearly this debate is, in some sense, merely about language.[9]

We can imagine a possible language, very similar to English, in which the word "cup" is used in such a way that glasses count as a kind of cup. We can also imagine a language in which the word "cup" is used in such a way that glasses are not a kind of cup. The only conceivable debate here is which of these possible languages is English. A is confused not about fundamental reality but about what the word "cup" means.

Now consider one of the central debates in contemporary metaphysics:

The Composition Debate

The question
When do fundamental particles compose composite objects?

The sides
- *Compositional nihilism*—Particles never compose composite entities. There are no such things as tables, only particles "arranged table-wise"; no such things as persons, only particles arranged "person-wise," and so on.
- *Compositional universalism*—For any set of particles, the members of that set—no matter how disparate and seemingly unrelated—compose an object. Universalists believe not only in "common sense" composite objects, such as table, rocks and planets but also in "crazy" composite objects, such as the object composed of Bill Clinton's nose, George Bush's left ear, and the planet Venus.

---

[8] Carnap 1950.
[9] Hirsch 2005: 69.

- *Restricted composition*—Only in certain quite specific circumstances do particles compose a composite object. Peter van Inwagen, for example, famously defends the view that particles compose only when they form a life.[10] So organisms exist, but tables, rocks, and planets do not.

Hirsch argues that the composition debate, like that over whether glasses are cups, is a merely verbal dispute, this time brought about by different possible meanings of terms pertaining to existence. We can imagine a possible language, very similar to English, in which the word "existence" is used in such a way that only particles "exist," or in such a way that only particles and organisms "exist." We can also imagine a possible language in which the verb to be is used in such a way that the sentence "There is an object composed of Clinton's ear, Bush's nose, and the Planet Venus" is true. The only possible disagreement concerns which if any of these imagined languages is English. Hirsch's answer is that none of them are; if we use existence terms in the way they are used in English, then it's true that there "are" tables, rocks, and planets, and false that there "is" an object composed of Clinton's nose, Bush's left ear, and Venus.

Karen Bennett argues that the composition debate, and other central debates in metaphysics, are problematic for a different reason: there's no way of working out which side is correct.[11] Following Lewis, a contemporary metaphysician tries to sell her theory at the "metaphysical marketplace" by boasting of its theoretical virtues of elegance, parsimony, and simplicity. Compositional nihilists, for instance, argue that their view is the most parsimonious: the only things that exist are particles. However, compositional nihilists don't want to reject common-sense talk as *though* there were composite objects. People who don't believe in witches don't talk about them as though they exist, but nihilists are happy to carry on talking about composite objects as though they exist; as Bennett puts it, nihilists never say "there are no toasters; revise your breakfast plans."[12] Thus, compositional nihilism involves an elaborate semantic account of how the sentence "There's a toaster in kitchen if you're feeling hungry" is correctly assertable while the sentence "There's a toaster on the moon" is not, even though neither is strictly speaking true.

---

[10] van Inwagen 1990.
[11] Bennett 2009.
[12] Bennett 2009: 58.

Bennett argues that the complexity involved in the nihilist's semantic theory perfectly cancels out the gains in parsimony involved in the nihilist's world view. The universalist has a much more simple and elegant semantic theory than the nihilist: the universalist can hold that the sentence "There's a toaster in the kitchen" is true just in case there's a toaster in the kitchen. But this gain in semantic simplicity is perfectly cancelled out by the lack of economy relative to nihilism: the universalist believes in a lot more stuff than the nihilist. Thus we have a perfect tie between the two views, with no way of deciding which is to be preferred.

Hirsch and Bennett have quite different views. Hirsch thinks that the dispute between the different sides of compositional debate is merely verbal. Bennett thinks that it is a genuine dispute concerning the nature of reality, just not one it's possible to resolve. But both agree that we have reached a stage in which these debates cannot be moved on. As Hirsch says:

> Of course ontologists do occasionally retract their positions, but, as Lewis remarks, a stage seems eventually to be reached in ontology when "all is said and done," when "all the tricky arguments and distinctions and counterexamples have been discovered," so that each position has achieved a state of "equilibrium." I'm assuming that in the ontological disputes under discussion the "all is said and done" stage has been reached.[13]

It is central to Hirsch's argument that this stage has been reached with respect to the debates he holds are merely verbal. Without going into all the details of how he argues for his position, we can appreciate that if there is no possible evidence (either empirical or from a priori reflection) that would cause proponents of either side of the composition debate to retract their view, then it is plausible that there is no fact of the matter as to which position is correct. It makes the composition debate look like the debate over whether glasses are cups; presumably nothing we could learn about the nature of glasses would settle this matter. Contrast this with the case of a dispute in empirical science in which there is some possible evidence that would cause one of the sides to retract their view.

---

[13] Hirsch 2005: 80–1.

Thus, it is a crucial premise for Hirsch that the "all is said and done" stage has been reached with respect to the central debates in metaphysics on the nature of material objects. In the case of Bennett, it is the conclusion of her argument, rather than a premise of her argument, that the "all is said and done" stage has been reached in many central debates. The debate is substantive, but there's just no way of working out which side is right.

Perhaps Bennett is right that nothing more can be said on these debates if we have available only the tools that contemporary metaphysicians make use of: roughly theoretical virtues and common sense.[14] Certainly no consensus to speak of has yet been reached. Or perhaps Hirsch is right that if the proponents on all sides of the composition debate have all relevant evidence before them and are still disagreeing, then we have good reason to think that these central debates are merely verbal. But I want to suggest that things look very, very different once we take on board a couple of the conclusions we have reached throughout this book. I want to suggest a way forward.

10.2 A Way Forward for Metaphysics

Suppose Jack and Jill know everything there is to know about the material constitution of the glass in front of them, and they still disagree about whether or not it is a cup. It is clear that there is no serious dispute here.

Now suppose Jack and Jill know everything there is to know about the nature of each kind of micro-level material entity in a given table-shaped region of space and how tokens of those kinds are arranged and related to each other, and suppose that everything that exists in that table-shaped region is grounded in facts concerning those micro-level material entities and their relationships. Let us further imagine that Jack and Jill are metaphysicians who disagree about whether or not there is a table in that table-shaped region of space.

As in the cup and glass case, it is hard to take seriously the idea that there could be a substantive disagreement here. After all, ex hypothesi both Jack and Jill have all the evidence that could possibly be relevant

---

[14] I am not especially sympathetic to Bennett's specific reasons for thinking that "all is said and done" stage has been reached. It is clear, however, that there is a lack of any significant consensus on these questions.

to determining whether or not there is a table: if there is a table it is grounded in facts about particles, and Jack and Jill have a complete understanding of all the particle-facts. What else could they be fighting over other than how to *describe* the case?[15]

However, the situation as just described does not match the real situation. Even if Jack and Jill are well-versed in what our best physics has to tell us about the nature of fundamental material entities—indeed, even if they are well-versed in the completed physics of the future—there is a still a massively significant aspect of the nature of fields and particles of which they are ignorant: their deep nature. Physics tell us about the causal structure of material entities, but leaves us completely in the dark regarding the concrete categorical nature that underlies that structure. It is crucial to Hirsch's case that all relevant evidence is in. But all relevant evidence is not in: we are ignorant of the deep nature of matter.

Indeed, it is extremely plausible that knowledge of the deep nature of matter would settle the composition debate as decisively as Google can settle a debate over the currency in Peru. It could turn out that the deep nature of matter is consciousness-involving, and that for any set of particles the members of that set form a subject of experience; hence, there is a subject of experience composed of Clinton's nose, Bush's left ear, and the planet Venus. Learning this would decisively settle matters in favor of the universalist. Perhaps it could even turn out that, when viewed in terms of its deep nature, only particles and organisms form unities, such that no one viewing reality in terms of its deep nature would be inclined to describe fundamental reality as containing tables.[16] While there is crucial evidence that cannot be accessed by those involved in the compositions debate, Hirsch's case that the debate is merely verbal collapses.

---

[15] Schaffer (forthcoming) argues that we need brute metaphysical principles to bridge the gap from the micro to the macro-level. However, in line with the grounding via analysis model outlined in section 2.2.2 and the grounding via essence model discussed in section 2.2.3, I am inclined to think that if one grasps the nature of the entities at both levels, then one can move a priori from micro to the macro (assuming the micro-level facts ground the macro-level facts). To the extent that the composition question is substantive, this is because of our ignorance of the deep nature of matter.

[16] Like Sider (2012), I am inclined to interpret the composition debate as not simply about what exists, but about what exists in fundamental reality. To put it in my terminology, it is a substantive question whether or not emergentism is true about composite objects. If the account I gave in section 2.2.2 of what it is for a table-shaped object to exist is correct, then the micro-level facts logically entail all that is required for a table-shaped composite object to exist. As a result, the question of whether or not there are tables is non-substantive. But the question of whether any or all composite objects, such as tables, are *fundamental* is substantive.

This still leaves Bennett's view that the debate, although substantive, cannot be settled. But Bennett, like the vast majority of contemporary metaphysicians, is trying to do metaphysics without a distinctive source of data beyond common sense and third-person observation. Looking at the current state of contemporary metaphysics, it is increasingly likely that these meager tools are unable to decisively settle any of the big questions they are being used to address. However, we learned in chapter 5 that there is a source of evidence, distinct from third-person data and common sense, that can potentially be used in metaphysical enquiry: our direct access to the essence of our conscious states. Indeed, it seems to me that the best strategy available to opponents of compositional nihilism is to try to use this source of evidence to establish the following: facts concerning o-subjects are something over and above facts concerning relationships between micro-level particles.

This crucial source of data is almost wholly neglected in contemporary metaphysics. In his recent defense of compositional nihilism, Theodore Sider spends less than a page considering what he calls "the Cartesian argument" against nihilism, roughly, that I know for certain that I exist and I am not plausibly a micro-level entity.[17] He quickly dismisses this on the grounds that we have no good reason to deny that sentences about my existence as a conscious being are true (or at least correctly assertable) in virtue of certain micro-level facts. Perhaps if we deny Phenomenal Transparency, then there is indeed no good reason to deny that the truth-conditions of o-phenomenal propositions could be satisfied by micro-level facts. But once we embrace Phenomenal Transparency, this becomes a great deal more difficult to make sense of, as we discovered in the discussion of the subject irreducibility problem in section 8.3.[18]

To sum up the proposal:

- Acknowledging our ignorance of the deep nature of matter removes the Hirschian concern that central debates regarding the nature of material objects are merely verbal.
- Our introspective grasp of the nature of consciousness provides an underexploited source of data that has the potential to resolve the stand-offs that concern Bennett.

---

[17] Sider 2013b.

[18] The subject irreducibility problem in section 8.3 isn't set up in terms of Sider's framework, but it can be easily set up that way, as I show in Goff (2015a, 2016b).

The datum of consciousness is a valuable source of data with the potential to transform metaphysical debates. Recognition of this fact could, I believe, lead to a radically new approach to metaphysics. In the next section I will sketch an argument for presentism as a case study to illustrate how this new methodology might work in practice.

10.3 A Phenomenological Argument for Presentism

Consider the following debate, which Hirsch also argues is merely verbal:

The Persistence Debate

The question
How do material objects persist through time?

The sides
- *Endurantism*—An ordinary material object (such as a rock, planet, or person) persists through time in virtue of being wholly present at each time at which it exists. On this view, ordinary material objects are extended in three dimensions.
- *Perdurantism*—An ordinary material object (such as a rock, planet, or person) persists through time in virtue of one temporal part of it being present at each time at which it exists. On this view, ordinary material objects are extended in four dimensions.

According to perdurantism the book in front of you is a four-dimensional spacetime worm, stretched out across time. What you are currently looking at is just one temporal slice of that worm. According to endurantism, what you have is in front of you right now is the entire book, not just one slice of it. The whole book also existed a moment ago and will exist a moment hence.

David Lewis objected to endurantism on the grounds that it is unable to account for the fact that objects change intrinsic properties.[19] Suppose you get extremely fed up with the nonsense being spouted in this book and decide to pulp it into an unreadable ball. It seems to follow that a single copy of my book is both book-shaped (as it exists

---

[19] Lewis 1986: 202–4.

yesterday) and unreadable-ball-shaped (as it exists today). How is this possible?

According to Lewis there are only three possible solutions:

- *Presentism*: Only the present moment exists. The state of affairs of the book being book-shaped no longer exists; the book has no shape other than the one that it has in the present moment: unreadable-ball-shaped.
- *Perdurantism* (Lewis's preferred view): Some temporal parts of the spacetime worm book are book-shaped, and some temporal parts are unreadable-ball-shaped. This is no more contradictory than the fact that some of my parts are hand-shaped and some are foot-shaped.
- *Relationism*: Shapes are, in fact, relationships material objects bear to times. Thus, the book bears the *being-book-shaped* relation to yesterday, and the *being-unreadable-ball-shaped* relation to today. The contradiction is removed: an object can consistently bear a single relation to one thing but not another; for example, I can be on the left of Susan but not on the left of Jerry.

Lewis rejects the first and third options and hence ends up with perdurantism by a process of elimination. His reasons for rejecting presentism are extremely weak. Lewis argues that (i) the presentist rejects persistence altogether, and that (ii) presentism is absurd as "no man, unless it be at the moment of his execution, believes that he has no future; still less does anyone believe that he has no past."[20] But although presentists deny the reality of the past, all sensible presentists will accept that there are *past truths* (expressed by sentences prefixed by the sentential operator "It was the case that . . .") and probable future truths (expressed using the sentential operator "Probably it will be the case that. . . .") If there are truths about the past then we can account for persistence in terms of them: I have persisted through time in virtue of the fact that it was the case that I existed at such and such prior times. And although most of us believe we have a future, for the presentist all this means is that we believe that it probably will be the case that we will exist at such and such future times.[21]

---

[20] Lewis 1986: 204.

[21] Many philosophers think it is a deep challenge for presentism of how to account for past truths without the reality of the past. I argue in Goff (2010b) that this a pseudo-problem. The charge that presentism is inconsistent with special relativity, however, is an important one. Ultimately empirical considerations should have more force in this matter than the philosophical considerations pertaining to the need to preserve our common-sense conception of time and the persistence of subjects

What about the third option? Lewis declares that it is absurd to think that shape is a relation. It is simply evident that an object's shape is an intrinsic feature of it rather than a relationship the object bears to things outside of itself.

Many have been unmoved by Lewis's conviction that shape is an intrinsic property. Plausibly shape *according to our folk concept of it* is an intrinsic property. But why should our folk concept not be revised in the light of scientific or metaphysical discoveries, just as our folk concept of solidity arguably has been? This reveals what a thin source of data common sense is. For almost all of our folk concepts, there seem no good grounds for holding them to be unrevisable. And once we are allowed to revise them, they can be molded to fit almost any metaphysical theory. The requirement that a theory accommodate freedom, value, shape, and solidity according to our exact folk conception of them would be very demanding; the requirement that a theory accommodate some watered-down version of these things, which captures merely a limited subset of our folk platitudes about them, is not. This is a significant factor in the failure of contemporary metaphysics to achieve consensus.

As luck would have it, there is one kind of folk concept that we know for certain is satisfied: direct phenomenal concepts. Not only that, but these concepts are transparent, revealing the complete essence of the properties they denote. If we have the intuition—as many do—that phenomenal qualities are intrinsic, then this is an intuition that we are entitled to take very seriously indeed. The strength of the Lewisian argument against relationism would be vastly improved upon if it were built on a deep intuition about the nature of consciousness.

Even when our intuitions about the nature of consciousness don't directly undermine a given metaphysical hypothesis, they can sometimes do so by working hand in hand with common sense. I am inclined to think that our understanding of consciousness, in conjunction with a little common sense, leads to a fairly strong argument for presentism, as I will now explain.

The one thing I know with certainty to exist—my conscious mind—is currently having an experience that represents a table with a laptop on it, beyond that a window, traffic outside, and a couple arguing in Hungarian in the next apartment. I am certainly not experiencing events of my

---

over extended periods of time. However, while we patiently wait for the unification of general relativity and quantum mechanics, which may decide the matter, it is arguably rational to go with the philosophical considerations.

childhood or of my life at the age of sixty-four. But according to perdurantism, I am a four-dimensional spacetime worm, stretched out over (I hope!) seventy or so years of time. That Goff-like spacetime worm is certainly not having the experience I have just been describing; if it is conscious at all it is having some kind of weird consciousness involving all of the experiences of my life. But that is not *my* consciousness; it is not the consciousness of that thing that right now I know with certainty to exist.

Spacetime worms that perdure for more than a few seconds can be said to "have" o-conscious states in the derivative sense of having temporal parts that have o-conscious states. But they don't directly instantiate o-conscious states in the sense that you and I directly instantiate o-conscious states; there is nothing that it's like to be a spacetime worm (or if there is, it's not what it's like to be an o-subject). Thus, for the perdurantist, spacetime worms persist through time but are not o-subjects, while brief temporal parts of spacetime worms are o-subjects but persist only through very brief periods of time. There is nothing in the perdurantist world-view that both persists through longish periods of time and is an o-subject.

In a recent article, Josh Parsons has drawn attention to this point but offers a solution: I am not a spacetime worm; rather I am a *temporal part* of a spacetime worm.[22] The thing that has my conscious experience, the thing I know with certainty to exist, is just one tiny slice of the Goff-like spacetime worm stretched over seventy years of time. This is the "stage theory" of the persistence of (or rather lack of persistence of) ordinary material objects.[23] It is a coherent view, and it might be true. But I hope to God it isn't. Because such temporal parts do not exist for very long at all. Human-like spacetime worms are stretched through fairly long periods of time, enveloping many temporal parts. But the temporal parts that could be plausibly thought to instantiate o-conscious states last no more than a couple of seconds each.

Thus, if Parsons is right, then my conscious mind, that thing I know with certainty to exist, won't be around in a couple of seconds' time. It will be replaced by some other conscious mind, which will be very similar to it, which will share its memories, but which won't be *me*: the thinking, feeling thing I know with certainty to exist right now. This is precisely the content of the fear of imminent death: the fear that *I* won't exist in the near future. If stage theory is true, then there is a very real sense in which

---

[22] Parsons 2015. We came up with this phenomenological argument against perdurantism independently.

[23] For further defense of the stage theory, see Sider (2001: 188–92).

I am dying every second.[24] We may one day have overwhelming empirical reason to believe such a picture of the world, but our humanity demands that we not lose touch with the fact that it is a radically sceptical scenario, different in degree but not in kind to solipsism or the hypothesis that I am a brain in a vat.[25]

We now have the basic components of a phenomenological argument for presentism:

A phenomenological argument for presentism

Premise 1—On average, o-subjects persist through several decades of time (common-sense commitment).

Premise 2—If o-subjects persist on average through several decades of time, then either presentism, relationism, or perdurantism is true (if Lewis is right that these are the only ways of accounting for the fact that objects change their intrinsic properties).

Premise 3—Relationism is false (supported by intuitions that consciousness is intrinsic rather than relational).

Premise 4—Perdurantism is false (supported by our introspective knowledge of what it's like to be an o-subject).

Conclusion—Therefore, presentism is true.

I do not take myself to have given anything like an adequate defense of this argument.[26] I merely wanted to illustrate that the datum of consciousness has potential applications in metaphysics beyond dealing with the mind–body problem.

In the final section I will outline a methodology that generalizes this consciousness-based approach to metaphysics.

10.4 Analytic Phenomenology

The Lewisian method I have just outlined starts metaphysical enquiry with only the data of common sense. This is to ignore a powerful source

---

[24] Of course I am speaking slightly loosely here: there is no single thing, such that that thing is dying every second. Rather there is a series of o-conscious minds existing in turn, such that every couple of seconds one of them ceases to exist.

[25] Offering a counterpart analysis of talk of my persistence (Sider 2001: 188–92) seems to me cold comfort.

[26] There is a huge literature on Lewis's argument; see Haslanger (2003) for an excellent starting point.

of data: carefully considered intuitions concerning phenomenal consciousness. It is justified to take carefully considered armchair intuitions as a guide to what is required from reality for our transparent concepts to be satisfied. In the case of direct phenomenal concepts, we have a class of concepts that are not only transparent but are also such that we know with an extremely high level of justification that they are satisfied. If armchair intuitions give us reason to think that reality must be such and such a way if there is phenomenal consciousness, then those armchair intuitions are reason to believe that reality really is that way. Hence, in the possibly unique case of reflection on phenomenal consciousness, armchair intuitions can get us all the way to reality.

I propose the following small but potentially revolutionary modification to the Lewisian method, as the basis of an approach that combines the rigor and resources of analytic metaphysics with a commitment to Phenomenal Transparency:

> *Analytic Phenomenology*—Start with common sense, empirical data, *and* carefully considered intuitions concerning the nature of phenomenal consciousness, and move on by appeal to theoretical virtue.

This does not give us an infallible method. No doubt compositional nihilists have responses to the subject irreducibility problem. Perhaps some will have a way of defusing the deep intuition that phenomenal qualities are intrinsic. And even if we could reach agreement on all the a priori intuitions about consciousness, we would still have to rely on common sense to get beyond solipsism. There is no guarantee that metaphysicians working in a framework that starts from Phenomenal Transparency would reach convergence in their views.

On the other hand, we have no reason to think they wouldn't. If the kind of serious, sustained, rigorous thought that has taken place in contemporary metaphysics in the last forty years was done *with an agreed source of data* (beyond common sense), who knows what could be achieved. Metaphysicians have spent too long, as it were, sitting by a microscope trying to work out the relative merits of various theories or the microscopic world, without actually *having a look in the microscope*. In this situation we may very well have reached Lewis's "all is said and done stage" while serious disagreement remains. It does not follow that serious disagreement will persist when we start looking through the microscope.

We can think of the history of metaphysics thus far as divided into two epochs. In the pre-Galilean epoch, lasting up to the sixteenth century, we tried to formulate a complete theory of the world all at once, without distinguishing the project of mapping the world's causal structure from the broader project. In the Galilean epoch that followed, we distinguished the more limited project of mapping causal structure and focused great resources on it.

In a sense, the second epoch went much better than the first, yielding a clear line of progress as well as stable consensus on big issues. In fact, as discussed in chapter 1, the Galilean project has gone so well that we have forgotten that it was only ever intended to be a partial description of reality. The visceral effect of technology on one's metaphysics is powerful. We can't help feeling an intense need to put all of our metaphysical faith in the scientific method that has produced it. Everything else seems too speculative and imprecise in comparison. This powerful influence has led to what will be looked back on as the deepest perversion in metaphysical thought: the conviction that the qualitative consciousness is nothing over and above causal structure.

It will be hard to move on from this to a "post-Galilean epoch." But if we ever do, there is the potential for a radically new approach to metaphysics, one not available until recent history. The consciousness-based approach of analytic phenomenology takes seriously two distinct sources of data:

- The findings of mature physical science concerning the causal structure of the material world.
- The direct first-person access each of us has to the nature of consciousness.

Aside from the extra source of data, analytic phenomenology could be indistinguishable from the familiar Lewisian approach. Rival hypotheses can evaluated in terms of (i) fit with the data and (ii) intrinsic theoretical virtues. As in science, a minimal amount of pre-theoretical common sense must also be respected; interpersonal verification of empirical data requires at the very least that each of us makes the anti-skeptical assumption that there are other minds. But the possession of a distinctive source of metaphysical data renders the analytic phenomenologist less reliant than the Lewisian on common sense, and, correspondingly, more open to revising ordinary thought for the sake of theoretical virtue.

Never in the history of human thought have three elements been in place: (i) mature natural science, (ii) serious systematic metaphysics, and (iii) broad agreement among the practitioners of metaphysics that consciousness must be taken seriously (the kind of seriousness expressed by the Consciousness Constraint articulated in section 1.1.1).[27] If one day each of these comes to pass, we could finally begin the serious, interdisciplinary task of formulating the most simple, elegant theory that is consistent both with the findings of natural science and with the evident reality of consciousness. A couple of hundred years of serious engagement with this project would result in the best guess at the nature of reality of which human beings are capable. I see no reason why it should not be possible to achieve consensus on central matters.

People worry that metaphysics hasn't got anywhere. But true post-Galilean metaphysics hasn't yet begun. It might not work, but it's worth a try.[28]

---

[27] Whether the seventeenth century counts as a time when these three elements were in place depends on how "mature" natural science has to be if it is to be helpful to metaphysics. Certainly, these elements haven't been present for a long time.

[28] The work of Barry Dainton is an example of the methodology I am trying to get at. A fine example of this is Dainton (2011b), in which he argues that the reality of time consciousness rules out certain metaphysical theories of time.

BIBLIOGRAPHY

Albahari, M. Forthcoming. "Beyond Cosmopsychism and the Great I Am: How the World Might Be Grounded in Universal 'Advaitic' Consciousness," in Seager forthcoming.

Alexander, S. 1920. *Space, Time and Deity*, London: Macmillan.

Alter, T. & Nagasawa, N. 2015. "What Is Russellian Monism?" in Alter & Nagasawa 2015.

Alter, T. & Nagasawa, N. (Eds.) 2015. *Consciousness in the Physical World*, New York: Oxford University Press.

Alter, T. & Walter, S. (Eds.) 2007. *Phenomenal Concepts and Phenomenal Knowledge*, New York: Oxford University Press.

Armstrong, D. M. 1968. *A Materialist Theory of Mind*, London: Routledge and Kegan Paul.

Armstrong, D. M. 1978. *A Theory of Universals*, Cambridge: Cambridge University Press.

Armstrong, D. M. 1983. *What Is a Law of Nature?* Cambridge: Cambridge University Press.

Armstrong, D. M. 1997. *A World of States of Affairs*, Cambridge: Cambridge University Press.

Armstrong, D. M., Martin, C. B., & Place, U. T. 1996. *Dispositions: A Debate*, edited by Tim Crane, New York: Routledge.

Augustine. 426/1998. *The City of God against the Pagans*, translated by R. W. Dyson, edited by G. B. Matthews, Cambridge: Cambridge University Press.

Balashov, Y. & Janssen, M. 2003. "Presentism and Relativity," *British Journal for the Philosophy of Science* 54: 2, 327–46.

Balog, K. 1999. "Conceivability, Possibility, and the Mind-Body Problem," *Philosophical Review* 108: 4, 497–528.

Balog, K. 2012. "Acquaintance and the Mind–Body Problem," in C. Hill & S. Gozzano (Eds.) *New Perspectives on Type Identity: The Mental and the Physical*, Cambridge: Cambridge University Press.

Bayne, T. J. & Chalmers, D. J. 2003. "What Is the Unity of Consciousness?" in A. Cleeremans (Ed.) *The Unity of Consciousness: Binding, Integration, Dissociation*, Oxford: Oxford University Press.

Bennett, K. 2009. "Composition, Colocation, and Metaontology," in Chalmers, Manley & Wasserman 2009.

Bennett, K. 2011. "By Our Bootstraps," *Philosophical Perspectives* 25: 27–41.

Ben-Yami, H. 2015. *Descartes' Philosophical Revolution: A Reassessment*, New York: Palgrave Macmillan.

Bird, A. 2007a. *Nature's Metaphysics: Laws and Properties*, Oxford: Oxford University Press.

Bird, A. 2007b, "The Regress of Pure Powers?" *Philosophical Quarterly* 57: 513–34.

Blackburn, S. 1990. "Filling in Space," *Analysis* 50: 62–65.

Block, N. 2006. "Max Black's Objection to Mind-Body Identity," in D. Zimmerman (Ed.) *Oxford Studies in Metaphysics II*, Oxford: Oxford University Press.

Block, N. and R. Stalnaker, 1999. "Conceptual Analysis, Dualism and the Explanatory Gap," *Philosophical Review* 108: 1, 1–46.

Bradley, F. H. 1935. "Relations" in his *Collected Essays*. Vol. 2, Oxford: Clarendon Press.

Bradley, F. H. 1897. *Appearance and Reality*, Oxford: Clarendon Press.

Brentano, F. 1874/1973. *Psychology from an Empirical Standpoint*, translated by A. C. Rancurello, D. B. Terrell, and L. McAlister. London: Routledge.

Broad, C. D. 1925. *The Mind and Its Place in Nature*, London: Routledge & Kegan Paul.

Brown, R. (Ed.) 2013. *Consciousness Inside and Out: Phenomenology, Neuroscience, and the Nature of Experience*, Dordrecht: Springer.

Brüntrup, G. 2016. "Emergent Panpsychism," in Brüntrup & Jaskolla 2016.

Brüntrup, G. & Jaskolla, L. (Eds.) 2016. *Panpsychism*, New York: Oxford University Press.

Cameron, R. 2008. "Truthmakers and Ontological Commitment: or, How to Deal with Complex Objects and Mathematical Ontology without Getting into Trouble," *Philosophical Studies* 140: 1.

Cameron, R. 2010. "Quantification, Naturalness and Ontology," in A. Hazlett (Ed.) *New Waves in Metaphysics*, New York: Palgrave-Macmillan.

Campbell, K. 1976. *Metaphysics: An Introduction*, Encino, CA: Dickenson.

Carnap, R. 1950. "Empiricism, Semantics and Ontology," *Revue International de Philosophie* 4: 20–40. Reprinted in *Meaning and Necessity: A Study in Semantics and Modal Logic*, 2d ed. Chicago: University of Chicago Press.

Carruthers, P. 2000. *Phenomenal Consciousness: A Naturalistic Theory*, Cambridge: Cambridge University Press.

Carruthers, P. 2004. "Phenomenal Concepts and Higher-Order Experiences," *Philosophy and Phenomenological Research* 68: 2, 316–36.

Chalmers, D. J. 1995. "Facing Up to the Problem of Consciousness," *Journal of Consciousness Studies* 2: 3, 200–19.

Chalmers, D. J. 1996. *The Conscious Mind: Towards a Fundamental Theory*, New York: Oxford University Press.

Chalmers, D. J. 2002. "Consciousness and Its Place in Nature," in his *Philosophy of Mind: Classical and Contemporary Readings*, New York: Oxford University Press.

Chalmers, D. J. 2003. "The Content and Epistemology of Phenomenal Belief," in Q. Smith & A. Jokic (Eds.) *Consciousness: New Philosophical Perspectives*, Oxford: Oxford University Press.

Chalmers, D. J. 2004. "Epistemic Two-Dimensional Semantics," *Philosophical Studies* 118: 153–226.

Chalmers, D. J. 2009. "The Two-Dimensional Argument against Materialism," in B. McLaughlin (Ed.) *Oxford Handbook of the Philosophy of Mind*, Oxford: Oxford University Press.

Chalmers, D. J. 2012. *Constructing the World*, Oxford: Oxford University Press.

Chalmers, D. J. 2015. "Panpsychism and Panprotopsychism," in Alter & Nagasawa 2015.

Chalmers, D. J. 2016. "The Combination Problem for Panpsychism," in Brüntrup & Jaskolla 2016.

Chalmers, D. J., Manley, D., & Wasserman, R. (Eds.) 2009. *Metametaphysics: New Essays on the Foundations of Ontology*, New York: Oxford University Press.

Churchland, P. M. 2013a. "Consciousness and the Introspection of 'Qualitative Simples,'" in Brown 2013.

Churchland, P. S. 2013b. *Touching a Nerve*, New York: W. W. Norton and Company.

Coates, P. & Coleman, S. (Eds.) 2015. *Phenomenal Qualities: Sense, Perception and Consciousness*, New York: Oxford University Press.

Coleman, S. 2006. "Being Realistic: Why Physicalism May Entail Panexperientialism," *Journal of Consciousness Studies* 13: 10–11, 40–52.

Coleman, S. 2012. "Mental Chemistry: Combination for Panpsychists," *Dialectica* 66: 1, 137–66.

Coleman, S. 2014. "The Real Combination Problem: Panpsychism, Micro-Subjects and Emergence," *Erkenntnis* 79: 1, 19–44.

Coleman, S. 2015. "Neuro-Cosmology," in Coates & Coleman 2015.

Coleman, S. 2016. "Panpsychism and Neutral Monism: How to Make Up One's Mind," in Brüntrup & Jaskolla 2016.

Conee, E. 1994. "Phenomenal Knowledge," *Australasian Journal of Philosophy* 72: 136–50.

Cutter, B. 2016. "Review of *Phenomenal Qualities: Sense, Perception and Consciousness*," *Notre Dame Philosophical Reviews*.

Dainton, B. 2011a. "Review of Consciousness and Its Place in Nature," *Philosophy and Phenomenological Research* 83: 1, 238–61.

Dainton, B. 2011b. "Time, Passage and Immediate Experience," in C. Callender (Ed.), *Oxford Handbook of Philosophy of Time*, Oxford: Oxford University Press.

Dancy, J. 2000. *Practical Reality*, Oxford: Oxford University Press.

Dasgupta, S. 2014. "The Possibility of Physicalism," *Journal of Philosophy* 111: 9, 557–92.

Dasgupta, S. 2016. "Metaphysical Rationalism," *Noûs* 50: 2, 379–418.

Dennett, D. 1991. *Consciousness Explained*, Boston: Little Brown.

deRosset, L. 2010. "Getting Priority Straight," *Philosophical Studies* 149: 1, 73–97.

deRosset, L. 2013. "Grounding Explanations," *Philosophers' Imprint* 13: 7, 1–26.

Descartes, R. 1645/1996. "Meditations on First Philosophy," in J. Cottingham (Ed.) *Meditations on First Philosophy with Selections from the Objections and Replies*, Cambridge: Cambridge University Press.

Diaz-Leon, E. 2008. "Defending the Phenomenal Concept Strategy," *Australasian Journal of Philosophy* 86: 4, 597–610.

Diaz-Leon, E. 2010. "Can Phenomenal Concepts Explain the Epistemic Gap?" *Mind* 119: 476, 933–51.

Diaz-Leon, E. 2014. "Do A Posteriori Physicalists Get Our Phenomenal Concepts Wrong?" *Ratio*, 27: 1, 1–16.

Diaz-Leon, E. Forthcoming. "Phenomenal Concepts: Neither Circular nor Opaque," *Philosophical Psychology*.

Dorr, C. 2008. "There Are No Abstract Objects," in T. Sider, J. Hawthorne, & D. W. Zimmerman (Eds.), *Contemporary Debates in Metaphysics*, Malden, MA: Blackwell.

Dowell, J. L. 2006. "The Physical: Empirical, Not Metaphysical," *Philosophical Studies* 131: 25–60.

Dretske, F. 1977. "Laws of Nature," *Philosophy of Science* 44: 248–68.

Eddington, A. 1928. *The Nature of the Physical World*, Cambridge: Cambridge University Press.

Ellis, B. 2001. *Scientific Essentialism*, Cambridge: Cambridge University Press.

Ellis, B. 2002. *The Philosophy of Nature: A Guide to the New Essentialism*, Montreal: McGill-Queen's University Press.

Feigl, H. 1960. "Mind–Body, Not a Pseudo-Problem," in S. Hook (Ed.) *Dimensions of Mind*, New York: New York University Press.

Feigl, H. 1967. *The "Mental" and the "Physical": The Essay and a Postscript*, Minneapolis: University of Minnesota Press.

Fine, K. 1994. "Essence and Modality," *Philosophical Perspectives* 8: 1–16.

Fine, K. 2001. "The Question of Realism," *Philosophers' Imprint* 1.

Fine, K. 2012. "A Guide to Ground," in F. Correia & B. Schneider (Eds.) *Metaphysical Grounding*, Cambridge: Cambridge University Press 2012.

Flanagan, O. 1991. *The Science of the Mind*, Cambridge, MA: MIT Press.

Foster, J. 1982. *The Case for Idealism*, London: Routledge and Kegan Paul.

Foster, J. 1991. *The Immaterial Self: A Defence of the Cartesian Dualist Conception of the Mind*, Oxford: Oxford University Press.

Frankish, K. 2016. "Illusionism as a theory of consciousness," *Journal of Consciousness Studies* 23: 11–12.

Frege, G. 1951. "On Concept and Object," translated by P. T. Geach, revised by Max Black, *Mind* 60: 168–80.

Galileo, G. 1623/1957. *The Assayer*, 1, in S. Drake (Ed.) *Discoveries and Opinions of Galileo*, New York: Anchor Books.

Geach, P. 1965. "Assertion," *Philosophical Review* 74: 449–65.

Goff, P. 2006. "Experiences Don't Sum," *Journal of Consciousness Studies* 13: 6, 53–61.

Goff, P. 2007. "Kirk on Empirical Physicalism," *Ratio* 20: 1, 122–29.

Goff, P. 2009. "Why Panpsychism Doesn't Help Explain Consciousness," *Dialectica* 63: 3, 289–311.

Goff, P. 2010a. "Ghosts and Sparse Properties: Why the Physicalist Has More to Fear from Ghosts than Zombies," *Philosophy and Phenomenological Research* 81: 119–39.

Goff, P. 2010b. "Orthodox Truthmaker Theory Cannot Be Defended by Cost/Benefit Analysis," *Analysis* 79: 1, 45–50.

Goff, P. 2011. "A Posteriori Physicalists Get Our Phenomenal Concepts Wrong," *Australasian Journal of Philosophy* 89: 2, 191–209.

Goff, P. 2012a. "A Priori Physicalism, Lonely Ghosts and Cartesian Doubt," *Consciousness and Cognition* 21: 742–46.

Goff, P. 2012b. *Spinoza on Monism*, London, UK: Palgrave Macmillan.

Goff. P. 2013. "Orthodox Property Dualism + Linguistic Theory of Vagueness = Panpsychism," in Brown 2013.

Goff, P. 2014. "The Cartesian Argument against Physicalism," in J. Kallestrup & M. Sprevak (Eds.) *New Waves in the Philosophy of Mind*, New York: Palgrave Macmillan.

Goff, P. 2015a. "Against Constitutive Russellian Monism," in Alter & Nagasawa 2015.

Goff, P. 2015b. "Real Acquaintance and Physicalism," in Coates & Coleman 2015.

Goff, P. 2016a. "The Phenomenal Bonding Solution to the Combination Problem," in Brüntrup & Jaskolla 2016.

Goff, P. 2016b. "Fundamentality and the Mind–Body Problem," *Erkenntnis* 81: 4, 881–98.

Goff, P. 2017a. "Panpsychism may be crazy, but it's also most probably true," *Aeon*, https://aeon. co/ideas/panpsychism-is-crazy-but-its-also-most-probably-true.

Goff, P. 2017b. "Panpsychism", in S. Schneider & M. Velmans (Eds.) *Blackwell Companion to Consciousness*, Oxford: Blackwell.

Goff, P. Forthcoming. "Cosmopsychism, Micropsychism and the Grounding Relation," in Seager Forthcoming.

Goff, P. & Papineau, D. 2014. "What's Wrong with Strong Necessities?" *Philosophical Studies*, 167: 3, 749–62.

Green, T. H. 1888. *Collected Works*, London: Longmans.

Griffin, D. R. 1998. *Unsnarling the World-Knot: Consciousness, Freedom, and the Mind-Body Problem*, Berkeley: University of California Press.

Harris, S. 2010. *The Moral Landscape: How Science Can Determine Human Values*, New York: Free Press.

Hartshorne, C. 1934. *The Philosophy and Psychology of Sensation*, Chicago: University of Chicago Press.

Haslanger, S. 2003. "Persistence through Time," in M. Loux & D. Zimmerman (Eds.) *The Oxford Handbook of Metaphysics*, Oxford: Oxford University Press, 315–54.

Hawthorne, J. 2001. "Causal Structuralism," *Philosophical Perspectives* 15: 361–78.

Hawthorne, J. & Nolan, J. 2006. "What Would Teleological Causation Be?" in J. Hawthorne (Ed.) *Metaphysical Essays*, Oxford: Oxford University Press.

Heil, J. 2003. *From an Ontological Point of View*, Oxford: Clarendon Press.

Heil, J. 2012. *The Universe as We Find It*, Oxford: Clarendon Press.

Hempel, C. 1980. "Comments on Goodman's Ways of Worldmaking," *Synthese* 45: 193–200.

Hill, C. 1997. "Imaginability, Conceivability, Possibility and the Mind-Body Problem," *Philosophical Studies* 87: 1, 61–85.

Hill, C. and McLaughlin, B. 1999. "There Are Fewer Things in Reality That Are Dreamt of in Chalmers's Philosophy," *Philosophy and Phenomenological Research* 59: 2, 445–54.

Hirsch, E. 2005. "Physical-Object Ontology, Verbal Disputes, and Common Sense," *Philosophy and Phenomenological Research* 70: 1, 67–97.

Horgan, T. 1984. "Jackson on Physical Information and Qualia," *Philosophical Quarterly* 34: 147–52.

Horgan, T. 1993. "From Supervenience to Superdupervenience: Meeting the Demands of a Material World," *Mind* 102: 408, 555–86.

Horgan, T. 2006. Materialism: Matters of Definition, Defense, and Deconstruction, *Philosophical Studies* 131: 1, 157–83.

Horgan, T. and Potrč, M. 2008. *Austere Realism: Conceptual Semantics Meets Minimal Ontology*, Cambridge: MIT Press.

Horgan, T. and Potrč, M. 2012. "Existence Monism Trumps Priority Monism," in Goff 2012b.

Howell, R. 2013. *Consciousness and the Limits of Objectivity: The Case for Subjective Physicalism*, Oxford: Oxford University Press.

Hume, D. 1748/2000. *An Enquiry concerning Human Understanding*, edited by Tom. L. Beauchamp, New York: Oxford University Press.

Jackson, F. 1982. "Epiphenomenal Qualia," *Philosophical Quarterly* 32: 127–36.

Jackson, F. 1986. "What Mary Didn't Know," *Journal of Philosophy* 83: 291–95.

Jackson, F. 1998. *From Metaphysics to Ethics: A Defence of Conceptual Analysis*, New York: Oxford University Press.

Jackson, F. 2007. "The Knowledge Arguments, Diaphanousness and Representationalism," in Alter & Walter 2007.

James, W. 1890/1981. *Principles of Psychology*, Vol. 1. Cambridge, MA: Harvard University Press.

James, W. 1904. "Does 'Consciousness' Exist?" *Journal of Philosophy, Psychology, and Scientific Methods* 1: 477–91.

Jaskolla, L. & Buck, A. J. 2012. "Does Panexperientialism solve the Combination Problem," *Journal of Consciousness Studies* 19: 9–10, 190–99.

Johnston, M. 1992. "How to Speak of the Colors," *Philosophical Studies* 68: 221–63.

Kim, J. 1989. "Mechanism, Purpose, and Explanatory Exclusion," *Philosophical Perspectives* 3: 77–108.

Kim, J. 1993a. "The Non-Reductivist's Troubles with Mental Causation," in J. Heil & A. Mele (Eds.) *Mental Causation*, Oxford: Clarendon Press; reprinted in Kim 1993b.

Kim, J. 1993b, *Supervenience and Mind: Selected Philosophical Essays*, Cambridge, MA: Cambridge University Press.

Kim, J. 1998. *Mind in a Physical World*, Cambridge, MA: MIT Press.

Kim, J. 2005. *Physicalism, or Something Near Enough*, Princeton, NJ: Princeton University Press.

Kirk, R. 1974a. "Zombies vs Materialists," *Proceedings of the Aristotelian Society* 48: 135–52.

Kirk, R. 1974b. "Sentience and Behaviour," *Mind* 83: 43–60.

Kirk, R. 2008. *Zombies and Consciousness*, Oxford: Oxford University Press.

Kirk, R. 2013. *The Conceptual Link from the Mental to the Physical*, Oxford: Oxford University Press.

Kriegel, U. 2008. *Subjective Consciousness*, New York: Oxford University Press.

Kriegel, U. 2013. *Phenomenal Intentionality*, New York: Oxford University Press.

Kripke, S. 1980. *Naming and Necessity*, Cambridge, MA: Harvard University Press.

Ladyman, J., Ross, D., Spurrett, D., & Collier, J. 2007. *Everything Must Go: Metaphysics Naturalised*, Oxford: Oxford University Press.

Lee, G. 2016. "Does experience have phenomenal qualities?" *Philosophical Topics* 44: 2, 201–30.

Leibniz, G. W. 1686/2012. *The Discourse on Metaphysics*, in P. Loptson (Ed.) *The Discourse on Metaphysics and Other Writings*, Calgary: Broadview Press.

Leibniz, G. W. 1714/2012. *The Monadology*, in P. Loptson (Ed.) *The Discourse on Metaphysics and Other Writings*, Calgary: Broadview Press.

Leuenberger, S. 2014. "Grounding and Necessity," *Inquiry* 57: 2, 151–74.

Levin, J. 2002. "Is Conceptual Analyses Needed for the Reduction of Qualitative States?" *Philosophical & Phenomenological Research* 64: 3, 571–91.

Levin, J. 2007a. "Nagel vs. Nagel on the Nature of Phenomenal Concepts," *Ratio* 20: 3, 293–307.

Levin, J. 2007b. "What Is a Phenomenal Concept?" in Alter & Walter 2007.

Levine, J. 1983. "Materialism and Qualia: The Explanatory Gap," *Pacific Philosophical Quarterly* 64: 9, 354–61.

Levine, J. 2001. *Purple Haze: The Puzzle of Consciousness*, New York: Oxford University Press.

Lewis, D. 1966. "An Argument for the Identity Theory," *Journal of Philosophy* 63: 17–25.

Lewis, D. 1970. "How to Define Theoretical Terms," *Journal of Philosophy* 67: 427–46.

Lewis, D. 1982. "New Work for a Theory of Universals," *Australasian Journal of Philosophy* 61: 343–77.

Lewis, D. 1986. *On The Plurality of Worlds*, Malden, MA: Blackwell.

Lewis, D. 1988. "What Experience Teaches," *Proceedings of the Russellian Society*, 13: 29–57.

Lewis, D. 1991. *Parts of Classes*. Cambridge, MA: Blackwell.

Lewis, D. 1994. "Reduction of Mind," in S. Guttenplan (Ed.) *Companion to the Philosophy of Mind*, Oxford: Blackwell.

Lewis, D. 1995. "Should a Materialist Believe in Qualia?" *Australasian Journal of Philosophy* 73: 1, 140–44.

Lewis, D. 2009. "Ramseyen Humility," in D. Braddon-Mitchell & R. Nolan (Eds.) *Conceptual Analysis and Philosophical Naturalism*, Cambridge, MA: MIT Press.

Loar, B. 1990/1997. "Phenomenal States." Originally published in J. Tomberlin (Ed.) *Philosophical Perspectives 4: Action Theory and Philosophy of Mind*, Atascadero, CA: Ridgeview; reprinted in substantially revised form in N. Block, O. Flanagan, & Guüven Guüzeldere (Eds.) 1997. *The Nature of Consciousness: Philosophical Debates*, Cambridge, MA: MIT Press.

Loar, B. 2003. "Qualia, Properties, Modality," *Philosophical Issues* 1: 113–29.

Locke, J. 1689/2008. *An Essay Concerning Human Understanding*, edited by Pauline Phemister, Oxford: Oxford University Press.

Lockwood, M. 1989. *Mind, Brain and the Quantum*, Oxford: Oxford University Press.

Lockwood, M. 1993. "The grain problem," in H. Robinson (Ed.) *Objections to Physicalism*, Oxford: Clarendon Press.

Loewer, B. 2001. "Review of J. Kim *Mind in a Physical World*," *Journal of Philosophy* 98: 315–24.

Lowe, E. J. 2000. "Locke, Martin and Substance," *Philosophical Quarterly*, 50: 201, 499–514.

Lowe, E. J. 2006. *The Four-Category Ontology: A Metaphysical Foundation for Natural Science*, Oxford: Oxford University Press.

Lowe, E. J. 2012. "What Is the Source of Our Knowledge of Modal Truths?" *Mind* 121: 484, 919–50.

Lycan, W. G. 1996. *Consciousness and Experience*, Cambridge, MA: MIT Press.

Mach, E. 1886. *The Analysis of Sensations and the Relation of Physical to the Psychical*, translated by C. M. Williams, Chicago: Open Court, 1984.

Malcolm, N. 1968. "The Conceivability of Mechanism," *Philosophical Review*, 77: 45–72.

Martin, C. B. 1980. "Substance Substantiated," *Australasian Journal of Philosophy* 58: 3–10.

Martin, C. B. 2007. *The Mind in Nature*, New York: Oxford University Press.

Martin, C. B. & Heil, J. 1998. "Rules and Powers," *Noûs* 32: 283–312.

Martin, M. G. F. 1997. "The Reality of Appearances," in M. Sainsbury (Ed.) *Thought and Ontology*. Milan: Franco Angeli.

Matthews, F. 2011. "Panpsychism as Paradigm?" M. Blamauer (Ed.) in *The Mental as Fundamental*, Frankfurt: Ontos Verlag.

Maxwell, G. 1979. "Rigid Designators and Mind-Brain Identity," in C. W. Savage (Ed.) *Perception and Cognition*, Minneapolis: University of Minnesota Press.

McClelland, T. 2013. "The Neo-Russellian Ignorance Hypothesis: A Hybrid Account of Phenomenal Consciousness," *Journal of Consciousness Studies* 20: 3–4, 125–51.

McGinn, C. 1989. "Can We Solve the Mind-Body Problem?" *Mind* 98: 391, 349–66.

McLaughlin, B. P. 1992. "The Rise and Fall of British Emergentism," in A. Beckermann (Ed.) *Emergence or Reduction*, Berlin: De Gruyter.

McLaughlin, B. P. 2001. "In Defence of New Wave Materialism: A Response to Horgan and Tienson," in C. Gillett & B. Loewer (Eds.) *Physicalism and Its Discontents*, Cambridge: Cambridge University Press.

Mellor, D. H. 1974. In Defense of Dispositions, *Philosophical Review* 83: 157–81.

Melnyk A. 2003. *A Physicalist Manifesto: Thoroughly Modern Materialism*, Cambridge: Cambridge University Press.

Melnyk, A. 2014. "Pereboom's Robust Non-Reductive Physicalism," *Erkenntnis* 79: 5, 1191–1207.

Mill, J. S. 1843. *System of Logic*, London: Longmans, Green, Reader and Dyer.

Molnar, G. 2003. *Powers: A Study in Metaphysics*, Oxford: Oxford University Press.

Montero, B. G. 2013. "Must Physicalism Imply the Supervenience of the Mental on the Physical?" 110: 2, 93–110.

Mørch, H. H. 2014. "Panpsychism and Causation: A New Argument and a Solution to the Combination Problem," PhD diss., University of Oslo.

Mumford, S. 2004. *Laws in Nature*, London: Routledge.

Nagasawa, Y. & Wager, K. 2016. "Panpsychism and Priority Cosmopsychism," in Brüntrup & Jaskolla 2016.

Nagel, T. 1974. "What's It Like to Be a Bat?" *Philosophical Review* 83: 435–50.

Nagel, T. 2012. *Mind and Cosmos: Why the Materialist, Neo-Darwinian Conception of Nature Is Almost Certainly False*, New York: Oxford University Press.

Nemirow, L. 1980. "Review of Nagel's *Mortal Questions*," *Philosophical Review* 89: 475–76.

Neurath, O. 1932/1983. "Sociology in the Framework of Physicalism," in R. S. Cohen & M. Neurath (Eds.) *Otto Neurath: Philosophical Papers*, Dordrecht, Boston and Lancaster: D. Reidel Publishing Company.

Ney, A. 2008a. "Defining Physicalism," *Philosophy Compass*, 3: 5, 1033–48.

Ney, A. 2008b, "Physicalism as an Attitude," *Philosophical Studies*, 138: 1–15.

Ney, A. 2015. "A Physicalist Critique of Russellian Monism," in Alter & Nagasawa 2015.

Nida-Rümelin, M. 1995. "What Mary Couldn't Know," in T. Metzinger (Ed.) *Phenomenal Consciousness*, Paderborn: Ferdinand Schöningh.

Nida-Rümelin, M. 1998, "On Belief about Experiences: An Epistemological Distinction Applied to the Knowledge Argument," *Philosophy and Phenomenological Research* 58: 1, 51–73.

Nida-Rümelin, M. 2007. "Grasping Phenomenal Properties," in Alter & Walter 2007.

Nida-Rümelin, M. 2016. "The Experience Property Framework: A Misleading Framework," *Synthese* (online version).

O'Connor, T. & Churchill, J. R. 2010. "Is Nonreductive Physicalism Viable within a Causal Powers Metaphysic?" in C. Macdonald & G. Macdonald (Eds.) *Emergence in Mind*, Oxford: Oxford University Press.

Papineau, D. 1993. *Philosophical Naturalism*, Oxford: Blackwell.

Papineau, D. 1998. "Mind the Gap," *Philosophical Perspectives* 12: S12, 373–89.

Papineau, D. 2002. *Thinking about Consciousness*, Oxford: Clarendon Press.

Papineau, D. 2006. "Comments on Galen Strawson: Realistic Monism: Why Physicalism Entails Panpsychism," *Journal of Consciousness Studies* 13: 10–11, 100–109.

Papineau, D. 2007. "Phenomenal Concepts and Perceptual concepts," in Alter & Walter 2006.

Parsons, J. 2004. "Distributional Properties," in F. Jackson & G. Priest (Eds.) *Lewisian Themes: The Philosophy of David K*, Oxford: Oxford University Press.

Parsons, J. 2015. "A Phenomenological Argument for Stage Theory," *Analysis* 75: 2, 237–42.

Pautz, A. 2015. "A Dilemma for Russellian Monists about Consciousness," Unpublished manuscript.

Pereboom, D. 2011. *Consciousness and the Prospects of Physicalism*, New York: Oxford University Press.

Pereboom, D. 2015. "Consciousness, Physicalism, and Absolutely Intrinsic Properties," in Alter & Nagasawa 2015.

Perry, H. 2001. *Knowledge, Possibility and Consciousness*, Cambridge, MA: MIT Press.

Putnam, H. 1960. "Mind and Machines," reprinted in his *Mind, Language, and Reality*, Cambridge, Cambridge University Press, 1975.

Putnam, H. 1967. "The Nature of Mental States," reprinted in his *Mind, Language, and Reality*, Cambridge, Cambridge University Press, 1975.

Putnam, H. 1973. "Meaning and Reference," *Journal of Philosophy* 70: 299–711.

Putnam, H. 1975. 'The Meaning of "Meaning"' in his *Mind, Language, and Reality*, Cambridge; Cambridge University Press, 1975.

Quine, W. V. O. 1948. "On What There Is," *Review of Metaphysics* 2: 21–38.

Robinson, H. 1982. *Matter and Sense*, Cambridge: Cambridge University Press.

Robinson, H. 1985. "The General Form of the Argument for Berkeleian Idealism," in Foster & H. Robinson (Eds.) *Essays on Berkeley: A Tercentennial Celebration*, Oxford: Clarendon Press.

Robinson, H. 1994. *Perception*, London: Routledge.

Robinson, H. 2016. *From the Knowledge Argument to Mental Substance: Resurrecting the Mind*, Cambridge: Cambridge University Press.

Roelofs, L. 2014. "Phenomenal blending and the palette problem," *Thought: A Journal of Philosophy* 3: 1, 59–70.

Roelofs, L. 2015. Combining Minds: A Defence of the Possibility of Experiential Combination, PhD diss., University of Toronto.

Rosen, G. 2010. "Metaphysical Dependence: Grounding and Reduction," in B. Hale & A. Hoffman (Eds.) *Modality: Metaphysics, Logic, and Epistemology*, Oxford: Oxford University Press, 109–36.

Rosenberg. G. 2004. *A Place for Consciousness: Probing the Deep Structure of the Natural World*, New York: Oxford University Press.

Royce, J. 1901. *The World and the Individual*, New York: Macmillan.

Russell, B. 1910. "Knowledge by Acquaintance and Knowledge by Description," *Proceedings of the Aristotelian Society* 11: 108–28.

Russell, B. 1921. *The Analysis of Mind*, London: George Allen and Unwin.

Russell, B. 1927. *The Analysis of Matter*, London: Kegan Paul.

Ryle, G. 1949. *The Concept of Mind*, Chicago: Chicago University Press.

Schaffer, J. 2007. "From Nihilism to Monism," *Australasian Journal of Philosophy* 85: 2, 175–91.

Schaffer, J. 2009a. "On What Grounds What," in Chalmers, Manley, & Wasserman 2009.

Schaffer, J. 2009b. "Spacetime the One Substance," *Philosophical Studies* 145: 1, 131–48.

Schaffer, J. 2010a. "The Least Discerning and Most Promiscuous Truthmaker," *Philosophical Quarterly* 60: 307–24.

Schaffer, J. 2010b. "The Internal Relatedness of All Things," *Mind* 119: 341–76.

Schaffer, J. 2010c. "Monism: The Priority of the Whole," *Philosophical Review* 119: 1, 31–76; reprinted in Goff 2012b.

Schaffer, J. 2012. "Why the World Has Parts: Reply to Horgan & Potrč," in Goff 2012b.

Schaffer, J. 2013. "The Action of the Whole," *Proceedings of the Aristotelian Society* 87: 67–87.

Schaffer, J. 2014. "Review of Sider's *Writing the Book of the World*," *Philosophical Review* 123: 125–29.

Schaffer, J. Forthcoming. "The ground between the gaps," *Philosophers Imprint*.

Schroer, R. 2010. "What's the beef? Phenomenal Concepts as Both Demonstrative and Substantial," *Australasian Journal of Philosophy* 88: 505–22.

Seager, W. 1995. "Consciousness, Information, and Panpsychism," *Journal of Consciousness Studies* 2: 272–88.

Seager, W. 2016. "Panpsychism Infusion," in Brüntrup & Jaskolla 2016.

Seager, W. (Ed.) Forthcoming. *The Routledge Handbook of Panpsychism*, London, New York: Routledge.

Shani, I. 2010. "Mind Stuffed with Red Herrings: Why William James' Critique of the Mind-Stuff Theory Does Not Substantiate a Combination Problem for Panpsychism," *Acta Analytica* 25: 4, 413–34.

Shani, I. 2015. "Cosmopsychism: A Holistic Approach to the Metaphysics of Experience," *Philosophical Papers* 44: 3, 389–437.

Shoemaker, S. 1981. "Absent Qualia Are Impossible—A Reply to Block," *Philosophical Review* 90: 581–99.

Shoemaker, S. 1982. "The Inverted Spectrum," *Journal of Philosophy* 79: 357–81.

Shoemaker, S. 2001. "Realization and Mental Causation," in C. Gillett & B. Loewer (Eds.) *Physicalism and Its Discontents*, Cambridge: Cambridge University Press.

Shoemaker, S. 2007. *Physical Realization*, Oxford: Oxford University Press.

Sider, T. 2001. *Four-Dimensionalism*, Oxford: Oxford University Press.

Sider, T. 2009. *Ontological Realism*, in Chalmers, Manley, & Wasserman 2009.

Sider, T. 2012. *Writing the Book of the World*, Oxford: Oxford University Press.

Sider, T. 2013a. "Symposium on *Writing the Book of the World*," *Analysis* 73: 4, 751–70.

Sider, T. 2013b. "Against Parthood," *Oxford Studies in Metaphysics* 8: 237–93.

Skiles, A. 2015. "Against Grounding Necessitarianism," *Erkenntnis*, 80: 4, 717–51.

Sklar, L. 1974. *Space, Time and Spacetime*. Berkeley: University of California Press.

Skow, B. 2005. *Supersubstantivalism. In Once upon a Spacetime*, PhD diss., New York University.

Skrbina, D. 2007. *Panpsychism in the West*, Cambridge, MA: MIT Press.

Smart, J.J.C. 1959. "Sensations and Brain Processes," *Philosophical Review* 68: 141–56.

Spinoza, B. 1677/1994. *Ethics, Demonstrated in Geometrical Order*, in E. Curley (Ed. and Trans.), *A Spinoza Reader*, Princeton: Princeton University Press.

Sprigge, T. L. 1983. *A Vindication of Absolute Idealism*, London: Routledge and Kegan Paul.

Sprigge, T. L. 2006. *The God of Metaphysics*, Oxford: Oxford University Press.

Sprigge, T. L. & Montefiore, A. 1971. "Final Causes," *Proceedings of the Aristotelian Society*, 45 (Suppl.), 149–92.

Stoljar, D. 2001. "Two Conceptions of the Physical," *Philosophy and Phenomenological Research* 62: 253–81.

Stoljar, D. 2006. *Ignorance and Imagination*, New York: Oxford University Press.

Strawson, G. 1986. *Freedom and Belief*, Oxford: Clarendon Press.

Strawson, G. 1994. *Mental Reality*, Cambridge, MA: MIT Press.

Strawson, G. 1987. "Realism and Causation," *Philosophical Quarterly* 37: 148, 253–77.

Strawson, G. 1989. 'Red and "Red,"' *Synthese* 78: 193–232.

Strawson, G. 1991. "The Contingent Reality of Natural Necessity," *Analysis* 51: 4, 209–13.

Strawson, G. 2003. "Real Materialism," in L. Antony & N. Hornstein (Eds.) *Chomsky and His Critics,* Oxford: Blackwell; reprinted in G. Strawson (Ed.) 2008 *Real Materialism and Other Essays*, New York: Oxford University Press.

Strawson, G. 2006a. "Realistic Materialism: Why Physicalism Entails Panpsychism," 13: 10–11.

Strawson, G. 2006b. "Panpsychism? Replies to Commentators and a Celebration of Descartes," *Journal of Consciousness Studies* 13: 10–11.

Strawson, G. 2008. "The Identity of the Categorical and the Dispositional," *Analysis* 68: 300, 271–82.

Stubenberg, L. 2015. "Russell, Russellian monism, and panpsychism," in Alter & Nagasawa 2015.

Taylor, J. H. 2013. "Physicalism and Phenomenal Concepts: Bringing Ontology and Philosophy of Mind Together," *Philosophia* 41: 1283–97.

Tooley, M., 1977, "The Nature of Laws," *Canadian Journal of Philosophy*, 7: 667–98.

Trogdon, K. 2013a. "An Introduction to Grounding," in M. Hoeltje, B. Schnieder, & A. Steinberg (Eds.) *Dependence: Basic Philosophical Concepts*, Munich: Philosophia Verlag.

Trogdon, K. 2013b. "Grounding: Necessary or Contingent?" *Pacific Philosophical Quarterly* 94: 4, 465–85.

Trogdon, K. 2016. "Revelation and physicalism," *Synthese* (online version).

Turausky, K. N.d. "Picturing Panpsychism: New Approaches to the Combination problem." Unpublished manuscript.

Tye, M. 1995. *Ten Problems of Consciousness: A Representational Theory of the Phenomenal Mind*, Cambridge, MA: MIT Press.

Tye, M. 2000. *Consciousness, Color, and Content*, Cambridge, MA: MIT Press.

Unger, P. 1980. "The Problem of the Many," *Midwest Studies in Philosophy* 5: 411–67.

Unger, P. 1999. "The Mystery of the Physical and the Matter of Qualities," *Midwest Studies in Philosophy* 23: 75–99.

Van Fraassen, B. 2002. *The Empirical Stance*, New Haven, CT: Yale University Press.

Van Inwagen, P. 1990. *Material Beings*, Ithaca, NY: Cornell University Press.

Van Inwagen, P. 1993. *Metaphysics*, Oxford: Oxford University Press.

Wilson, J. 1999. "How Super-Duper Does Supervenience Need to Be?" *Philosophical Quarterly* 82: 33–52.

Wilson, J. 2005. "Supervenience-Based Formulations of Physicalism," *Nous* 29: 426–59.

Wilson, J. 2006. "On Characterising the Physical," *Philosophical Studies* 131: 1.

Wishon, D. 2015. "Russell on Russellian Monism," in Alter & Nagasawa 2015.

INDEX

Ability Hypothesis, as a response to the knowledge argument, 69. *See also* knowledge argument
acquaintance, 66, 69–70, 115, 122, 168
Acquaintance Hypothesis, as a response to the knowledge argument, 69. *See also* knowledge argument
Albahari, Miri, 228n19, 241–42
analytic phenomenology, 256, 270–72
  definition of, 271
anti-subject-summing argument
  Coleman's, 187, 192, 198, 228
  conceivability, 173, 176
  James's, 172
  See also combination problem; subject-summing problem
a posteriori identity/necessity, 82–84, 86, 99–100, 123
appearance property, 86–91, 141, 146
Aristotle, 12n16, 32, 42n26
Armstrong, David M., 44, 83n9, 140n6, 222, 223n8, 237, 240n38
Armstrong-Dretske-Tooley conception of natural laws, 185n21, 232n24, 249n53, 250n54
aspect, primitive metaphysical notion of, 221–32, 234–37, 239–41, 249
Augustine, 111n8
austerity problem, 135

Balog, Katalin, 119n20, 122
behaviorism, 143n11
  analytic, 67
  metaphysical, 137
Bennett, Karen, 50n37, 261–63, 265
Berkeley, George, 24
Bradley's regress, 222

Canberra plan, 129
categorical nature/property, 17, 31n13, 57, 128, 131, 137, 140–41, 143, 144n16, 169, 171, 184, 202–3, 205, 208, 231, 254, 256, 264

causal closure, 18–19, 243–44
  micro-level, 153–58, 163
causal exclusion problem, 43, 153, 155, 158, 205, 209, 237–38, 240–41, 248–49, 251
causal powers, 19, 37, 41, 57, 60, 127, 131, 137–40, 144n16, 231–32, 246–50, 252
causal structuralism, 31, 137–41, 150, 176
causal theory of names, 92
certainty, 3n3, 14, 107, 111–13, 118, 120–22, 268–69
Chalmers, David, 7, 10, 15, 47n31, 56n49, 72n10, 76, 78, 81–82, 84, 86–91, 96, 100–1, 107n2, 115n14, 129, 145, 194, 204–6, 208, 229n21
Churchland, Patricia, 5–8, 187, 202n11
Churchland, Paul, 202n11, 243
CIS. *See* Conceivable Isolation of Subjects
CIS+. *See* Conceivable Isolation of Subjects
co-consciousness, 212–13
Coleman, Sam, 158, 187–92, 198, 200–1, 228, 242. *See also* anti-subject-summing argument: Coleman's
combination problem, 20, 165–66, 171–73, 179n17, 186, 213n24, 228, 230
  bottom-up, 165–66, 209, 218
  spatial relations response, 181, 183, 185
  top-down, 165–66, 193, 218
  See also anti-subject-summing argument; mental combination (mental composition/phenomenal combination); subject-summing problem
compositional nihilism, 217, 239n36, 260–62, 265, 271
compositional universalism, 260, 262, 264
computational property, 239–41
conceivability, 161
  negative ideal, 81–82, 88
  positive, 81
  and possibility, 77, 81, 85–88, 95–96, 99–101, 104–6, 123–25, 128, 176, 230

Printed in the USA/Agawam, MA
September 26, 2017

659316.052